Digital Practices

Also by Susan Broadhurst

LIMINAL ACTS: A Critical Overview of Contemporary Performance and Theory

PERFORMANCE AND TECHNOLOGY: Practices of Virtual Embodiment and Interactivity (*co-edited with Josephine Machon*)

700.1
B780

Digital Practices

Aesthetic and Neuroesthetic Approaches to Performance and Technology

Susan Broadhurst

LIBRARY ST. MARY'S COLLEGE

WITHDRAWI

© Susan Broadhurst 2007

All rights reserved. No reproduction, copy or transmission of this publication may be made without written permission.

No paragraph of this publication may be reproduced, copied or transmitted save with written permission or in accordance with the provisions of the Copyright, Designs and Patents Act 1988, or under the terms of any licence permitting limited copying issued by the Copyright Licensing Agency, 90 Tottenham Court Road, London W1T 4LP.

Any person who does any unauthorised act in relation to this publication may be liable to criminal prosecution and civil claims for damages.

The author has asserted her right to be identified as the author of this work in accordance with the Copyright, Designs and Patents Act 1988.

First published 2007 by
PALGRAVE MACMILLAN
Houndmills, Basingstoke, Hampshire RG21 6XS and
175 Fifth Avenue, New York, N.Y. 10010
Companies and representatives throughout the world

PALGRAVE MACMILLAN is the global academic imprint of the Palgrave Macmillan division of St. Martin's Press, LLC and of Palgrave Macmillan Ltd. Macmillan® is a registered trademark in the United States, United Kingdom and other countries. Palgrave is a registered trademark in the European Union and other countries.

ISBN-13: 978–0–230–55313–2   hardback
ISBN-10: 0-230-55313-3   hardback

This book is printed on paper suitable for recycling and made from fully managed and sustained forest sources. Logging, pulping and manufacturing processes are expected to conform to the environmental regulations of the country of origin.

A catalogue record for this book is available from the British Library.

A catalog record for this book is available from the Library of Congress.

10   9   8   7   6   5   4   3   2   1
16   15   14   13   12   11   10   09   08   07

Printed and bound in Great Britain by
Antony Rowe Ltd, Chippenham and Eastbourne

For my mother …

We shall not cease from exploration
And the end of all our exploring
Will be to arrive where we started
And know the place for the first time.

(T.S. Eliot, Four Quartets)

Contents

List of Illustrations   ix

Acknowledgements   xi

1 The Digital: A Preliminary View   **1**

Theoretical overview   2
Digital performance   10

2 Selective Aesthetic Approaches   **19**

Merleau-Ponty   19
Lyotard   24
Derrida   29
Deleuze   37

3 Neuroesthetics   **47**

Visual perception   47
A neuroesthetic approach   52
Art and perception   57
Consciousness and the digital   60

4 Live Performance and the Digital   **69**

Intelligence, interaction, reaction and performance:
    The Jeremiah project   69
Digital dance, evolution and chance:
    Merce Cunningham's *BIPED*   77
Virtuality, cybernetics and the post-human:
    Stelarc's obsolete body   86

5 Digital Sound, New Media and Interactive Performance   **99**

Optik: Contact, impulse and electro-acoustic sound   99
Palindrome: 'Intermedia', collaboration
    and interaction   110
Troika Ranch: An electronic disturbance   117

6 Digital Film   **131**

The *Matrix* trilogy: 'Bullet time', simulation and
    virtual cinema   132
Star Wars prequels: The digital force of ILM
    in Phantom Menace, *Attack of the Clones* and
    Revenge of the Sith   146

7 Bioart   **161**

Transformation and communication: Eduardo Kac's
    transgenic art   161
Wetware and GMOs: Critical Art Ensemble's
    recombinant theatre   168
Butterflies, FISH and functional portraits:
    Marta De Menezes's aestheticizing of evolution   177

8 Conclusion: Digital Practices   **185**

Bibliography   196

Index   211

List of Illustrations

Figure 3.1 Area V4 of the brain. Photo courtesy of
Professor Semir Zeki. From the Laboratory of
Neurobiology at UCL, www.vislab.ucl.ac.uk   56

Figure 4.1 Elodie and Jeremiah from *Blue Bloodshot
Flowers* (2001). Director: Sue Broadhurst;
Technology: Richard Bowden. Image:
Terence Tiernan   70

Figure 4.2 Elodie and Jeremiah from *Blue Bloodshot
Flowers*. Image by Sally Trussler and Richard
Bowden   72

Figure 4.3 Jeremiah and Director, *Blue Bloodshot Flowers*.
Image by Terence Tiernan   74

Figure 4.4 Merce Cunningham Dance Company performs
'BIPED' at the Lincoln Center Festival (1999).
Credit: ©Stephanie Berger   78

Figure 4.5 *MUSCLE MACHINE*. Gallery 291, London (2003).
Photographer: Mark Bennett. STELARC   94

Figure 4.6 *Extra Ear – ¼ Scale* (2003). The Tissue Culture &
Art (Oron Catts & Ionat Zurr) in collaboration
with Stelarc. Biodegradable polymer and human
chondrocytes cells, 3cm × 1.5cm × 1.5cm.
Photography by Ionat Zurr   95

Figure 5.1 Optik perform *Xstasis* (2003), Montreal, Canada.
Photo: Alain Décarie   100

Figure 5.2 Optik perform *Xstasis* (2003), Montreal, Canada.
Photo: Alain Décarie   108

Figure 5.3 Demonstration of EyeCon System. Palindrome IMPG
(2000), Dancer: Aleksandra Janeva.
Photo: Jürgen Henkel   113

Figure 5.4   This image shows a real-time video effect
             linked to a technology that responds to the
             touch of two dancers. From the Palindrome opera
             Blinde Liebe, (2005). Dancers: Aimar Perez Gali,
             Helena Zwiauer   114

Figure 5.5   *Solo4>Three* (2003). Dance and Choreography:
             Emily Fernandez. Interactive video system:
             Frieder Weiss. Photo credit: Ralf Denke   116

Figure 5.6   Danielle Goldman in *Surfacing* (2004). Photo:
             Richard Termine   123

Figure 5.7   The Company in *Future of Memory* (2003).
             Photo: Richard Termine   124

Figure 5.8   Motion tracking leaves three-dimensional traces
             of the performers' movements in Troika Ranch's
             16 [R]evolutions (2005). Performers: Johanna
             Levy & Lucia Tong. Photo: Richard Termine   126

Figure 5.9   Colour and multiplicity are introduced to imply
             evolutionary change in *16 [R]evolutions*
             (Performers: Johanna Levy & Daniel Suominen –
             photo A.T. Schaeffer)   127

Figure 7.1   *GenTerra*. Performance at St. Norbert Art and Culture
             Center, Winnipeg, Manitoba, Canada (2001)   173

Figure 7.2   *GenTerra*. The photo was taken at the Darwin Centre,
             Natural History Museum, London (2001)   174

Figure 7.3   Marta de Menezes, *Nature?* Live *Bicyclus anynana*
             butterfly with modified wing pattern. Part of
             *Genes and Genius: The Inheritance of Gregor
             Mendel*, The Mendel Museum (2005)
             © Marta de Menezes   179

Acknowledgements

I would like to give special thanks to Josephine Machon, Alan Petersen, Catherine Waldby and Paul Woodward for their professional expertise. I would also like to thank family, particularly Pat Denton, together with James, Suzanne and Louisa; friends, including Hervé Constant, Jacqui Day, Michael Newling, Ros Porter, Sue Ramus; and colleagues Steve Dixon, Barry Edwards, Rachel Fensham, Frédéric Fol Leymarie and Stelarc for their entertainment, friendship and helpful advice. Also, special thanks to Paula Kennedy and Christabel Scaife at Palgrave Macmillan for their support in the publishing process.

Many thanks to Semir Zeki from Imperial College, London, for kindly allowing me to include his image of 'Area V4'. I would also like to thank Terence Tiernan, Stephanie Berger, Stelarc, Ionat Zurr and Oron Catts from TCA; Barry Edwards from Optik; Mark Coniglio and Dawn Stoppiello from Troika Ranch; Robert Wechler, Frieder Weiss and Emily Fernandez from Palindrome, Steve Kurtz from CAE; and Marta De Menezes for permission to include their images, and thanks to Paul Verity Smith for his technical assistance.

The book's cover image is by Richard Termine and is from Troika Ranch's *16 [R]evolutions* (2005). The performer is Lucia Tong.

Extracts from chapter 4 have previously been published in *The Drama Review* and *Digital Creativity*. Extracts from chapter 7 have been published in *Body, Space & Technology* and extracts from chapter 8 have also been published in *Performance Research*.

1
The Digital: A Preliminary View

In recent years, new performance practices have emerged that prioritize such technologies as motion tracking,[1] artificial intelligence,[2] 3-D modelling and animation, digital paint and sound, robotics, interactive design and biotechnology. These practices have emerged within the context of a broad-based technological infiltration in all areas of human experience and in a variety of ways, with implications that are seemingly both ontological and epistemological. This chapter provides a preliminary view of and signals what is indicated by digital practices. I am arguing that due to the preponderance of performance practices which utilize the above technologies, a retheorization of aesthetics and perception as a whole is needed.

Significant questions relate to the use of sophisticated technologies within contemporary art and performance practices. Since, as I have argued elsewhere, language without the body does not 'mean' at all, as corporeality provides language with meaning under sociocultural and thus temporal constraints (Broadhurst 1999b, 17), what then are the implications for a virtual body? Therefore my overall question is: as digital technologies are becoming increasingly prominent in art practices, does the resultant physical/virtual interface give rise to a new aesthetics? What are the theoretical and practical implications of this?

It is my belief that tensions exist within the spaces created by this interface of body and technology. These spaces are 'liminal' in as much as they are located on the 'threshold' of the physical and virtual. Since no body (not even a naked body) escapes (re)presentation altogether (Broadhurst 1999a, 103), the virtual body (as any other body) inscribes its presence and absence in the very act of its performance, leaving gaps and spaces in its wake. I suggest it is within these tension-filled spaces that opportunities arise for new experimental forms and practices.[3]

Therefore, firstly and most importantly, the utilization of digital technology is crucial to this performance.

My aim is to explore and analyse the effect this technology has on the physical body in performance, especially in relation to the problem of (re)presenting the 'unrepresentable', that is, the sublime of this physical/virtual interface (or liminal space). The sublime is the tension between joy and sorrow – the delight of having a feeling of totality inseparable from the pain of not being able to present an object equal to this idea of totality. Spectators are not simply engaged in passive contemplation but are called to do what, according to Kant, cannot be done, to 'present the unpresentable' (1978, 119), to surpass what is possible for something else, to strive continually towards a judgement that can never be guaranteed. The sublime indicates that there can never be security in mere contemplation, for the signs presented demand much more than this.

As a development of my previous theorization on liminality (Broadhurst 1999a, 1999b, 2004b), I believe that aesthetic theorization is central to this analysis.[4] However, other approaches are also valid, such as those offered by recent research into cognitive neuroscience,[5] particularly in relation to the emergent field of 'neuro-esthetics', where the primary objective is to provide 'an understanding of the biological basis of aesthetic experience' (Zeki 1999, 2).

In theorizing from the above varied perspectives it is not my intention to provide an overarching theorization for performance and technology, nor is it to relate various theories to each other and find some common thread. Instead, by taking certain ideas and concepts I am suggesting something in the way of a tool-kit that would be useful in articulating the multilayeredness of digital performance practices. Moreover, in analysing digital practices it is not my intention to coin a new genre of art and performance; rather, I aim to focus on a variety of practices that utilize sophisticated new and existing technologies. As Derrida notes in his discussion on 'The Law of the Genre' (1980), 'every text participates in one or several genres, there is no genreless text ... yet such participation never amounts to belonging' (211–12).

Theoretical overview

For Maurice Merleau-Ponty, in his aesthetic theorization, consciousness is always already 'embodied', just as perception is already interpreted or 'stylized' by a horizon of human undertakings that extrapolates meaning. This pre-reflective stance is guided by an 'operative intentionality' that prioritizes gesture, sexuality and even silence. His 'ontology of the flesh' provides a phenomenological focus on the body-subject (Merleau-Ponty 2000), a focus implied but never developed by Husserl or Heidegger. For Merleau-Ponty consciousness cannot be fully explained by an autonomous intrinsic or *a priori* condition for abstract cognition. Without the complex 'intertwining' (Entrelacs) and 'chiasm' (chiasme)[6] between pre-theoretical, lived experience and conceptual judgement there would always be the inevitable dualism of mind/body opposition – an influence from Descartes that is still prevalent today. Therefore, instead of the Cartesian cogito, 'I think, therefore, I am,' Merleau-Ponty shows that 'to be a body is to be tied to a certain world' and 'our body is not primarily *in* space; it is of it' (1962, 148).

Our body is already in the world; it is not a body in itself which could be objectified or universalized. Rather, perception is always embodied within a specific context or situation.[7] Perception is an active process of meaning construction involving not only visual perception but all the senses, together with the total physical environment in which the body is situated and an embodied 'intentionality' towards the world. For instance, when I hold an object in my hand and view it from different angles, my intentionality is directed towards that object. Moreover by learning new skills and utilizing technology, humans change the world they live in.

It is my belief that an application of Merleau-Ponty's embodied perspective on cognition and interaction would enable an analysis of the elements of physical and virtual interaction, so central to digital practices. His theorization on perception is essential to this embodied experience, as are the ramifications of new technological knowledge and skills for 'having' and creating 'a world'.

Jean-François Lyotard posits two radically different territories: one of communication and discourse and the other of form, colour and the visual. One is determined by linguistic-philosophical closure and the other, the 'figural', is indeterminate and disruptive of discursive systems and of signification in general. Instead of a conceptual interpretation of meaning there are flows and drives of 'intensities' which continually displace the identity of the reader. According to Lyotard, 'the aim was the elimination of the game of good/evil in favor of that of intensities' (van Reijen and Veerman 1988, 277).

Lyotard in his later writings premised a revision of the Kantian sublime primarily from a linguistic perspective (1988, 1991).[8] However, his linguistic bias lacks a satisfactory account of non-verbal signification. For it is only by a broader analysis that a more appropriate interpretation can be achieved that would allow for the prominence of the 'body' (physical and virtual). And it is by such means that the sublime, which exceeds the linguistic and is 'an outrage to the imagination' (Kant 1978, 90–1), can be presented in and through such performances as those of the digital. Given the limitation of and in presentation, Lyotard believes that the task of a critical politics is, nevertheless, to present the unpresentable, to present the fact that the unpresentable exists and that it concerns our future (Lyotard 1988, 166).

Lyotard's theorization on figure, discours and libidinal economy and his writings on industrial and post-industrial technosciences, together with his experimentation in the arts, are important in an analysis of digital practices. The figural, as the figuration not of representational art but instead of creativity and elusiveness, is important since this mirrors many of the practices of the digital, placing the performances within the context of a libidinal economy. Intensities are also useful in analysing various modes of the digital, given its diverse elements, which often escape meaningful interpretation. Likewise, Lyotard's emphasis on post-industrial technoscience relates to the aesthetics of digital practices.

For Jacques Derrida, the deconstruction of art runs parallel to his ongoing project of deconstructing tradition, particularly the logocentric discursive bias prevalent in Western philosophy. In *The Truth in Painting*, Derrida compares Cézanne's declaration: 'I OWE YOU TRUTH IN PAINTING AND I WILL TELL IT TO YOU' (Derrida 1987, 2) with the notion of the truth of art as it is found in Kant, Hegel and Heidegger. He claims that the philosophy of art presupposes the existence of works of art. As Derrida mentions, this is already to assume that art as a concept, 'has a unity ... and an originary meaning, an *etymon*, a truth that is one and naked ... and that it would be sufficient to unveil it *through* history' (20). This supposition of the unity of art over time supports an ontological view of art that has an originary meaning and a single truth – in short, a philosophy of identity, which Derrida seeks to challenge.

Derrida's writings on deconstruction and identity, presence and absence and contamination of the 'live' by the virtual and the virtual by the 'live' are central to digital practices. Since in these performances there is a continual formation and deformation of identity together with the destabilization and problematization of originary meaning, in *Memoirs of The Blind: The Self-Portrait and Other Ruins*, Derrida describes machines that 'sound out' rather than see, via echoes and waves. They operate 'anoptically' – that is, without seeing, through a blind transcription of 'coded' signals (Derrida 1993, 32). This 'superequipped surveillance' is anoptic rather than 'panoptic' (Foucault 1986), searching into the darkness where objects are sounded out rather than illuminated, 'instruments ... that sound out ... that allows one to know ... where one no longer sees ... the *scanner's* computer blindly transcribing the coded signals of the photoelectrical cells' (Derrida 1993, 32). In a similar way the algorithmic coded information from motion sensors 'track' instead of see.

In exploring ways of theorizing the aesthetics of digital practices, the writings of Gilles Deleuze are invaluable, particularly in his notion of 'desire', which is seen as an affirmative process of 'flows' and 'lines of flight', and in his belief that the play of 'difference and repetition' has supplanted that of the 'same and representation' (Deleuze 1994). The Oedipus complex for Deleuze, together with Felix Guattari (1984, 1999a), inevitably leads to the belief in an original event or 'trauma' which for them is ultimately reductive. Unlike Jacques Lacan, they refute the idea of desire as being based on lack. For Deleuze and Guattari, desire is always in movement, made up of different elements depending on the situation,[9] and is seen as 'machine-like'. The phrases 'desiring machines' and 'body without organs' (BwO) emphasize the theory's horizontality (Lechte 1994, 104). The 'BwO' is a term borrowed from Artaud. It signifies not an organic body but one like the body politic that is always in the process of formation and deformation as is the performance practice of the digital.

Deleuze's notion of 'intensity' or hierarchy of forces describes elements at the limit of perception and is described in terms of pure ontological difference (1994, 144) that prefigures 'actual' entities (246). Intensities cannot be directly perceived; instead, they can only be felt, sensed or perceived in the 'quality' they cause (144). Intensities are imperceptible because 'a perceived difference' is a difference that has 'already been identified, reduced, or contracted' (Colebrook 2002b, 27). For this reason, intensities are outside of, but implicated in, our experience of them. Deleuze uses the term 'extensity' or 'extensive' difference to describe the way intensities are homogenized in everyday perception and experience (1994, 230).[10] Art shatters everyday perception because it draws attention to singular 'intensities'.

In digital practices, due to the hybridization of the performances and the diversity of media employed, various intensities are at play. It is these imperceptible intensities, together with their ontological status, that give rise to new modes of perception and consciousness.[11]

Other approaches, which provide a very different perspective in an analysis of the digital, are those offered by recent research into cognitive neuroscience and consciousness. Computer modelling and brain scanning have been crucial to this emergent field of cognitive neuroscience which centres on how mental activities are carried out by the brain.

Recent discoveries in neurobiology, artificial intelligence, cognitive science and medicine have converged, providing for the first time more information about how the brain goes about thinking and perceiving. It is my intention to explore the area of cognitive neuroscience in relation to visual perception and imagery, and question whether this discipline can be useful as part of an interpretative framework from which to articulate performance practice. Writers such as Stephen Kosslyn and Olivier Koenig (1992) have investigated this relatively new area of research. Integrating very different sorts of information and ideas they demonstrate that the emerging field of cognitive neuroscience is much more than the sum of its parts.

For Kosslyn and Koenig, 'vision is not a single process' (1992, 52). The identification of a stimulus consists of much more than is obvious from its visible properties. Nowhere is this more clearly illustrated than in the broad and diverse range of aberrations that frequently transpire following brain damage. One such account is vividly described by Oliver Sacks in his discussion of how one man's vision was so disturbed that he 'mistook his wife for a hat' (Sacks 1986).

The ability to identify appears to arise from the joint action of a number of brain subsystems working together, something that is only attained with great difficulty (if at all) by a computer. What relevance do these subsystems have for our perception of performance practices, particularly those that feature not only a physical body but also a virtual body? And not only a physical space but also a virtual space?

Mental abilities, such as language, memory, thought and visual imagery, have complex underlying structures. Cognitive neuroscience seeks to improve our understanding of these structures by defining 'component processes and specifying the way that they work together' (Kosslyn and Koenig 1992, 3). This approach is a description of mental events from a functional perspective. In other words *'the mind is what the brain does'*, and facts about the brain are needed to characterize these events. For Kosslyn and Koenig, this approach is described by the term *'Wet Mind'*. This is distinguished from the *'Dry Mind'* approach of cognitive psychology, where the metaphor of the computer is central and mental events are examined and explored without any regard for the brain itself (4). The central aim is not to replace a description of mental events by one of mere brain activity but rather integrate both approaches to provide a description of how the brain gives rise to mental activities.

Vision is fundamental to many cognitive abilities and plays a critical role in visual cognition and reading, and the act of perceiving is an important focus of cognitive neuroscience. Perception is differentiated from imagery in so much as in the former, a perceived object is physically present whereas for the latter objects are 'seen' which are not being actually viewed and these images can be changed at will. Memory also plays a role since visual images are built on visual memories. Although these images are immediate and transient, they can be used at different times to form new imagery. In fact, visual imagery is important to cognition due to its ability to create and be creative (Kosslyn and Koenig 1992, 129). The ability to perceive the world around us seems so effortless as to be taken for granted. However, given what is involved this is no mean feat. A common fallacy is to assume that an image is inside the eyeball, our vision system providing us with no more than a window with which to view the world. According to V.S. Ramachandran and Sandra Blakeslee, to begin to understand perception, it is necessary to get rid of the idea of 'images in the brain' and replace it with one of 'symbolic description of objects and events in the external world' (1999, 66). An example of a symbolic description is this written paragraph which you are reading. However, what is meant by symbolic description in the brain is not marks on a page but rather the language of nerve impulses and synapses.[12] The brain contains multiple areas for processing images which is also composed of intricate networks. Any object or event evokes a unique pattern of activity in relation to that object or event. To understand visual processes, it is necessary to decipher the code encrypted by the brain. Perception then involves much more than replicating an image that provides an objective view on the world, since our perception can change even when the image on the retina stays the same. In fact, every act of perception involves making a judgement (67).

It is important to note that an act of judgement is central to both cognitive neuroscientific and aesthetic approaches to perception. Just as in aesthetic theorization we cannot escape the structure of complex judgements,[13] in making judgements from a neuroesthetic perspective there needs to be an assumption that there is a certain amount of stability of physical properties. Ramachandran and Blakeslee argue that due to evolution and also early childhood learning 'stable physical properties' are incorporated into the visual areas of the brain (68) – which means that certain assumptions or hidden knowledge about what we see can be elicited when we view an image. Using an image of a leopard, they argue that when we see a set of dots moving together, the dots usually belong to a single object, such as a leopard. So if we see the same group of dots moving together and coming towards us it is perfectly reasonable for our visual system to again assume that the dots belong to this object and that is what is seen. As Ramachandran and Blakeslee remark, 'no wonder Herman von Helmholtz (the founding father of visual science) called perception an "unconscious inference"' (68).

What implications does a cognitive neuroscientific approach to perception have in an analysis of digital practices? Certainly, the performances, due to their hybridity and multiplicity of codes, are unique and may well destabilize perception, since they contain no apparent 'stable physical properties'. Consequently, it would prove difficult, if not impossible, to make any 'unconscious inference'.

One of the most fascinating debates in recent years has centred on consciousness and what it consists of. In some Platonist interpretations, consciousness is seen as the soul or spirit; that is, the soul becomes a self through life experience. Although on a secular level this does not need to be a religious experience, it is the case that these terms are frequently used to describe a distinctly human trait and awareness, not supposed to be shared by other life forms. However, this was denounced by Gilbert Ryle in his influential book *Concept of Mind* (1976), where consciousness is seen as the 'Ghost in the Machine'. In short, for Ryle, consciousness is no more than an 'epiphenomenon of brain activity' (Lodge 2002, 4–5). This view is shared by Ramachandran and Blakeslee, when they investigate the assumed gap between mind and brain that 'poses a deep epistemological question – a barrier that simply cannot be crossed'. They argue that there is no such divide between 'mind and matter, substance and spirit'. Rather, this barrier is apparent only and comes about as a result of language due to a mistranslation from one language to another (1999, 231). Interestingly, this dispute has parallels with the debate surrounding the Cartesian mind/body duality. However, here the mechanistic view of consciousness denies the notion of a mind/body split, claiming that mind and body are both in their essence materialistic, whilst the idealist interpretation supports the mind/body split.

Francis Crick focuses on understanding the neurobiological basis of consciousness, marrying the molecular and cellular aspects of neurons,[14] observations in neuroanatomy and psychological studies of behaviour in an attempt to scientifically investigate just what consciousness is.[15] For Crick, in his controversial writings, emotions, memories, sense of personal identity and free will are in fact no more than the behaviour of a vast assembly of nerve cells and their associated molecules. Crick is confrontational in his approach and challenges religion with the suggestion that in a scientific view, the soul is just one more manifestation of brain physiology (Crick 1994).

A key term in consciousness studies is *qualia* (Latin), which is 'the subjective content associated with a conscious sensation' that according to Crick and Koch, 'does exist and has its physical basis in the brain' (2001, 194), or as Ramachandran and Blakeslee rather more colourfully describe it, '"qualia" simply means the raw feel of sensation such as the subjective quality of "pain" or "red" or "gnocchi with truffles"' (1999, 229). However, not everyone agrees that qualia even exists. For Daniel Dennet in *Consciousness Explained* (1991), qualia can be best understood in functional or causal terms and human consciousness is merely the operation of a 'virtual machine implemented in the parallel architecture of a brain' (210).

Nevertheless, a central dilemma for qualia or subjective sensation is how it can be described in such terms as 'the firing of neurons'. In short, how is it possible to reconcile first-person sensations with third-person accounts of those sensations, how to reconcile the subjective with the objective. For Crick and Koch (1998), although it is not possible to convey with words the exact nature of subjective experience, it is possible to convey a *'difference'* between 'subjective experiences' – for example, to distinguish between the colours 'red and orange'. The implication of this is that a conscious experience can perhaps only ever be explained in relation to another conscious experience. Not all researchers find it so easy to close this divide since one of the main problems is the actual location of subjective sensation within the brain, which is still a part of ongoing exploration and investigation. One 'hypothesis is that there are special sets of "conscious" neurons distributed throughout cortex ... and associated systems ... that represent the ultimate neuronal correlate of consciousness (NCC)' (Crick and Koch 2001, 194).[16]

Parallel to the examination of consciousness are advances in computing. For instance, the advanced programming of neural networks leads to an exciting and enhanced potentiality for artificial forms of intelligence. These neural networks are based on an evolutionary model. As David Lodge mentions, 'neural networks are programs which evolve on their own,' imitating the countless connections or synapses between neurons within the brain (2002, 7). Although this interrogation has developed in quite sophisticated ways there remains a lot of work yet to be done in this area. One of the problems is the sheer number of possible neuronal connections in the brain: more 'than there are atoms in the universe' (8).

A study of consciousness has important implications for an analysis of digital practices, not least of which is the centrality of the technology that informs it. For instance, an evolutionary model of neural networks, such as that on which artificial intelligence is based, mirrors the neuronal synapses of the human brain. However, a similar dilemma to the one posed by an aesthetic attempt to theorize the 'unpresentable' or sublime remains evident, since articulating subjective sensation from a neuroscientific perspective continues to be highly problematic.

In positing a premise that can address digital practices, it is my intention to survey both aesthetic and cognitive neuroscientific approaches to perception, since I believe that current critical theorization is deficient in its present form. In assessing a 'neuroesthetic' approach, it is not my intention to find a definitive and determinate biological explanation for how we perceive art and performance. Rather, it is the means of adding to and perhaps supporting aesthetic theories of perception, which resist closure since the digital by its very nature is open to a multilayered system of interpretation. In the following chapters, I will discuss these approaches in more detail together with their implications for performance.

Digital performance

An important trait of the following digital practices is the centrality of non-linguistic modes of signification, since in much of this performance significatory modes are visual, kinetic, gravitational, proximic, aural and so on. The sublime is also central to such an analysis due to the experimental aspects of these works and the accompanying feelings of disquiet produced by a striving to present the unpresentable. These feelings of disquiet relate to Kant's notion of 'negative pleasure'. In discussing the sublime, he writes, 'the sublime does not so much involve positive pleasure as admiration or respect, i.e. merits the name of a *negative pleasure*' [my stress] (1978, 91).

There is also an accentuation on the chthonic[17] or primordial, though this is not a feature shared by all digital practices. Other aesthetic features are heterogeneity, experimentation, indeterminacy, fragmentation, a certain 'shift-shape style' and repetition. Also there is the free use of 'defamiliarizing' devices, such as the juxtaposition of disparate elements, that in creating a distancing effect cause the audience to actively participate in the activity of producing meaning. This insistence on free creativity, invention and experimentation correspond to such Dionysian features as immediacy, disruption and excess (Nietzsche 1956), digital practices becoming what can only be seen as *Gesamtkunstwerke* (collective works of art).

Additional traits are hybridization, pastiche, an exploration of the paradoxical and open-ended nature of reality and a rejection of the notion of an integrated personality in favour of the deconstructed, posthuman subject. There is also an emphasis on montage and collage.

According to Roger Copeland, 'montage, unlike the inherently less manipulative aesthetic of collage, fuses its separate components into a single entity and the resulting juxtaposition ... is imposed upon the viewer ... when the juxtaposition is separated by a gap of space and time, then we begin to enter the world of collage' (2002, 20). The above features together with a range of technologies are emphasized in a variety of ways in different practices. For instance, in live art and performance, motion capture and interactive technologies are prioritized. One such performance would be *Blue Bloodshot Flowers* (Broadhurst, 2001), featuring an 'avatar' called Jeremiah that reacts and interacts with a physical performer and the audience by the means of visual surveillance technology.[18] Jeremiah is programmed with artificial intelligence to a certain extent. Therefore, although he(it) has emotions that react to certain stimuli, he is capable of demonstrating random behaviour that can be fairly disruptive during a performance, adding a further dimension to the experience of working with a virtual body. This aspect of the performance questions traditional notions of origin and identity since Jeremiah's identity is in no way fixed and his origins are dubious.

Another such performance is a work from Merce Cunningham, *BIPED*, initially performed in 1999,[19] where pre-recorded dancing avatars are rear-projected onto a translucent screen, giving the effect of a direct interface between the physical and virtual bodies. Moreover, Cunningham's use of motion capture, in collaboration with Shelley Eshkar and Paul Kaiser, displaces the boundaries of physicality in a fairly radical way. Virtual bodies are generated by physical movement through the mediation of digital technology and the creative input of digital designers. Hand-drawn abstract images and figures by Eshkar, animated by motion-capture data provided by real dancers, are seen together with the live dancers on stage, bringing into question notions of identity formation and deformation.

Similarly, Stelarc combines the physical and virtual, so much so that the virtual becomes an actual extension of the physical, as in his work *Hexapod*, a six-legged walking robot, now developed into the *Muscle Machine* (2003a). Another project, entitled *Movatar* (2000), is an inverse motion capture system which allows an avatar to perform in the physical world by accessing and actuating a host body, thus becoming increasingly autonomous and unpredictable, becoming in fact artificial life. According to Stelarc, 'technology transforms the nature of human existence' (2004a). In Stelarc's performances, as in other digital practices, the body is coupled with a variety of instrumental and technological devices that instead of being separate from the body become part of that body, at the same time altering and recreating its experience in the world.

These performance practices explode the margins between the physical and virtual and what are seen as dominant traditional art practices and innovative technical experimentation. They also share certain aesthetic features, such as innovation, indeterminacy, marginality and an emphasis on the intersemiotic.[20]

Digital sound emphasizes heterogeneity and the experimental. As I have argued elsewhere, 'digital sampling' creates exciting new hybrid styles of music which previous technologies have been unable to do and can be described as being at the 'creative edge of contemporary music'.[21] Real-time interactive performances that utilize digital sound technology are prolific at the present time. One of the reasons for this increase is the development of musical instrument data interface (MIDI) and such programming environments as Max/MSP that have the special advantage of being interactive with visual and network technologies.

A performance group who utilize this sound technology is Optik, whose performances prioritize the use of interactive sound. On 26 October 2001, Optik gave a performance of *An Experiment in Telepresence* in the Karman Theatre in Sao Paulo, Brazil. Open to the public it was scheduled to start at 9 P.M. At the same time a percussionist was in London in a music studio. The local time in London was 12 midnight (2 hours ahead of Sao Paulo). The performance consisted of the contact/impulse-driven movement piece interacting with sound. Images of the performance were sent to London, whilst the sound was directed to Brazil. The performer's movement reacted to the sound as much as the sound interacted with images from the performers, creating a continuous loop of reaction and interaction.

Other digital sounds include the performances of Palindrome, who focus on the interface and interaction between virtual sound and the physical body. The title of their performance *Seine hohle Form* (roughly translated as 'its hollow form') signifies the challenge of creating a musical work that only exists when a dancer moves. The choreography is influenced by the live production of sound through the use of sensors and real-time synthesis, and these movements in turn shape the resulting music. There are no musical cues for the dancers, since without their movements the music is either non-existent or missing key elements (Rovan, Wechsler and Weiss 2001).

Similarly, Troika Ranch aim to create dynamic art works by fusing traditional elements of music, dance and theatre with interactive digital technology. They are pioneers in their use of *MidiDance*, a software created by Mark Coniglio, which can interpret physical movements of performers. As a result that information can be used to manipulate media in a variety of ways, such as the playback of musical notes or phrases and the projection of pre-recorded or live video imagery which then accompanies the physical performer in real time. For them, linking the actions of a performer to the accompanying sound and visual imagery provides a new creative potential for performance.

Digital sound, like other digital technology, brings traditional assumptions of reproduction and representation into question. These performers can be said to be innovative in their attempt to literally 'reproduce' and not 'represent' their disruptive sounds and figurative visual imagery since what is recorded by means of digital technology is a set of instructions for recreating the original performance rather than a transcription of that performance. Therefore, the 'recording' is an original performance; it is literally 'reproduced again' and not 'represented'. This shatters the distinction between 'live' and 'recorded' performance as well as that between 'original' and 'reproduction'.

In film, there is an emphasis on the use of new technologies that can produce a plethora of visual and aural special effects. Although strictly speaking not being experimental in its presentation as are the other digital practices discussed in this book – that is, being mainstream popular entertainment events as opposed to marginal and mainly localized practices – digital film's innovative perspective lies in its design and development of much sophisticated technology that is then later used in live interactive performance. The use of paint box, animation, motion capture and 3-D modelling are central to digital film. Contemporary films that employ such new technologies are notably Andy and Larry Wachowski's *The Matrix* (1999) and its sequels, *The Matrix Reloaded* (2003) and *The Matrix Revolution* (2003); and George Lucas's *Star Wars* prequels: *Episode I: Phantom Menace* (1999), *Episode II: Attack of the Clones* (2002) and *Episode III: Revenge of the Sith* (2005).

The Matrix films are exemplary of the digital with their manipulation of imagery and use of both montage and collage; the chthonic is also strongly referenced. The emphasis is on the desire for a return to the seemingly primordial, the city of Zion, a utopia beyond artificial intelligence ('the matrix') where the organic reigns supreme. The name Zion, of course, also carries biblical connotations. Moreover, according to Samuel Kimball, 'autochthony' (the birth of humans directly from the earth, not by physical means) 'informs the entirety of *The Matrix*'. However for Kimball, there is ambivalence in the mythic reference since the films' storyline 'violently resists' this myth while their 'imagery and techniques recreate' it (2001, 176).

The exterior shots are digitally reworked, particularly the use of colours. For instance, the sky is depicted as being white instead of the brilliant blue of an Australian sky (where the film was shot). Also there is an overt use of green filters in the 'reality' shots, creating a defamiliarizing distancing effect and at same time seducing the spectator with its highly self-referential stylistic features. Another factor in the films' lighting and colour approach is dictated by the use of a special slow-motion photographic technique dubbed 'bullet time' that has the ability to capture both super-slow and high-speed motions at the same time on film – a technique needed to demonstrate Neo's (a.k.a. Thomas Anderson) increasingly skilful manipulation of virtual time and space (Probst 1999, 36).

In George Lucas's *Star Wars* prequels, human actors mingle with digital characters and animatronic models as they wander through the computer-generated and digital matte-painted landscapes of intergalactic cities and planets. Live performance is merged with 2-D and 3-D elements to create complex characters and intricate environments. Notably, the garden planet of Naboo, which is the focus of much of the action, at least in the first two films, together with Coruscant, a polis of high-rise buildings and spaceports; Kamino, a storm-filled watery planet; Mustafar, a tumultuous volcanic world; and many more of the intergalactic settings that are assembled from live-action footage, miniature sets, digital models and background digital paint-box effects.

Lucas's special effects studio with its utilization of such digital tools as Mocap or motion capture, high-definition (HD) cameras, previsualization techniques, Zenviro (camera-mapping tool), blue screen composite imaging, 3-D modelling and animation, matte digital paint and many more, has paved the way for new kinds of film-making. For instance, in *Episode III*, Zenviro was used to create a science fiction environment but it could just as easily simulate a different mixture of reality and fantasy or indeed an actual environment.

According to Robert Romanyshyn, technology allows us to 'increasingly practice a distancing and detached vision' (1989, 117), a way of viewing the world without believing ourselves to be implicated. As J.P. Telotte suggests, computer-generated imagery takes this notion even further by allowing film-makers to '"reproduce" that which has never been "produced", that which has no existence separate from the movies' (2001, 146). Again, Jean Baudrillard believes that new forms of technology and information have become central to a shift from a productive to a reproductive social order in which simulations and models increasingly constitute the world, so that distinctions between the real and appearance are increasingly erased. On this account, this must inevitably lead to the 'hyperreality' of art as it finds only its 'own empty essence' (1988, 187). I am suggesting that digital practices indicate an increased potentiality for new artistic creativity rather than emptiness; instead of a 'scene of nihilism', they indicate a redefinition of 'meaning'.

In biotechnological art and performance practices, technologies – such as those involved with reproduction and genetic engineering – are prominent. The Human Genome Project, a public consortium, and Celera Genomics, a private company, jointly announced a rough draft of the human genome, the human molecular 'blueprint', in 2000. Although it was expected that this would provide a dramatic breakthrough in increasing our understanding of human development, it was quickly realized that in fact the work in understanding the various levels of the genome's operations was just beginning. Since then various debates relating to cloning, ownership of DNA and genetic engineering together with the implications of new plant and animal life forms have appeared increasingly in the public forum. Various new biotechnical artworks (bioart) reflect concerns relating to these recent developments in genomics.

One such artwork is Alba the GFP (green fluorescent protein) Bunny (2000), a genetically engineered rabbit that glows green when illuminated with the correct light. For Eduardo Kac, 'transgenic art ... is a new art form based on the use of genetic engineering techniques to transfer synthetic genes to an organism or to transfer natural genetic material from one species into another, to create unique living beings' (1998). Kac concentrates on exploring the 'fluidity of subject positions in the post-digital age', by means of a combination of 'robotics and networking', 'telepresence', 'biotelematics' and 'transgenics' (Kac 2005a).

Critical Art Ensemble (CAE) are bioartists, who through their 'recombinant theatre', have made technology, wetware [22] and transgenics [23] the focus of their work. Originally they worked with multimedia but since 1996, they have concentrated on responding to the debates surrounding biotechnology. As tactical mediaists the group have presented various interactive performance projects. These projects are underpinned by their concerns with the representation, development and deployment of social policies regarding this technology. One of their works, *Flesh Machine* (1997–8), focuses on eugenics in the discourse and practice of current reproductive technologies, featuring the genetic screening of audience members and the diary of a couple going through in vitro fertilization. Another work, *Society for Reproductive Anachronisms* (1999), engages the audience in dialogue about the problems of medical intervention in reproduction.[24] Their more recent performances, *GenTerra* (2001–5) and *Free Range Grain* (2004), have attempted to critically evaluate and respond to concerns regarding genetic engineering and the creation and release of new life forms into the ecosystem.

Another artist who works with biotechnology is Marta de Menezes, who has for her project *Nature?* (2000) reprogrammed patterns on butterfly wings by injecting the pupa in development. These pattern transformations relate only to the phenotype and not the genotype, thus disappearing at the end of the life cycle. In her work *Functional Portraits* (2002b), she utilizes Functional Magnetic Resonance Imaging (fMRI) to visualize in real time the operation of the brain. In doing so de Menezes attempts to demonstrate the correlation between neuronal activity and the related sensation, thought or action.

Finally, in the digital, the physical and virtual are accentuated and hence, current theory needs to be adjusted to allow for this technical interface and accompanying corporeal prominence. Conventional ways of interpreting performance and art practices have been dominated by the transference of linguistic interpretation to the non-linguistic. This makes the body a secondary phenomenon. However, in many art forms, the body is primary and yet transient (Broadhurst 1999b, 2004b). Unless the immediacy of the body (both physical and virtual) is made the focus of interpretation, such performances as the digital cannot be fully appreciated. It is only by such a broader analysis that a more suitable interpretation of the digital can be achieved which would allow for the prominence of the 'body', however transitory or virtual.

Notes

1. 'Magnetic or optical motion capture has been used widely in performance and art practices for some time now. This involves the application of sensors or markers to the performer or artist's body. The movement of the body is captured and the resulting skeleton has animation applied to it. This data projected image or avatar (Hindu: manifestation of a deity or spirit) then becomes some part of a performance or art practice' (Broadhurst 2002, 159).
2. 'The consensus ... is that AI is about the design of intelligent *agents*. An agent is an entity that can be understood as perceiving and acting on its environment. An agent is rational to the extent that it can be expected to achieve its goals, given the information available from its perceptual processes' (Jordan and Russell 2001, lxxv).
3. See Broadhurst (2002, 2004a).
4. Liminality, from *limen* (Latin: literally threshold) is a term most notably linked to Victor Turner who writes of a no-man's-land betwixt-and-between, a site of a 'fructile chaos ... a storehouse of possibilities, not by any means a random assemblage but a striving after new forms' (Turner 1990, 11–12). My own use

of the term includes certain aesthetic features described by Turner, but emphasizes the corporeal, technological and chthonic (Greek: back to the earth) or primordial. Other quintessential features are heterogeneity, the experimental and the marginalized. Therefore, *liminal* performance can be described as being located at the edge of what is possible (Broadhurst 1999a, 12).

5. 'The term alone suggests a field of study that is pregnant and full of promise. It is a large field of study uniting concepts and techniques from many disciplines ... At the heart of cognitive neuroscience ... lies the fundamental question of knowledge and its representation by the brain ... Cognitive neuroscience is thus a science of information processing ... one can identify key experimental questions ... How is information acquired (sensation), interpreted to confer meaning (perception and recognition), stored or modified (learning and memory) ... and to communicate (language)?' (Albrecht and Neville 2001, li).

6. According to Stephen Priest, the relationship between the 'visible' and 'invisible' is 'one of "intertwining" and "chiasmus". It is an intertwining because the flesh of the world is an inextricable mix of the visible and invisible. It is chiasmic because visible and invisible are an isomorphic reversal of one another' (2003, 10). However, 'chiasm' also refers to the crossover of the optic nerves and Merleau-Ponty makes metonymical use of this term in his discussion of the visible and invisible particularly in 'The Intertwining – The Chiasm', *The Visible and the Invisible* (2000, 130–55).

7. For Merleau-Ponty, 'to perceive is to render oneself present to something through the body. All the while the thing keeps its place within the horizon of the world ... in putting each detail in the perceptual horizons which belong to it. But such formulas are just so many enigmas unless we relate them to the concrete developments which they summarize' (1974b, 226).

8. For Lyotard, signs are not, in their reference and signification, validatable by cognition; instead, they imply that something which should be put into phrases cannot be phrased (1993b, 56).

9. For instance, 'the earth is the primitive, savage unity of desire ... the great unengendered stasis ... the earth is already ... a social machine, a megamachine, that codes the flows of production' (Deleuze and Guattari 1984, 140–2).

10. Colebrook suggests that, in extensive or everyday perception, the world is organized 'into distributed blocks', 'extended objects' that are 'mapped on to a common space' (2002a, 38).

11. For Deleuze and Guattari, 'experimentation has replaced all interpretation'. No longer is there a 'Self' who thinks and recalls; rather, 'there is a glowing fog, a dark yellow mist' that has affects and experiences movement.' It is no longer an organism that functions but a BwO that is constructed' (1999a, 162).

12. A synapse is where neurons make contact with other neurons. See Ramachandran and Blakeslee for a fuller discussion of synapses (1999, 8).

13. According to Kant, since the aesthetic is a result of 'reflective' not 'determinant' reason, when it comes to making aesthetic judgements every example must precede the rule (1978, 35). That is, rules are created on each occasion, which can in no way be determined beforehand. This has exciting consequences for technologically informed as for other experimental performances, since aesthetic judgements need to be revised on each and every occasion, and no set judgement can exist.

14. A neuron has a cell body with a multiplicity of tiny branches called dendrites, which receive information from other neurons. It also has a primary axon for sending data and axon terminals for communication with other cells. Each neuron makes between a thousand and ten thousand synapses with other neurons that can either be excitable or inhibitory (Ramachandran and Blakeslee 1999, 8).

15. In 1953, a paper appeared in *Nature* proposing the double-helical structure for DNA (Deoxyribonucleic Acid). The paper was authored by Francis Crick and James Watson and took the world by storm. The paper suggested a mechanism for explaining how genes are transferred with precision from cell to cell and across generations. However, in recent years, Crick's research has been devoted mainly to the study of consciousness.

16. The neural correlate of consciousness (NCC) generally refers to the correlation between neuronal activity and the sensation, thought or action that relates to that mental activity.

17. Chthonic is a Greek term meaning under the earth.

18. I directed *Blue Bloodshot Flowers* in 2001. It was presented at the 291 Gallery, East London, and involved the direct real-time interaction mainly between a virtual, artificially intelligent performer and a physical performer. However, after the scripted performance, audience members also interacted with the avatar.

19. I attended a performance of *BIPED* at the Barbican Centre, London, in October 2000.

20. A significatory practice which involves such non-linguistic modes as those provided by the semiotics of corporeal gesture: kinetic, visual, aural, haptic, gravitational, proximic and tactile. See Broadhurst (1999a, 1999b, 2002, 2004a, 2004b).

21. For a more detailed discussion see Broadhurst (1999a, ch. 4).

22. A term relating to the interface of digital technology and living biological systems. The origins of the term are unclear but gained widespread usage following Rudy Rucker's novel of the same name (1989).

23. A transgenic is a person, plant or animal whose genetic structure has been altered through introducing other-specie DNA into its genome.

24. CAE created the Society for Reproductive Anachronisms (SRA) in order to have an inexpensive, highly mobile means to speak to the issues raised in *Flesh Machine*.

2
Selective Aesthetic Approaches

In surveying the following contemporary aesthetic theorization my aim is to provide interpretive strategies that would be capable of addressing sophisticated technological art practices. It is my belief that Lyotard, Merleau-Ponty, Deleuze and Derrida, although varied in their approach, have much to contribute to such an analysis.

Merleau-Ponty

> Vision is not the metamorphosis of things themselves into the sight of them; it is not a matter of things' belonging simultaneously to the huge, real world and the small, private world. It is a thinking that deciphers strictly the signs given within the body.
>
> (Merleau-Ponty 1974a, 292)

Much critical theorization in recent times has focused on the body and much of this emphasis has been directly attributable to the work of Maurice Merleau-Ponty. As Horst Ruthrof argues, by shifting the perspective from Husserl's phenomenology of idealization to the 'primacy' and 'phenomenology of perception', Ruthrof instituted the 'corporeal turn' so crucial to contemporary theory and practice (1997, vii). This theoretical emphasis on the corpus is important since within the following digital practices the body, both physical and virtual, is pivotal.

For Merleau-Ponty, the 'perceiving mind is an incarnated mind' and perception is not simply the result of the external world on the body: 'what recent psychologists have come to formulate: the lived perspective, that which we actually perceive, is not a geometric or photographic one' (1964, 14). There is no perception in general; there is only perception as it is 'lived' in the world. As a result, the perceiving subject is always

19

changing, always going through a process of rebirth; 'my body *obeys* the pregnancy ... flesh responding to flesh ... This definition of pregnancy as implying motivity ... a sense by transcendence' (Merleau-Ponty 2000, 209). Digital practices such as Stelarc's performances amply demonstrate this since he shows 'to be a body is to be tied to a certain world' (Merleau-Ponty 1962, 148).

Replacing objective notions of embodiment by embodied experience allows Merleau-Ponty to go beyond the limited subject/object ontology not by returning to a reductionist dualism of binary oppositions, which would simply prioritize one term over another, but rather by attempting to understand the interplay of the biological and physical, 'the inside and outside'. Merleau-Ponty asks us to reflect on the consciousness of lived experience: 'Consciousness ... is not a matter of 'I think that' but "I can"' (1962, 137). The body is seen not as an objectifiable entity, instead, 'I am not in front of my body, I am in it, rather I am it'. The body interprets itself and it is to be 'compared, not to a physical object, but rather to a work of art ... It is a focal point of living meanings' (Merleau-Ponty 1962, 150–1). Here, Merleau-Ponty is suggesting that perception is not only intertwined with the scientific and rationalistic but also with the 'aesthetological', the 'mute' artistic, the 'primordial' (1974b, 209). An instance of this is provided by bioart practices where 'we are witnessing the birth of a new form of art: art created in test-tubes' (De Menezes 2005c).

If the body is also seen as an intertwining of movement and vision then 'we cannot imagine how a *mind* could paint; it is by lending his body to the world that the artist changes the world' (1974a, 283). Exemplary of this is the physicality and independent decision-making process of Optik's individual performers within that performance practice which for director Barry Edwards provides a way into the 'exploration of consciousness' (1999, 193).

According to Merleau-Ponty the senses translate each other and are mutually and immediately comprehensible without the intervention of idea or concept (1962, 253), leading to a synaesthetic perception of the world.[1] Binocular sight in a similar way becomes monocular providing a 'synthesis' of stereoscopic vision (233). Touch is emphasized since it is important to our perception of colour which is itself dependent on our ability to distinguish textured areas, 'a thing would not have this colour had it not also this shape, these tactile properties' (319).

In Merleau-Ponty's later writings, 'Eye and Mind' (1974a) and *The Visible and The Invisible* (2000), he emphasizes the 'flesh of the world' rather than a lived perceiving body (2000, 248). 'Flesh', a concept that 'has no name in any philosophy'(147), is a quintessential term for

Merleau-Ponty.[2] It denotes a position, which is both subject and object and simultaneously a subjectivity that is 'divergent' from itself, in short, an inscription of pure difference (249). Flesh also refers to a notion of 'reversibility' which refers to the body's ability to act as a perceiving subject and at the same time to be an object of perception. For instance, the handshake is reversible since, 'I can feel myself touched as well and at the same time as touching' (149).

Merleau-Ponty posits the notion of 'massive flesh' as being incapable of rational thought or conceptualization but is rather a pre-subjective, pre-discursive, elemental body,[3] which exists before 'I' am there:

> My personal existence must be the resumption of a prepersonal tradition. There is, therefore, another subject beneath me, for whom a world exists before I am here, and who marks out my place in it.
> (Merleau-Ponty 1962, 254)

Merleau-Ponty distinguishes between the 'lived' body or 'I' body from the objective body. He argues that the lived body is made of an elaborate network and contexts that make up the perceptual field whereas the objective body is merely a biological entity. The former is a cultural identity produced by perception. The latter being an object which offers itself up to biology. However, flesh in itself is implicated in both: 'Is my body a thing, is it an idea? It is neither, being the measurement of the things' (Merleau-Ponty, 2000, 152).

For Merleau-Ponty, the body is a system of possible actions. When we point to an object, we refer to that object not as an object represented but as a specific thing towards which we 'project' ourselves (1962, 138), in fact a 'virtual body' with its phenomenal 'place' defined by task and location (25). This emphasis on a virtual body has resonance with and points to a deconstruction of the physical/virtual body of digital practices, a body of potential creativity. This theorization provides useful tools in exploring the interface between the physical and virtual so integral to such digital practices as the *Star Wars* prequels (1999–2005) where the relationship between both could perhaps be seen as one of invention and potentiality.

Merleau-Ponty was heavily influenced by the psychoanalytical theory of Jacques Lacan in his analysis of the visual self. Lacan in turn appropriated Merleau-Ponty's chiasmic ontology of the visible and invisible, renaming them in terms of the 'the eye' and 'the gaze' (Jay 1993, 353). The intertwining and chiasm (metonymically referring to the optical chiasma – that is, the crossover of the optic nerves) of body, experience and preconception work together in the act of perceiving. According to Martin Jay, 'we are always in the middle of a multilayered process ... best understood as chiasmus' (319).

As a development of his previous post-Cartesian phenomenological approach in *The Structure of Behavior* (1963) and *Phenomenology of Perception* (1962), Merleau-Ponty's later work indicates that perception is not an intentional act but rather simply a being in the world or a 'being at' in the world, 'the seeing and the visible, the touching and the touchable ... is not an act, it is a being at ... the reflexivity of the body, the fact that it touches itself touching, sees itself seeing ... does not go beyond a sort of *imminence*, it terminates in the invisible' (Merleau-Ponty 2000, 249).

For Merleau-Ponty, visibility always involves non-visibility, 'when I say then that every visible is invisible ... this must not be understood in the sense of a *contradiction* ... it is the visibility itself that involves a non-visibility' (Merleau-Ponty 2000, 247). Invisibility is not the inverse of visibility since that would lead to only an 'objective' absence. According to Merleau-Ponty, 'when we speak of the flesh of the visible, we do not mean to do anthropology, to describe a world, covered over with all our own projections'. Instead, what is meant is a carnal being of 'several leaves or faces' (136). However, the invisible is what consciousness does not see. It is not 'for reasons of principle' that it is not seen. Rather, it is because it is consciousness it does not see and what it does not see is the act of perceiving in its 'corporeity' and 'flesh wherein the *object* is born' (248).[4]

In another seemingly fundamental development or even shift from his earlier theorization, Merleau-Ponty explores the interaction of language and perception. Although the primacy of signification had always been the focus of his work, language itself is now emphasized. Merleau-Ponty was notably influenced by the linguistic work of de Saussure, placing emphasis on the concept of parole rather than langue, on speech enactments rather than the system of language itself. Language was seen crucially as the 'living present' in speech (Lechte 1994, 31). Although art has the power to evoke primordial perceptual experience, its 'mute "thinking" sometimes leaves us with the impression of a vain swirl of significations' that refute meaning (Merleau-Ponty 1974a, 310). Language on the other hand lifts the 'veil' of meaning not by a sum of statements but as 'a verbal chain woven', as an endless chain of signification (Merleau-Ponty 2000, 199). In a sense, 'language is everything, since it is the voice of no one, since it the very voice of the things, the waves, and the forests' (155). The exact relationship between speech and vision is not clearly defined and remains fairly elusive. According to Merleau-Ponty, silent or mute vision in becoming speech and speech in turn conveying meaning 'inscribes' the invisible into the visible by virtue of reversibility, which supports both vision and speech eventuating in 'an almost carnal existence of the idea' (155–6). As with the visible and invisible, the 'mute' and language are seemingly not mutually exclusive; for just as perception needs language to be expressed, language requires the pre-discursive to bring it into existence in the first place.[5]

Merleau-Ponty's theorization on the visible and invisible together with his notion of flesh provides useful tools in exploring the interface between the physical and virtual so integral to the digital. Of particular relevance is his emphasis on intertwining and chiasm; divergence and reversibility; the focus on the 'lived' perceptual body, especially the tactile and kinaesthetic; together with the primordial and pre-discursive (chthonic). Instead of either the physical or the virtual being prioritized in much of this performance, the relationship between both could perhaps be seen as an intertwining, an instance of 'massive flesh' with all that term implies, a system of inventiveness and 'possible actions'.

For Merleau-Ponty, instrumentation is mutually implicated with the body in an epistemological sense. The body adapts and extends itself through external instruments. Giving the example of a blind man's stick, he claims that the stick ceases to be an object for the man. Instead it extends the scope of the tactile, providing a parallel to sight. The stick becomes not merely a medium to locate the position of things but rather an extension of the man's own reach. To have experience, to get used to an instrument is to incorporate that instrument into the body. 'Habit expresses our power of dilating our being in the world, or changing our existence by appropriating fresh instruments' (Merleau-Ponty 1962, 143). Habit is neither intellectual nor an involuntary action but the body as 'mediator of a world'. The experience of the corporal schema is not fixed or delimited but extendable to the various tools and technologies which may be embodied. Our bodies are always open to and intertwined with the world. Instruments appropriated by embodied experience become part of that altered body experience in the world. In this way, 'the body is our general medium for having a world' (146). An example of this is found in Palindrome's performance *Seine hohle Form* (2000) where the performer has a crucial role in creating the media and that media then becomes part of the performance.

Technology then would imply a reconfiguration of our embodied experience. For instance, in Troika Ranch's performances, the MidiDancer, which allows the gesture of a performer to be 'amplified and translated' into an alternative medium, implies such a reconfiguration. When the meaning aimed at cannot be reached by the body alone, it builds its own instruments and projects around itself a mediated world (Merleau-Ponty 1962, 146). Rather than being separate from the body, technology becomes part of that body and alters and recreates our experience in the world. This intertwining of body, technology and world is crucial in an analysis of digital practices. Rather than the abandonment or subjugation of the physical body with the introduction of technology into performance, I would suggest that technology and instrumentation extend the body by altering and recreating its embodied experience. The body in turn creates new technologies and instrumentation to bring potential creativity and mediation into its corporeal world.

Lyotard

> What do we want of art today? ... Well for it to experiment ... what do we want of philosophy? To analyze these experimentations ... to reflect according to opacity.
>
> (Lyotard 1989d, 193)

For Lyotard, a certain form of art because it is not formed in terms of established social organizations practices a critical politics that no other political activity has succeeded in practicing. In discussing the relationship between aesthetics and politics, Lyotard states that: 'we have to deal with an entire problematic which in a certain sense remains 'aesthetic'. This no longer refers to the aesthetic of the beautiful ... but rather to an aesthetic of the sublime' (Lyotard 1988b, 298). Warning against the complete aestheticization of the political, Lyotard claims that, 'it would be desirable to rethink the political' from other than the belief of 'doing good'. Rather to 'begin from the Kant of the second *Critique* or from Levinas ... That would allow at least ... the avoidance of politics in terms of fabrication and fashion' (299). Aesthetic ideals do not replace political ideals but a certain form of art serves to deconstruct certain kinds of traditional thinking. Digital practices, in a similar way, deconstruct certain traditional assumptions.

Art, then, has a double status, in order to fulfill its critical function as art, Lyotard demands that it must be art and anti-art at the same time. Critical discourse is a derivative of art and must consequently develop the tools and concepts, which have originated in art. Therefore, the aesthetic precedes the critical. This critical activity together with a continual search for and reinvention of the rules of games and of the possibility of a political approach that resists all attempts to reduce, resolve, regulate or repress heterogeneity, is further attested to by what Lyotard calls the 'differend'.[6]

For Lyotard then, the ultimate task of a critical arts practice is to present the unpresentable, to present the fact that the unpresentable exists and that it concerns our future. Therefore, '"our" destination ... is to supply a presentation for the unpresentable, and therefore, in regard to Ideas, to exceed everything that can be presented' (Lyotard 1988a, 166). The unpresentable or 'sublime' for Lyotard, is seen as a response to art deprived of rules and limits (1986a, 8). This can also be said to correspond to the digital where artistic rules are likewise 'dissolved' and disseminated. *Blue Bloodshot Flowers* (2001), which centred on the real-time interaction between a physical and virtual performer, was such an attempt 'to exceed everything that can be presented', as also are the performances of Troika Ranch and Palindrome amongst many others.

This 'joyful sublime', as 'a contradictory feeling ... of both pleasure and displeasure', allows us to confront the new techno sciences by concerning itself with such things as the unrepresentability of technology and the indefinability of the multinational corporations (Lyotard 1986b, 10), together with technology's very real links to the military establishment. According to Lyotard:

> The spirit of the times is definitely geared to what is pleasing, and the task of art remains that of the immanent sublime, that of alluding to an unpresentable which has nothing edifying about it, but which is inscribed in the infinity of the transformation of 'realities'.
>
> (1993a, 128)

Central to Lyotard's philosophical endeavour is the relationship between art and critical discourse and how art offers critical perspectives on discursive systems. In *Discours, figure* (1971), Lyotard defends the perceived world against the dominance of language. In his opening argument, he claims that the 'given' is not a 'text' and that there is within it a 'constitutive difference', which is to not to be 'read' but to be 'seen'. And this difference and the 'immobile mobility' that reveals it, is continuously being forgotten in the 'process of signification' (9).

Lyotard posits two radically different territories, one of communication and discourse and the other of form, colour and the visual. One being determined by linguistic-philosophical closure and the other, the 'figural', being indeterminate and 'disruptive of discursive systems and destructive of signification in general, a radical exteriority to discourse, what discourse is unable to say' (Carroll 1987, 30). Instead of a conceptual interpretation of meaning there are flows and drives of 'intensities' which continually displace the identity of the reader (or spectator). The aim is to eliminate oppositions in favour of intensities and it is useful in a description of such digital practices as Stelarc's *Fractal Flesh* and *Ping Body* (1995–8), Troika Ranch's digitally interactive dance theatre, and the *Star Wars* prequels, where their diverse elements often escape meaningful interpretation. According to Lyotard, 'the aim was the elimination of the game of good/evil in favour of that of intensities' and more provocatively, even the 'event is construed as intensity' (Lyotard 1988b, 277).

For Lyotard, the figural is not the figuration of representational art but is instead the visual elements that create illusive but evocative phenomena, which need not necessarily, translate as representation or meanings. In his description of the figural as the *'l'inconscient renversé* (unconscious overturned)', he emphasizes the unconscious processes and traces that are revealed in dreams and parapraxis (slips of the tongue and so on) not as themselves but in altered forms (Turim 1984, 95). Lyotard distinguishes between the 'figure-image', which violates the perceptual recognition of the outlines of objects, for example, in Cubism; the 'figure-forme' that disrupts the space of visibility itself in which such outlines might be recognized, for example, abstract expressionism; and finally, the 'figure-matrix' that is neither visible nor readable but is pure difference itself (Lyotard 1971, 279).

Lyotard in the opening section of *Discours, figure* is clearly indebted to Merleau-Ponty's attempt to move beyond the Cartesian metaphysical subject/object divide, not by a process of dialectics but by going beneath this dualism to uncover what in 'our mute life ... that compound of the world and ourselves which precedes reflection' is 'reduced to our idealizations and syntax' (Merleau-Ponty 2000, 102). However, Lyotard ultimately criticizes Merleau-Ponty for his refusal to engage with such artists as Duchamps and Cubists, whilst valorizing the work of Cézanne.[7] For Lyotard, there is the added aversion to an attempted restitution of a primordial state anterior to the mind/body divide together with the perceived 'nostalgia for any *voyure* anterior to the chiasm'. Instead of such a reconciliation, Lyotard calls for a 'deconciliation', with the figural being not tied to the 'visible' but to the 'Id of desire', and not the 'figural of desire but to its operations' (Jay 1993, 566).[8]

In *Discours, figure* there is a premise of '"an unsuppressible gap" between the sensible and intelligible', which 'is expressed in terms of the "letter" and the "line", between a graphic and figural space' (Dews 1984, 43). Although for Lyotard, 'the letter is threatened, invaded by the line' (1989e, 48); rather, than merely presenting a simple opposition to discourse, the figural indicates heterogeneity and a disruption of discourse that disallows any systematics of full cohesion.[9] He writes, 'I did not try in *Discours, figure* to oppose language and image. I was suggesting that a (discursive) principle of readability and a (figural) principle of unreadability shared one in the other' (Lyotard 1984, 17).

Lyotard, in his approach, is critical of both phenomenological and structuralist approaches to meaning whilst continuing to utilize their theoretical tools. For Lyotard, the phenomenological project is 'fundamentally contradictory' in its effort to capture a pre-linguistic world due to its designation of a 'pre-logical signified' which in being itself is forever incomplete, as it is dialectically referred back from being to meaning by way of 'intentional analysis' (1971, 44). Whilst in structuralism, any sense of the referential dimension of language is omitted in its understanding of language as a closed system of signifiers representing signifieds. For Lyotard there remains the question of how the almost visual property of language can be explained in this closed 'system of langue' (32).[10]

For Lyotard, libidinal economy is premised on the notion that individuals are connected to each other, objects and even the sociopolitical by forces of desire, its impetus being intensities and drives, rather than signification. This approach provides a critique of the way that such drives are mobilized within capitalist structures for profit whilst at the same time preserving images of individuality and organic togetherness. This emphasis on a libidinal force of desire, which is pure 'difference itself', seriously countermands Lacan's argument of an unconscious structured as language. According to Lyotard, in 'The Dream-Work Does Not Think', Lacan identifies metaphor with the Freudian notion of 'condensation' and metonymy with 'displacement' (Lyotard 1989e). However, for Lyotard, there is a certain futility in bringing everything back to the linguistic 'as the model for all semiology', when it is 'clear that language, at least in its poetic usage, is possessed ... by the figure' (30).

The figural for Lyotard is not that of representational art but is instead concerned with innovation, experimentation and ambiguity and it is important since it mirrors many digital practices such as the performances of Optik, Troika Ranch's *The Future of Memory* (2003) and films such as *The Matrix* trilogy (1999–2003), situating these performances firmly within the context of a libidinal economy. In a satirical aside, Lyotard claims that, 'if we have religious souls like Freud and Lacan, we produce the image of a grand signifier forever completely absent – the image of a grand zero ... whose obviously unpronounceable name will be translated in a libidinal economy by that of Kastrator' (1989f, 2).

A libidinal economy is central to the belief that 'industrial and postindustrial technosciences ... implies the meticulous programming, of beautiful images'. In fact, these images are not only beautiful, but 'too beautiful', not as an indeterminate sentiment but rather as the result of 'the infinite realization of the sciences, technology and capitalism' (Lyotard 1993a, 122). As too are the images of such digital practices as de Menezes's *Nature?* (2000), where the complex and colourful patterns on butterfly' wings are reprogrammed by microsurgical modification.

Lyotard, in writing about experimental cinema, coins the term 'Acinema', to describe strategies of 'mobility' and 'immobility', which in contrast to traditional representational cinema that 'acts as the orthopedic mirror analyzed by Lacan', destroys the illusion of unity and coherence (1989a, 176). 'Excessive movement' which defamiliarizes in a non-recuperative way (172), creates 'lyric abstractions' (177). Metaphorically using the image of pyrotechnics to illustrate this strategy, Lyotard presents a pleasure derived from drives and intensities that is non-utilitarian and non-productive. Influenced by Freud's *Beyond the Pleasure Principle*, Lyotard points to such a pleasure as a joining together of life and death instincts (171).

In contrast, immobility produces films which Lyotard likens to 'tableaux vivants'. This cinema defamiliarizes by a lack of movement, fixing a frame for a longer time than normal, it causes the spectator to be aware of that image which itself can be abstract and difficult to interpret, giving rise to 'the most intense agitation' (177–8). The use of mobility and immobility as a strategy has a certain resonance in some digital practices. For instance, in *The Matrix* trilogy, the use of a special slow-motion photographic technique has the ability to capture both super-slow and high-speed motions at the same time on film, a technique needed to demonstrate Neo's increasingly skilful manipulation of virtual time and space.

Lyotard's emphasis on figure, discourse and libidinal economy has been gradually displaced by his theorization on the differend. The sublime now centring on a linguistic model whose main premise is the incommensurability of phrase regimes; 'symbolization, then, does not occur here through a substitution of object, but through permutations of instances in the respective phrase universes, and without recourse to a direct presentation' (Lyotard 1988a, 132–66). In *The Differend*, Lyotard makes some explicit semiotic reference only in a brief sentence where he argues that, 'a wink, a shrugging of the shoulder ... can be phrases' (70). It is my belief that this shift in theorization is ultimately restrictive due to its emphasis on the linguistic; since for many art practices, such as the digital, an analysis is needed that can go *beyond* but also include language.

Lyotard's theorization on figure, discourse and libidinal economy together with his writings on industrial and post-industrial technosciences, and experimentation in the arts are valuable in an analysis of digital practices. The figural, as not the figuration of representational art but instead of creativity and elusiveness, is important since this mirrors many of the practices of the digital, placing the performances within the context of a libidinal economy. Equally, Lyotard's analysis of a 'nihilism of convened, conventional movements' (Lyotard 1989a, 167) and his emphasis on post-industrial technoscience relates to the aesthetics of digital practices.

Derrida

> The live transmission, no matter how direct it "technically" appears, is immediately caught in a web of all kinds of intervention. It is framed, cut, it begins here, is interrupted there ... As soon as we know, "believe we know" ... the field of perception and of experience in general is profoundly transformed.
>
> (Derrida and Stiegler 2002, 40)

> I don't know what perception is and I don't believe anything like perception exists ... I believe that perception is interdependent with the concept of origin and of centre.
>
> (Derrida 1972, 272)

Derrida describes machines that 'sound out' rather than see, via echoes and waves. They operate 'anoptically' – that is, without seeing, through a blind transcription of 'coded' signals, searching into the darkness where objects are sounded out rather than illuminated, 'instruments ... that sound out ... that allows one to know ... where one no longer sees ... the *scanner's* computer blindly transcribing the coded signals of the photoelectrical cells' (Derrida 1993, 32). In a similar way the algorithmic coded information from motion sensors from such performances as Palindrome, Troika Ranch and Cunninghams *BIPED* (2000a) 'track' instead of see.

Derrida in his theoretical enterprise is not attempting to construct a 'new' aesthetics or provide an alternate theory of art. Rather, he is concerned with how art resists even its own theorization and for this reason he attempts through various strategies to push the question of art beyond itself and its representation. His questioning of art together with its theory, takes the form of a critical dialogue with the major philosophies of art. According to Derrida, how can philosophy be taken seriously if it can be undermined by such 'low' forms of art and literature as that of Genet? Or as he puts it more succinctly, 'how could ontology lay hold of a fart?' (1986, 58), thereby also demonstrating Derrida's refusal to prioritize any of the senses (visual, aural, tactile, olfactory) and instead he emphasizes their interconnectedness as does digital practices.

In a direct attack on phenomenology, particularly on Husserl, Derrida claims that

> As soon as we admit this continuity of the now and not-now, perception and non-perception, in the zone of primordiality ... we admit the other into the self-identity of the *Augenblick*; non-presence and non-evidence are admitted in the *blink of the instance*. There is a duration to the blink, and it closes the eye.
>
> (Derrida 1973, 65)

For Derrida, the 'primacy of perception' so central to phenomenology suggests the possibility of immediacy, which privileges presence at the same time forgetting the contamination of perception by its intertwining with language. Not only is presence privileged in visual perception but also in aurality. Since, 'this inwardness of life with itself, which has always made us say that speech [*parole*] is alive, supposes, then that the speaking subject hears himself [*s'entende*] in the present' (78). Derrida's intention is not only to challenge phenomenology but conventional Western philosophy as a whole with its 'metaphysics of presence'. It is Derrida's belief that Husserl along with other philosophers depends on a theory of presence. There is the assumption that pure expression can be present in an unmediated and therefore certain way. This is also the view of many artists and performers, including Critical Art Ensemble, in their discussion on 'pedagogy' where they believe that 'performance, spectacle and *presence*' is required (2000b, 144). However, Derrida denies this possibility with its belief in a single definable moment and in doing so he questions the foundation and grounding of traditional philosophy.

One of Derrida's main concerns is that the assumption of presence has given primacy to speech over writing. In this way the voice is regarded as evidence of immediate full presence whilst writing is delegated to a secondary transcript of speech. Derrida insists that his position on writing (*écriture*) is not a defence of that term in the traditional sense. He argues

> What is being pursued ... is a certain displacement of writing, a systematic transformation and generalization of its 'concept'. The old opposition between speech and writing no longer has any pertinence as a way of testing a text that deliberately deconstructs that opposition. Such a text is no more 'spoken' than it is 'written', no more *against* speech that *for* writing, in the metaphysical sense of these words.
>
> (Derrida 1981a, 181)

'Writing' does not refer to the empirical process of writing but rather to the structure of writing, which is always inhabited by the 'trace'. For Derrida, the trace is 'the *pure* movement which produces difference ... It does not depend on any sensible plenitude, audible or visible, phonic or graphic. It is, on the contrary, the condition of such a plenitude' (1976, 62).

Within metaphysics, the difference between two terms is perceived from the perspective of one of the terms, the term of plenitude from which the second term is held to derive. The first term is not recognized as appearing in opposition to another lesser term. The problematic of the trace articulates the recognition of that privileged term in a difference of opposition that could not appear as such without the opposition that gives it form. Therefore, the trace explains why a concept of plenitude of presence can be thought only within binary conceptual structures. For example, in placing AI at its centre, *The Matrix* (1999) demonstrates literally that there can never be presence without absence; since within its narrative artificial intelligence technology is initially prioritized over human intelligence yet the AI was created by humans. As the plotline continues, the organic in the form of Neo subverts and replaces the centre (AI) at the same time remaining contaminated by its technology.

Deconstruction is central to most digital practices, yet has been accused by many of being a self-defeating method since it can transgress metaphysics only by continuing to speak the language of that tradition. Therefore, the necessity of utilizing the resources from what is to be deconstructed is the very condition in which deconstruction can successfully intervene in the discourse of metaphysics. As Derrida argues, 'we cannot give up this metaphysical complicity without also giving up the critique we are directing against this complicity' (1978a, 281).

This is important for the digital since much of it appears to be complicit with what it seeks to deconstruct. This apparent complicity with dominant means of digital representation whilst trying to destabilize identity, underpins areas of concern regarding the commodification and consumerism of technology since much of it is provided by multinational corporations. For instance, Stelarc is viewed by many as being a strong advocate for an optimistic post-human future. However, whilst appearing to be complicit with dominant means of digital representation, Stelarc's performance attempts at the same time to destabilize those structures by identifying concerns that affect us all. Similarly, artists Oron Catts and Zurr from TCA believe their 'role is to reveal inconsistencies in regard to our current attitudes to life' and draw attention to inconsistencies between 'our Western cultural perceptions and the new techno scientific understanding about life' (2003). However, as with other bioartists, by manipulating life forms, there is always the risk of them being seen to be complicit with the same biotechnological knowledge and techniques that they seek to expose.

Deconstruction does not engage in the annulment or neutralization of opposites; rather, it aims at foregrounding the asymmetrical nature of its object of enquiry such as philosophy. Derrida insists that 'in a classical philosophical opposition we are not dealing with peaceful coexistence of a *vis à vis*, but rather with a violent hierarchy' (1981b, 41). Rodolphe Gasché stresses the double nature of Derrida's deconstruction in order to distinguish it from 'deconstruction-as-criticism' and to differentiate between Derrida's notion of writing and the normal 'everyday sense' of the term.[11]

According to Derrida, the fictions of plenitude and oppositions can only be thought because they both contain traces of the other and thus are always already contaminated. Therefore, the purity of a concept is merely a fiction. The general structure of reference as trace accounts for the fact that all concepts appear in opposition to other concepts and are formed by the difference in which they appear (Derrida 1976, 62). In this way, speech is as much contaminated by writing as writing is by speech. Speech can no more provide an unmediated truth about being anymore than writing can. This privileging of the voice in metaphysics is known as 'phonocentrism'. Derrida also uses the term 'logocentrism' as a replacement for metaphysics, pointing to Western philosophy's reliance on an essence, a foundational truth, which seeks full plenitude in the relation of a 'transcendental signifier' to a 'transcendental signified'; that is, a *logos* such as the Word, God, Matter or Idea.

An artist and writer who sought to evade phonocentrism was Antonin Artaud. As Derrida writes, Artaud's theatrical writing is a '*writing* of the body itself' (1978a, 191) and also a critique of the logocentrism of

Western society.[12] In his essay, 'The Theatre of Cruelty and the Closure of Representation' (1978a), Derrida enacts a complex dialogue with Artaud's writing, culminating in a demonstration of its inherent contradictions. Artaud was opposed to the logocentrism of theatre with its belief in the possibility of a full and perfect embodiment of thought in language.[13] According to Derrida, '*Artaud wanted to erase repetition in general*' (245), and was searching for a theatre of 'pure presence as pure difference ... a present which does not repeat itself' (247–8). Derrida argues that Artaud's theatre of cruelty is an impossibility (of which Artaud was himself, seemingly very much aware). For no matter how spontaneous or immediate any act of theatre might seem it must always to a certain degree involve repetition. Derrida concludes that in attempting to find the primitive essence of theatre, Artaud is faced only with difference and the fact that theatre can only ever be a mimesis, a representation or a fiction, by virtue of it remaining theatre. Although Artaud's theoretical postulations relate in many ways to digital practices, particularly in his notions of immediacy, fragmentation and indeterminacy, together with his accentuation of the non-verbal, his emphasis on a certain essentialism together with his belief in an unchanging, fixed nature of relations is irreconcilable with the aesthetic features of the digital.

For Derrida, the notion of difference means not only to differ but also to defer. To encompass both meanings, the quasi-concept 'differance' was coined. This theoretical development was also a response to Ferdinand de Saussure and structuralists, such as Claude Lévi-Strauss, for whom writing was again believed to be secondary to speech and even a deformation of language itself. A distinction interrogated by Derrida who noted that de Saussure et al. had utilized a notion of idiomatic writing that attempted to deny all complexities, writing being seen as a merely' graphic device that supported speech. Differance is not simply deferring because an act of delay does not necessarily entail a movement of difference. Therefore, together with deferring, differance implies difference; at the same time Derrida's concern with phonocentrism is highlighted since differance although sounding identical to difference, when spoken, is not the same when written (in French the verb *différer* means to both differ and defer). A strategy in keeping with Derrida's emphasis that speech has no more relation to an immediate presence than writing does.

Differance is used by Derrida in order to provide a critique of the notion of differentiation and it is also an 'undecidable', a quasi-concept that 'grounds' philosophical contradictions, aporias and inconsistencies. It is the non-unitary ground for all possible kinds of differentiation, differing and deferring.[14] By insisting on the difference among differences, Derrida avoids resolving them in a logical unity thereby, promoting the plurality of difference, of discordance, that culminates not in contradiction but remains a contradiction without eventual dissolution.

Other undecidables are 'The supplement', which 'occupies the middle point between total absence and total presence' (1976, 150–7); 'Iterability' which marks the relation between repetition and alteration and so acts as a critique of pure identity, displacement is implied as it 'alters, something new takes place' (Derrida 1977, 173–5); and 'Re-mark' that contains the necessity of repetition and cuts across other undecidables. It suggests everything is marked, forever leaving new traces and supplements on signification. Every concept always carries a mark with it that can be followed and that also identifies it as belonging to something else (Derrida 1981a, 265).[15]

Undecidables are important in a theorization of digital practices since they help to explain how identity can never be fully established, how new genres are formed and how unstable these formations are. This is because in any rigorous analysis of an origin, there is found only 'difference', 'supplement', 'margin', and 'trace'. For instance, Cunningham's *BIPED* (2000a) with its interface and interaction between physical and virtual bodies, can be seen to displace fixed categories of identity. In the performance each carries a 'trace' of the other, given that the virtual performers are the digital reincarnation of the human bodies. Any search for an ultimate origin is frustrated. In fact, the origin merely reveals itself as yet another signifier for a further chain of signification, a signification that always involves dispersion and dissemination, without origin and without end. According to Derrida:

> What interests me is this re-mark ... is absolutely necessary for and constitutive of what we call art, poetry or literature. It underwrites the eruption of *techné* which is never long in coming ... Can one identify a work of art ... especially a work of discursive art, if it does not bear the mark of a genre.
>
> (1980, 211)

For Derrida, writing is always inhabited by *techné*, 'it is difficult to avoid the mechanist, technicist and teleological language at the very moment when it is precisely a question of retrieving the origin and the possibility of movement, of the machine, of the *techné* of orientation in general. In fact ... it is essentially impossible' (1991, 48).

This can be compared to Heidegger's claim that in contrast to technical language, which never questions its 'identity' ('mathematics is not more rigorous than historiology, but only narrower' (1978, 195)), poetic language is continually questioning human destiny and human being (1971, 74). Heidegger, it can be seen, does very clearly differentiate between technical and non-technical language. Just as he writes of an 'era of technicity', the era of the 'Gestell' (usually translated as 'enframing' or 'scaffolding'). The modern *techné*, in contrast to the original Greek meaning of the term that was a poetic and revealing art (1977, 27), causes us to refute the revelation that art can bring us. For Heidegger, in attempting to overcome this alienation and assure 'our redemption', art and technology must be reintegrated (1977, 35).

Derrida interrogates art in terms of its borders and the effects on it of forces coming from 'outside' its borders. Effects that interfere with its integrity, self-knowledge and representation. Derrida considers the notion of a fixed border to be a sign of critical dogmatism, 'from Plato to Hegel, to Husserl and Heidegger. This requirement presupposes a discourse on the limit between the inside, and outside of the art object, here a *discourse on the frame*. Where is it to be found?' (Derrida 1987, 45). In short, for Derrida, there can be no clearly defined 'technical language', anymore than there can be any language not contaminated by technicity. He writes,

> The way in which I tried to define writing implied that it was already … a teletechnology, with all that this entails of an original expropriation … this specificity does not … substitute, the prosthesis, teletechnology, etc., for immediate or natural speech. These machines have always been there … even when we wrote by hand, even during so-called live conversation.
>
> (Derrida 2002, 37–8)

In a similar way, a 'live' image broadcast on a television channel can never be uncontaminated by its 'censor, frame, filter' (40). 'And yet the greatest compatibility … seems to be asserting itself, *today*, what appears to be most alive … and the differance or delay, the time it takes to exploit, broadcast, or distribute it' (38). Since what is produced 'live' by this technology is '*produced before being transmitted*' (40). And no matter how direct it 'technically' might appear, it is the result of various kinds of interventions. The live or direct is never intact.

In a similar way, a 'live' image digitally broadcast on a television as with Optik's *In the Presence of People* (2000), relayed to another monitor in a different location, can never be uncontaminated since what is produced live by this technology is *'produced before being transmitted'*. And no matter how immediate or direct it 'technically' might appear, it is the result of various kinds of intervention. However, knowing or believing that the 'live or direct' is possible, is enough to transform 'the field of perception and experience in general' (Derrida 2002, 40).

Derrida's theory of metaphor is also important in an analysis of the digital, because it points to Western philosophies as our mythologies; that is, our unacknowledged metaphorical texts.[16] Since Derrida deconstructs metaphor, he is able not only to introduce its opposite, the proper or literal, but also to move to the more general level of metaphoricity as a structure that accounts for the difference between the figural and the proper. Metaphor cannot be regarded as a substitute for the concept, in the sense of supplanting it as a ground principle. For there is no ground, only signification, with metaphoricity as a general condition of all textuality. Derrida claims that, 'since everything becomes metaphorical, there is no longer any literal meaning and, hence, no longer any metaphor either' (1981a, 258). When everything turns out to be metaphorical, both metaphor and the proper disappear and for this reason Derrida introduces the notion of quasi-metaphoricity. According to Derrida, 'metaphors. The word is written only in the plural. If there were only one possible metaphor ... there would be no more true metaphor' (1982, 268).

The employment of wide, jarring metaphors is a central characteristic of much of the digital where the colourful and figurative use of language and the juxtaposition of metaphors often evoke surreal images. This is accompanied by the interaction of the physical and virtual that also creates inclusive, jarring metaphors. This mixture of wide metaphors produce a synaesthetic effect caused by the interplay of various mental sense impressions, which continually frustrate the expectations of any simple closure and thus promotes active spectatorial participation. For instance, the employment of wide, jarring metaphors is a central characteristic of *Blue Bloodshot Flowers* and also depicts the violence that pervades the *Matrix* films. For Larry Wachowski, commenting on his film, 'there are many incredible and beautiful images in violence' (Probst 1999, 34). The use of metaphors within these practices evokes surreal images of sex, violence and death.

Finally, Derrida's theorization on deconstruction, presence and absence, identity formation and deformation, metaphysical complicity, metaphoricity and the contamination of the virtual with the 'live', and the 'live' with the virtual, is central to digital practices. In these performances there is a continual formation and deformation of identity together with the destabilization and problematization of originary meaning. In addition to questioning accepted conventions of authorship, ownership and intertexuality, digital technology brings traditional assumptions of reproduction and representation into question given that for example in every performance of *Blue Bloodshot Flowers*, the avatar Jeremiah, as any other digital technology, is 'original' and literally 'reproduced again' and not 'represented'.

Deleuze

> Desire is not bolstered by needs ... needs are derived from desire: they are counterproducts within the real that desire produces. Lack is a countereffect of desire.
>
> (Deleuze and Guattari 1984, 27)

Throughout his work, including his later collaboration with Guattari, Deleuze's experiential enterprise is directed towards the rethinking and reconstruction of ontology itself. Orthodox tools of philosophy: being, object, qualities and dualisms, are replaced by the 'concepts of planes', 'becoming', 'intensities', 'flows' and 'connections'. Rigid binary oppositions such as man/woman, nature/nurture are eschewed in favour of a 'continuum of interacting embodied subjectivities' and 'machinic assemblage of bodies, of actions and passions' (Deleuze and Guattari 1999a, 88). All of which are pivotal in an aesthetic theorization of the various art forms and performances of digital practices, such as the *Star Wars* prequels with their blurring of the borders between good and evil, and light and dark. Similarly, in Cunningham's *BIPED* (2000a) both physical and virtual bodies continually become other and various imperceptible intensities exist that give rise to new modes of perception.

Deleuze's commitment throughout his work is to the belief that that philosophy should be a 'critical enterprise of demystification'. This is contrasted to his view of orthodox philosophy whose thinking is 'sedentary' in that its categorization is restrictive and rigid. Such traditional thinking privileges a philosophy of representation and identity, which is directly opposed to 'difference and repetition'. In short, what can be 'known' *a priori* about the conditions for all possibility of experience cannot explain the difference between rational conceptualization and sensory intuition. To counteract this thinking, Deleuze proposes a 'nomadology' which resists the conceptual inflexibility of thinking identity in orthodox terms.[17]

Deleuze influenced by Nietzsche ('philosophers must distrust those concepts most they did not create themselves', Deleuze and Guattari 1999b, 6) and Spinoza, 'who knew full well that immanence was only immanent to itself ... a plane traversed by movements ... filled with intensive ordinates' (48), posits nomadic thought as an anti-dialectical tool to refute the Hegelian recuperation of negation and difference. Thought is seen as rhizomatic (root-like) rather than arboreal (tree-like). 'The rhizome is an anti-genealogy ... not amenable to any structural or generative model. It is a stranger to any ideas of genetic axis or deep structure' (Deleuze and Guattari 1999a, 11–12). It is an 'acentred, nonhierarchical, nonsignifying system ... without an organizing memory or central automaton, defined solely by a circulation of states' (21). The rhizome has no beginning or end, it is always in the middle or between things, it is 'alliance' and its 'fabric' is 'the conjunction, "and ... and ... and". This conjunction carries enough force to shake and uproot the verb "to be"' (25).[18]

Arborescent systems, on the other hand, 'are hierarchical systems with centres of significance and subjectification, central automata like organized memories' (Deleuze and Guattari 1999a, 16).[19] For Deleuze, thought is seen as rhizomatic rather than tree-like, its movement is one of affirmative differentiation and becoming, rather than a sedentary stasis of sameness and being.

Deleuze, influenced by Nietzsche, posits the nomadic as an anti-dialectical tool to refute the Hegelian recuperation of negation and difference. An approach that is rhizomatic (root-like) rather than arboreal (tree-like) (Deleuze 1999a, 11–12).

Such a tool is central to digital practices; for instance Critical Art Ensemble claim that digital technology has allowed power itself to go 'nomadic' through electronic networks. Therefore, resistance must go digital too (1994, 16).

The Deleuzian approach is one of 'radical empiricism' (Deleuze and Guattari 1999b, 47), an ethical or political approach to thought rather than a philosophical one. It is based on experience rather than ideas and in contrast to a philosophy of idealism where experience is viewed as being mediated through ideas; experience for the empiricist is unmediated and immediate. Quintessentially, experience cannot be thought of as an experience of some individual subject but rather as a 'multiplicity of worlds'.

An effect of this empirical approach is that ideas are extended by experience, the subject being constructed from experience but also always becoming. 'Social machines' are collective assemblages that extend experience. Experience is not grounded in a body as such but rather in its connections. *'There is only desire and the social, and nothing else'* (Deleuze and Guattari 1984, 29). A 'desiring machine' is no more than the connections of an experience. The body is made up of a variety of desiring machines, parts unrelated to any whole but connected to other desiring machines within the body and within the social world: for instance, the flow of milk between a breast-machine and a mouth-machine, or a flow of words between a mouth-machine and an ear-machine. The flows may be flows of actual physical matter or energy. The experience of this connection creates an expectation of desire, a need to again experience this connection, making desire in this way productive. We only have an idea of what it is to be human after bodies habitually form these connections and cause us to reflect on some general idea of subjectivity.

One of the key motifs running through Deleuze and Guattari's work is the concept of a 'machine'. Originally appropriated from a Lacanian term, the machine denotes a shift away from the organic and human towards a timeless entity with no identity, intent or even end; in fact, a model of pure machinic production, always in the process of becoming and making new connections.

With its emphasis on the emergence of social formations, this 'radical empiricism' is clearly an ethics. It shows the formation of social assemblages from bodies and their connections:

> On a first, horizontal, axis, an assemblage comprises two segments, one of content, the other of expression ... a *machinic assemblage of bodies* ... a *collective assemblage of enunciation* ... on a vertical axis, the assemblage has both *territorial sides*, or reterritorialized sides, which stabilize it, and cutting *edges of deterritorialization* which carry it away.
>
> (Deleuze and Guattari 1999a, 88)

For Deleuze and Guattari, Oedipalization is one of the principle methods of limiting desire in capitalist societies and psychoanalysis enforces this constraint. All social relations are reduced to commercialization and commodification. Desire is 'deterritorialized' or de-codified, thus subverting traditional relations of the social, cultural and economic, such as class-structure, religious beliefs and kinship systems. At the same time desire is 'reterritorialized' by transforming production into equivalence-form ensuring via the Oedipal complex that desire is concentrated within the individualized nuclear family. Commodified desire regulated by capitalism extends to the social. 'Schizophrenics', those who escape Oedipalization, are not reterritorialized, but neither do they have means of acting on their desire.

In contrast to the Lacanian notion of desire based on 'lack', desire for Deleuze and Guattari is related to 'production' or 'desiring-production'. Desire is unconscious and is part of the object desired and also the social field in which it appears. There is no object of desire without a desiring consciousness that reflects that desire. And far from the object generating 'desire-as-lack', desire produces the object desired.

> Desire has nothing to do with a natural or spontaneous determination; there is no desire but assembling, assembled, desire. The rationality, the efficiency, of an assemblage does not exist without the passions the assemblage brings into play, with the desires that constitute it as much as it constitutes them.
>
> (Deleuze and Guattari 1999a, 399)

Deleuze and Guattari present desiring-production in terms of a psychological model where desire is confronted in essentially a direct manner. For example, some psychotics view various parts of the body as being separate entities and sometimes as invading or 'persecution machines'. Similarly, schizophrenics in a catatonic state, appear to exist in 'bodies without organs'.

According to Deleuze, 'beyond the organism, but also at the limit of the lived body, there lies what Artaud discovered and named: the body without organs' (2003, 44). The body without organs or BwO is 'the field of immanence of desire' (Deleuze and Guattari 1999a, 191) and is an 'intense and intensive body' (Deleuze 2003, 44). Not only an individualized body but by extension and assemblage, it can also be a social body, such as that of capital. It produces and disseminates intensities. 'It is not space nor in space, but matter that will occupy space to that or that degree ... which corresponds to the produced intensities' (Deleuze and Guattari 1999a, 153).

The body does not have organs but (liminal) 'thresholds or levels' (Deleuze 2003, 45). It is produced by desiring machines and these machines work best at the moment 'they break down' (Deleuze and Guattari 1984, 8). It is at that moment during desiring production that 'everything freezes into place ... the automata stop dead and set free the unorganized mass' of BwO (8–9) that has '*no mouth, no tongue, no teeth, no larynx, no esophagus, no belly. No anus*' (8).

A conflict develops between the BwO and desiring machines leading to a '*repulsion*' of the desiring-machines. For Deleuze and Guattari, 'this is the real meaning of the paranoiac machine' where the BwO experiences desiring machines as 'an over-all persecution apparatus'. However, the 'paranoiac machine' is 'merely an avatar of the desiring-machines', a virtual projection that occurs when the desiring machines can no longer be tolerated by the BwO (9). Desiring machines and the body without organs can be seen as two sides of the same coin, or 'two states of the same "thing", a functioning multiplicity one moment, a pure, unextended zero-intensity the next' (Bogue 1989, 93). A continual play of attraction and repulsion takes place between the desiring-machines and the BwO in the process of producing desire.

Just as the BwO has replaced the 'organism', 'experimentation' has replaced 'interpretation'. Flows of intensity (fluids, conjunctions of affects) have replaced subjectivity; becomings (becoming-animal, becoming-woman) have replaced history. In *Genesis* (1999), Eduardo Kac, whose bioart projects focus on interspecies relations, explores issues that relate to the cultural impact of biotechnology. His work reflecting the notion that, 'in a way we much start at the end: all becomings are already molecular. That is because becoming is not to imitate or identify with something or someone' (Deleuze and Guattari 1999a, 272).

No longer are there acts to explain, dreams or phantasies to interpret, rather there are 'colours, sounds, becomings and intensities' (Deleuze and Guattari 1999a, 162); all of which are central to many digital practices such as *Blue Bloodshot Flowers* (2001), due to the hybridization of the performance and the diversity of media employed, as well as to much contemporary non-digital performance. The self no longer feels, acts and reflects; instead it has affects and experiences. For Deleuze and Guattari, 'there is an essential difference between ... the phantasy, an interpretation which must itself be interpreted, and the motor-program of experimentation. The BwO is what remains when you take everything away' (151).

Deleuze and Guattari's notion of BwO is important in an analysis of digital practices. For instance, the avatars from *BIPED* do not have organs but only 'thresholds or levels' and are timeless entities with no identities, intents or even ends. They are models of pure machinic production always in the process of becoming and making new connections; neither, 'virtual' nor 'actual' but 'possible'. And in Troika Ranch's *The Future of Memory* (2003), *The Chemical Wedding of Christian Rosenkreutz* (2000), *The Electronic Disturbance (1996), 16 [R]evolutions* (2005), and to a lesser extent *Surfacing* (2004), the ebb and flow between the organic and electronic is also in a continual process of becoming and making new connections.

Deleuze and Guattari, argue that art, by necessity, exposes the spectator to a flow of life that is experienced rather than conceptualized.
'Sensation is ... on a plane of composition ... these are not the elements
of ideas that we contemplate through concepts but the elements of matter that we contemplate through sensation' (1999b, 212). On the plane
of composition there is 'a universe of affects and percepts' whilst the
plane of immanence of philosophy is constituted from 'immanence or
concepts'. Affects and percepts are produced through art and unlike
concepts are experienced, 'art thinks no less than philosophy but it
thinks through affects and percepts' (66). Affects are not feelings, 'they
go beyond the strength of those who undergo them' (164), they are
'sensations' and 'instincts'.[20] For instance, harmonies of tone or colour
are affects of music and painting. Deleuze in writing on modern music
claims that

> Certain modern musicians oppose the transcendent plan(e) of organ-
> ization ... to the immanent sound plane ... Or rather it is a question
> of a freeing of time ... an electronic music in which forms are
> replaced by pure modifications of speed ... which affirms a process
> against all structure and genesis, a floating time against pulsed time
> or tempos, experimentation against any kind of interpretation.
>
> (Deleuze and Guattari 1999a, 287)

Similarly, in his writings on cinema, Deleuze claims that new affects are
created and new possibilities for perception are produced. Flows and connections of images are not fixed in time and do not combine to make
complete wholes (Deleuze 1986, 18). Instead, cinema represents a challenge to perception and rather than offering a theory on cinema, philosophy responds to the new perceptive forces resulting from this new art
form (Deleuze 1989, 41). New possibilities for perception are likewise produced by the fragmented images created by many digital practices.

Percepts, on the other hand, are sensations received; images, sounds,
touch and so on, which may or may not be a true representation of what
is sensed. However, percepts are not perceptions they are independent of
who is experiencing them. Both percepts and affects are *beings* whose
validity lies in themselves. Far from the spectator construing a work of
art as an effect of their own perceptions and feelings, the spectator is no
more than 'a compound of percepts and affects'. The work of art exists
in and for itself and is pure sensation (Deleuze and Guattari 1999b, 166).

The notion of 'intensity' describes elements at the limit of perception
and is described in terms of a pure ontological difference (Deleuze 1994,

144) that prefigures 'actual' entities (246). Intensities cannot be directly perceived; instead, they can only be felt, sensed or perceived in the 'quality' they cause (144). For this reason, intensities are outside of, but implicated in our experience of them. For instance, 'sensation is not qualitative and qualified, but has only an intensive reality, which no longer determines with itself representative elements, but allotropic variations' (Deleuze 2003, 45).

Deleuze uses the term 'extensity' or 'extensive' difference to describe the way intensities are homogenized in everyday perception and experience (1994, 230). Art shatters everyday perception because it draws attention to singular 'intensities'. Attention is drawn to this 'virtual flow of intensities' since art like any other 'thing' is only actualized thorough the act of perception. According to Deleuze and Guattari, art and artists are continually 'adding new varieties to the world' and in doing so create new modes of perception and experience (1999b, 175).

Unlike conceptual becoming which is the 'action by which the common event itself eludes what it is,' aesthetic-becoming is the 'action by which someone or something is ceaselessly becoming-other'. Art does not 'actualize the virtual event', rather, it embodies the event or gives it 'a body, a life, a universe' that is neither 'virtual' nor 'actual' but 'possible' (177).

This potential embodiment is central to digital practices where both physical and virtual bodies continually become-other and where, various imperceptible intensities are at play. It is these intensities, together with their ontological status that give rise to new modes of perception and consciousness. For Deleuze and Guattari, no longer is there a '"Self" ... an organism that functions but a BwO that is constructed' (1999a, 162). Their view of art as 'sensation' – as a 'force' that ruptures everyday opinions and perceptions 'to make perceptible the imperceptible forces' (1999b 182), provides a means of theorizing the unpresentable or sublime of digital practices. Similarly, their notions of 'difference', 'rhizomes', 'affects', 'intensities', 'bodies without organs', and desire as affirmation prove to be useful tools in an analysis of digital practices with its emphasis on experimentation, virtuality and alterity.

Notes

1. According to Merleau-Ponty, 'synaesthetic perception is the rule, and we are unaware of it only because scientific knowledge shifts the centre of gravity of experience, so that we have unlearned how to see, hear, and generally speaking, feel' (1962, 229).

2. 'The flesh we are speaking of is not matter. It is the coiling over of the visible upon the seeing body ... it draws this relationship and even this double relationship from itself, by dehiscence or fission of its own mass' (Merleau-Ponty 2000, 146). (Fission is the act of splitting or breaking into parts. Dehiscence is a term for fruit bursting open spontaneously to release its seeds.)

3. 'To designate it [flesh], we should need the old term "element", ... in the sense of a *general thing*, midway between the spatio-temporal individual; and the idea, a sort of incarnate principle ... The flesh is in this sense an element of Being' (Merleau-Ponty 2000, 139).

4. According to Merleau-Ponty, the invisible is composed of four 'logically' distinct layers. Firstly, what is not actually visible but could be; secondly, the existentials of the visible; thirdly, the tactile or kinesthetic and finally, the Cogito or the sayable (257). In short, 'pure transcendence, without an ontic mask' (229). For Derrida, commenting on the 'nonvisible', it 'does not describe a phenomenon that is present elsewhere, that is latent, imaginary, unconscious, hidden or past; it is a "phenomenon"' (1993, 52). However, Merleau-Ponty appears to suggest that this invisible 'other' of the visible also provides an opening into the unconscious processes of consciousness. It is the 'invisible of this world' which renders the world visible, 'its own and interior possibility' (Merleau-Ponty 2000, 151). In a certain sense the invisible could almost be seen as the sublime or unpresentable of the visible. However, for Merleau-Ponty, primarily the relationship between the visible and invisible is one of intertwining and chiasm, and is described in various terms, such as a 'hinge', or a 'fold', realized by a 'doubling up' into 'inside and outside' (2000, 264).

5. 'The structure of its mute world is such that all the possibilities of language are already given in it' (Merleau-Ponty 2000, 155).

6. The 'differend' (*différend*) is described as 'distinguished from a litigation ... [it] would be a case of conflict between (at least) two parties, that cannot be equitably resolved for lack of a rule of judgement applicable to both arguments ... A wrong results from the fact that the rules of the genre of discourse by which one judges are not those of the judged genre or genres of discourse' (Lyotard 1988a, xi).

7. According to Lyotard, for Merleau-Ponty 'the eye's relation to the visible which is the relation of Being to itself' finds expression in the work of Cézanne, yet at the same time, the 'experimentations' of Duchamps or the Cubists are diminished because they are 'unaware' of the 'paradoxical arrangements' that relate to the whole and which alone can restore the 'being as movement'. In Lyotard's opinion, Merleau-Ponty, by rejecting works of alterity and heterogeneity, remains ultimately 'monotheistic' in his approach (Lyotard 1989d, 189).

8. Although interestingly enough, the clearest notion of the figural for Lyotard is found in the works of Cézanne and Klee, their innovation is located in their departure from discursive modes, each offering different ways of demonstrating the figural. Cézanne's work avoids representational recuperation by resisting the 'already known' order with an immobility whose function recalls that of hallucinatory drugs' (Lyotard 1989c, 161). Klee's art on the other hand, is an almost 'direct writing of fantasies' and an abstraction that 'distills the energy of a trace, of a line, of points that connect' (Turim 1984, 96).

For Lyotard, this rejection of representation places their art within the context of a libidinal economy.

9. This notion of heterogeneity is similar to Bataille's notion of excess, which in its transgression of what is knowable, prevents assimilation of alterity into any coherent order (see Julian Pefanis 1991, 86).

10. Appropriating the psychoanalytical term *anamnesis* (the recollection of past events), Lyotard, in relation to the 'visible', claims, 'the anamnesis of a patient in analysis is at least a matter of language; that of the working painter remains ... in the realm of vision ... The sentimental *we* demanded and promised by aesthetics is an Idea. It cannot be shown. It marks the limits of an anamnesis of the visible, of the sensible' (1989b, 231–9).

11. 'Two moments are thus characteristic of deconstruction: a *reversal* of the traditional hierarchy between conceptual oppositions ... and a *reinscription* of the newly privileged term ... The deconstructed term ... is no longer identical with the inferior term of the initial dyad'(Gasché 1979, 192–3).

12. Also see 'to Unsense the Subjectile', where Derrida discusses Artaud's paintings and drawings: 'This spatial work would be first of all a corporeal struggle with the question of language' (1998, 65).

13. For Derrida, Artaud's 'Theatre of Cruelty' was a refusal of theatre's role as repetition: 'The stage will no longer operate as the repetition of a *present*, will no longer re-present a present that would exist elsewhere and prior to it, absent from it, and rightfully capable of doing without it: the being-present-to-itself of the absolute Logos, the living present of God' (Derrida 1978b, 237).

14. 'As distinct from difference, differance thus point out the irreducibility of temporalizing ... With its *a*, differance more properly refers to what in classical language would be called the origin or production of differences and the difference between differences ... neither a *word* nor a *concept* ... which indicates the closure of presence, together with the closure of the conceptual order and denomination, a closure that is effected in the functioning of traces' (Derrida 1973, 130–2).

15. Further undecidables are the 'margin', the 'pharmakon', and the 'hymen' (Gasché 1986, 244).

16. See Derrida for a detailed discussion of metaphor and metaphoricity (1982, 209–71).

17. 'History is always written from the sedentary point of view and in the name of a unitary State apparatus, at least a possible one, even when the topic is nomads. What is lacking is a Nomadology, the opposite of history' (Deleuze and Guattari 1999a, 23).

18. Among its characteristics are that any point of a rhizome can be connected to anything else and must be (Deleuze and Guattari 1999a, 7). It has the added principle of 'multiplicity', which is neither subject nor object, only 'determinations, magnitudes, and dimensions' that cannot increase without change in nature. A rhizome may be broken or shattered but will start up again either 'on one of its old lines or on new lines' (9).

19. The tree is 'filiation' and 'imposes the verb "to be"' (Deleuze and Guattari 1999a 25) and is already the 'image of the world ... This is the classical book, as noble, signifying, and subjective ... the book imitates the world, as art imitates nature: by procedures specific to it that accomplish what nature cannot

or can no longer do. The law of the book is the law of reflection, the One that becomes two ... Binary logic is the spiritual reality of the root-tree' (5).

20. Sensation is what determines instinct whereas instinct is the transition from one sensation to another. The quest is for the best sensation 'not the most agreeable ... but the one that fills the flesh at a particular moment' (Deleuze 2003, 39–40).

3
Neuroesthetics

This chapter examines a neuroesthetic approach linking performance, art and technology, with recent neuroscientific research on cognition and behaviour in order to provide some understanding of the biological underpinnings of aesthetic experience. At the same time such research provides a further perspective in an analysis of the digital. Much topical work in this emergent area focuses on the visual rather than other perceptual events and as such visual perception is emphasized in the following discussion.

Visual perception

> It is difficult for many people to accept that what they see is a symbolic interpretation of the world – it all seems so much like "the real thing".
>
> (Crick 1994, 84)

How do we perceive? How do we see? How do we understand what we see? And how can we recollect an image that we can picture in perfect detail when the visual stimulus is no longer before us? One of the many common mistaken beliefs concerning the ability to see is that somehow light enters the brain and produces an image which someone in our brain makes sense of. Although light does stimulate the very sensitive photoreceptors located on our retina, it does not enter the brain. The only information that the brain receives comes from electrical impulses at varying frequencies, as signals from our senses. The signals need to be made sense of according to rules and regulations based on a complex interaction of neural activity, experience and knowledge. As scientific research progresses bringing increased knowledge of how visual imagery is constructed; there is even more of a distinction between 'perceived appearances' and 'accepted realities', or between what we *see* and what we *know* and believe we see (Gregory 1998, 2), which ultimately leads to a questioning of the very nature of our consciousness, identity and being.

Perception is differentiated from imagery in as much as in the former a perceived object is physically present. In the latter, perceived objects are not being actually viewed and these images can be changed at will. Memory also plays a role since visual images are built on visual memories. Although these images are immediate and transient, they can be used at different times to form new imagery. In fact, visual imagery is important to cognition due to its ability to create and be creative (Kosslyn and Koenig 1992, 129).

Visual imagery is also central to many digital practices, for instance, memory and the act of remembering are explored in Troika Ranch's *The Future of Memory* (2003) by means of a multilayered collage of imagery and sound; the technology acting as a 'metaphor for memory' itself.

One key aspect concerning vision is that with all the exploration and work that has been done by scientists, psychologists, theorists and philosophers in this area, there is still 'no clear idea of how we see anything' (Crick 1994, 24). Although we all take visual awareness for granted we do not know just how the brain makes sense of what it sees. It is true that fragments of this process can be understood. For instance there is certainly some idea of the location of various visual operations in the cortex of the brain but there are still simple questions that as yet cannot be answered. For instance: How do we see colour and make sense of it? How do we recognize a familiar face? What allows us to see motion?

Quite a lot of hypotheses have been formulated about these processes mainly as a result of what happens when things go wrong. For example there is a condition (prosopagnosia) where familiar faces cannot be recognized or another condition (achromatopsia) where the ability to see colour fails and for these unfortunate individuals the world is seen in different shades of grey (Zeki 1999, 72). Abnormalities such as these are usually caused by injury to or lesions in the brain. Exploration of these damaged areas has given a clear indication where various visual functions occur but we are still left with questions of how we make sense of what we see. I will return to this discussion below.

Another important point is that we can never have direct knowledge of objects in the world since what our brain makes sense of is not an image but a symbolic interpretation and as we are all aware interpretations can sometimes be wrong. What we see is not what is actually in front of us but what out brain believes to be there, coloured by our knowledge and experience as in the example from chapter 1, where a leopard is recognized on the assumption of what a group of dots coming towards us might mean.

For Semir Zeki, vision is an active process, a search for constancies (1999, 6), a certain assumption of the stability of physical properties being viewed. There is a need for us to be able to discount changes and variations in order to categorize objects. He gives the example of the greenness of a leaf. The colour green is a composition of light made up of wavelength and energy that produces a code which the brain is able to decipher. There is no actual colour as such, only wavelengths of light that our visual system makes sense of and as far as we know only primates, birds, reptiles and some insects have the ability to see colour at all. The wavelength composition of a leaf changes constantly depending on the light factor. For instance, a leaf viewed at dusk would produce a different light reflection from that produced at midday. There is no unique code for any colour yet the brain is still able to decide that the leaf is green whatever the time of day. This 'discounting of the illuminant' is an example of Helmholtz's notion of 'unconscious inference' where certain assumptions of hidden knowledge concerning what we see can be elicited when we view an object (Zeki 1999, 6).

According to Zeki, '*we see in order to be able to acquire knowledge about the world*' (1999, 4). In his exploration of art and the brain, Zeki links the workings of the brain to visual arts since visual art is itself a function of the brain. Since the brain is only interested in acquiring knowledge from a constant world this acquisition does not come easily. The world is continually changing and objects appear from different vantage points, distances, light and depth, yet the brain can still make sense of these objects. For Zeki, art being an extension of the function of the visual brain is also a search for essentials and stability even when it appears at its most disruptive.

As with other cutting edge experimental art, in perceiving digital practices such as those of Palindrome, where there are an unusual and diverse range of media codes present, there is indeed a need for the brain to attempt to find essentials and stability in order to make sense of the images before it. However, due to the multilayered nature of much of this performance, a certain defamiliarization effect is produced. And although there is a need to continually attempt to recognize and make sense of elements within the works, the audience is repeatedly frustrated by the juxtaposition of disparate elements and the concomitant lack of closure or resolution. Instead of a harmonious sense of well-being there is rather a tension between joy and sorrow. The delight of having an idea of the totality of feeling together with the pain of not being able to fully present an object equal to that idea; the inability to 'present the unpresentable' (Kant 1978, 35).

In the Kantian tradition, pure reason concerned with understanding and practical reason relating to nature are seen as separate spheres with the aesthetic as a further realm bridging this divide. Although Kant himself criticized any notion of fixture and closure in his claim that 'the concept never stands within safe limits' (1911, 584–5), to all intents and purposes these spheres are assumed on the whole to be distinct aspects of being. However, this assumed discreetness is brought into question by some neuroscientists, including Zeki who refute the notion of a master area of the brain that would be capable of understanding what is being perceived. For Zeki, the concept of a master area in the brain is a 'logical and neurological problem', in as much as there would still be the question of who was "looking" at the image from the master area' (1999, 65).

Specialized visual areas do not connect anatomically with any individual area that can process or understand what is being viewed. Rather, there are multiple connections with other visual areas. Also no visual area is a recipient only; all areas receive and send signals (Zeki 1999, 71). Therefore, it would seem that the visual system is capable of both seeing and understanding and as such is fairly autonomous. This of course raises questions of consciousness and as would be expected, Zeki argues for a consciousness that is not one unified whole but rather made up of various microconscious events; each one tied to the activity of different cells in the processing system of vision. A process where there is no final stage in the cortex of the brain but instead the generation of microconsciousnesses at different times and locations not to give a unified perception of an image but rather to give us a unified percept of ourselves (67).

Bioartists like Marta de Menezes seek to explore neurons as living objects since they are believed by many to form the basis of consciousness itself. In her most recent work, *Tree of Knowledge* (2004–5), she uses a combination of cell imaging and tissue-culture technologies in order to create 3-D living sculptures using as art medium the neuronal cells themselves. I will discuss consciousness and the questions it raises below.

Different regions of the cortex can be mapped according to their primary function though it needs to be remembered that these areas are not completely discrete, and can and do interact together.[1] Vision certainly involves more than one region though these areas are functionally different. Nevertheless, the primary area of vision is located at the back of the head, the somatosensory region (touch) is at the top and hearing as may be expected is at the side. The frontal area is thought to be concerned with high-level cognition such as long-term planning, though its exact function is not known for certain. Areas of the brain interact in unexpected ways and may cause unforeseen consequences if damage or disease occurs (88). It is this unpredictability of brain interaction that is important in the perception of such multilayered performances as digital practices, since unforeseen consequences may also arise as a result of the unusual combination of perceptual codes proffered by such works.

In a widespread study by Ramachandran on the phenomenon of the 'phantom limb,' where amputees experience sensations from a limb that is no longer present, MEG (magneto encephalography) was employed to locate these sensations. Astonishingly, the body-surface maps on the brains of four arm amputees were found to have altered. Not only were the hand areas missing from the right hemispheres of the brain but those areas had also been invaded by sensory input from the face and from the upper arm. This correlated to the actual bodily experience of one of the patients who sensed his phantom hand when his face or upper arm was stroked. This finding challenges the accepted view that the circuitry of the brain is fixed and unchanging since as this evidence shows, new functionally effective pathways can and do emerge in adult brains within a short period of time following injury (Ramachandran and Blakeslee 1999, 29–31).

A further instance of regional encroachment on supposedly fixed functionally localized areas of the brain has been provided by Helen Neville in her study on deafness. Neville posited that in completely deaf people, parts of the visual system take over areas of the auditory during the brain's development since normal sound related activity is absent (1990, 71–91; 1995, 219–34). In hearing people, the normal auditory input appears to preclude any visual invasion of the auditory regions of the cortex (Crick 1994, 113). This again reinforces the argument that altered sensory experience such as deafness, loss of limb or blindness, does produce functional reorganization of the cortical sensory system.

A key question relating to perception is that if functionally effective pathways of the brain are not as fixed as previously thought, could they also be affected by the unusual and diverse stimuli of such art practices? Some of these art practices are discussed in the following chapters and exemplified by the work of Stelarc, where the body is coupled with a variety of instrumental and technological devices that instead of being separate from the body become part of that body, at the same time altering and recreating its experience in the world.

A neuroesthetic approach

> The eye is a simple optical instrument. With internal images pro-
> jected from objects in the outside world, it is Plato's cave with a lens.
> The brain is the engine of understanding. There is nothing closer to
> our intimate experiences, yet the brain is less understood and more
> mysterious than a distant star.
>
> (Gregory 1998, 1)

Although the eye is thought of as the organ of vision, it is in fact the brain
that does the 'seeing', or to be more accurate its visual cortical areas. Of
course without the eye, vision is impossible and damage to it is commonplace, with the effects well documented. Not so well documented is
damage to the visual cortex, which also leads to various forms of blindness. It is only relatively recently that the brain has been thought to be
involved in the act of seeing at all and instead of 'the visual world being
impressed on the "retina" of eye', the eye merely filters visual signals and
registers transformations in light intensity or wavelengths of light and
transmits this information to the cortex of the brain (Zeki 1999, 14).

Humans have virtually total binocular vision, where the left half of
each retina projects to the left visual cortex and the right half of the
retina projects to the right visual cortex. Therefore, the right visual cortex receives all the input from the left visual field, and the left visual cortex receives input from the right. Binocular vision is also important in
assessing depth of vision where cells in the visual cortex can compare the
input from the two. Digital performances such as *Dead East, Dead West*,[2]
an experimental sound and movement-based piece, use 3-D technologies in an attempt to replicate this stereoscopic effect on 2-D imagery.

The retina as well as being a filtering device also processes information
to a certain extent. The cells that send signals from the eye to the brain
are called ganglion cells; they are situated at the back of each eye and are
cell bodies of the optic nerves. A ganglion cell will respond vigorously to
a small dot of light in one particular part of the visual field – its 'receptive field' – depending on where the eye is focused. In contrast, the
larger the dot of light becomes the less vigorous is the response from the
ganglion cell. In other words, the retina when processing data coming
into the eye partially eliminates redundant information preferring to
send only what is interesting to the brain, that is, areas of the visual
field where light distribution is not constant or uniform (Crick 1994,
124). However, as complex as the retina is, it does not have the necessary apparatus to eliminate unnecessary information that represents the

essentials of an object; instead, most of this more sophisticated equipment is located in the cortex of the brain (Zeki 1999, 14).

Salomon Henschen, an early twentieth-century neuro-pathologist, showed that the retina of the eye is not linked to the whole of the cerebral cortex, but instead to a fairly localized area now generally known as the 'primary visual cortex' or area 'V1' (Zeki 1999, 15). Adjacent areas of the retina connect with V1, recreating a visual map of the retina on the cortex. Connections between the retina and the primary visual cortex are genetically determined, the necessary visual apparatus being present at birth. However, to be able to function at all, this system needs to be exposed to the visual world. For whatever reason, if cells in the visual brain are deprived of this crucial exposure in the early period of life they become dysfunctional and are unable to fully respond to visual stimuli, if they can respond at all. Deprivation of exposure later in life does not carry such serious consequences (93–4).

It is now known that there are many areas outside V1, at least 20 distinct visual areas and approximately seven more that are partially related to vision (Crick 1994, 149) – regions that are specialized to deal with various aspects of a visual scene. Their names are also usually shortened and numbered, for example, 'V2', 'V3', 'V4' and 'V5' (sometimes called 'MT' – middle temporal); other abbreviations are used for many more visual areas.[3]

An important issue currently being debated concerns the involvement of the primary visual cortex during imagery. Some studies have found activation in V1 when a visual image is summoned to memory. Kosslyn posits a type of processing called 'depictive imagery' that relies on high-resolution representations and allows the reorganization, reinterpretation or comparison of shapes. According to Kosslyn, this type of imagery relates to 'what most people seem to mean when they say they are "seeing with the mind's eye"' (Kosslyn and Thompson 2000, 982). This activity takes place in V1 and in other areas of the medial occipital cortex (MOC). Moreover, a small image formed in response to the name of an object activates V1, since this area is concerned with central vision, whereas more peripheral regions are activated for a larger image (Kosslyn, Thompson and Alpert 1995, 469–68).

V1 and V2 are concerned with orientation, movement, disparity and colour (Crick 1994, 147). In V1, cells are grouped together that receive different attributes of vision; one of these groups are the 'blob' cells – specifically concerned with colour; they are small groups of high metabolic activity whose cells differentiate between different wavelengths of light (Zeki 1999, 60). Nearly all the neurons in V2 receive input from both eyes unlike V1 whose map is of the opposite side of the visual field (Crick 1994, 140). However, V2's receptive fields are usually larger than those of V1, and can respond in less obvious ways. Although it is possible to specify which features are demonstrated by individual visual areas, it does not mean that they are the only attributes of those areas. For that matter, there may be no clear indication just what such features mean. For example, to know that V2 appears to have some concern with colour gives us no clear idea whether the neurons within this area allow us to see colour or merely draw the brain's awareness to what the colour actually looks like (146).

What is known is that colour is perceived before form, which in turn is perceived before motion – the period of time between the perception of colour and motion of an object is approximately 60–80 milliseconds (Zeki 1999, 66). This again suggests that the perceptual systems themselves are functionally specialized leading to the brain registering a change in the colour of an object before a change in direction of that same object. The consequence of this is that the brain over very short periods of time is unable to combine what happens in real time; instead, it unifies the results of its own processing systems though not in real time. Nevertheless all visual attributes are combined to provide us with an integrated experience. Since perception is a conscious act and perceives at least two attributes at varying time, this indicates that not only are there separate consciousnesses for each attribute but that 'different consciousnesses are asynchronous with respect to one another' (67).

Digital practices such as Palindrome's shadow performances, as a result of their multilayered, distorted and delayed effects, challenge the notion of an 'integrated experience' by making perceptible this sequential anomaly; at the same time they ensure the audience's active participation in the production of meaning.

Since V1 is the gateway to the visual brain, if injury or disease occurs the consequence is total blindness with an unusual exception, which I will discuss below. However, if surrounding areas are diseased or injured, there is instead, an inability to perceive certain aspects of the visual scene corresponding to the injured specialized area with some surprising results. One such condition is prosopagnosia – the inability to recognize familiar faces – that usually results from a lesion in a very specific part of the brain, the fusiform gyrus,[4] which is on the underside of the occipital lobe towards its junction with the temporal lobe. Interestingly, the right non-dominant hemisphere takes a leading role in face perception (Zeman 2002, 216).

It is not surprising that a large area of the human brain is devoted to face recognition, since interaction and communication are largely dependent on the ability to identify the facial characteristics of other humans, and to decipher their expressions. In fact, so sophisticated is the ability of humans to recognize facial expressions that even very slight differences are perceived and made meaningful. In the performance of *Blue Bloodshot Flowers*, it proved remarkable just how much information could be gleaned by the audience from Jeremiah's facial expressions on very little evidence, leading to a variety of emotions being projected by these spectators onto the avatar. Similarly, the ultimate high-resolution facial capture scene from *The Matrix: Revolutions* (2003), when Neo punches Agent Smith in the face, depends on facial recognition for its high impact.

The V4 complex primarily concerned with colour is located in the fusiform gyrus. Damage to this area causes a condition known as achromatopsia, where the individual does not see actual colour but only shades of grey. This is due to the resultant inability to accept the ratio of different light wavelengths from the receptive field of vision and its surrounding areas, a function very necessary to generate colour. And of course, colour cannot be divorced from form, since there must be a border to distinguish colour, even if the brain processes both attributes separately (Zeki 1999, 195). Though colour is a property of the brain and not of the external world it is still dependent on a physical reality outside the brain; 'the science of colour is therefore a mental science' that also makes use of 'optics' and 'anatomy'.[5] The key areas of the cortex that seem to be concerned with colour are specialized cells in V1, V2 and the colour centre V4, together with locations in the temporal lobe. Motion is similarly detected in V1 and V2 and the motion centre – V5 and also in other surrounding specialized areas.

The fusiform gyrus, in addition to accommodating V4, is also the location of the number area, which represents visual numbers. In fact both areas are adjacent to each other. This has surprising repercussions for a certain subgroup of individuals who whilst being otherwise normal, experience sensations in modalities other than the modality that is being directly stimulated (Ramachandran and Hubbard 2001, 4). This mingling of the senses is known as synaesthesia (from the Greek *syn*: joining and *aisthesis*: sensation), and presents in a variety of ways, for example, some individuals visualize colours when they view numbers. Others see colours in response to a tone, for instance, a musical note may evoke a distinct colour. Various explanations have been given for this phenomena, but recent evidence suggests that synaesthesia is a genuine perceptual phenomenon (3).[6]

Recent studies have suggested links between synaesthesia and creativity. An important effect is that it improves memory and recall. According to

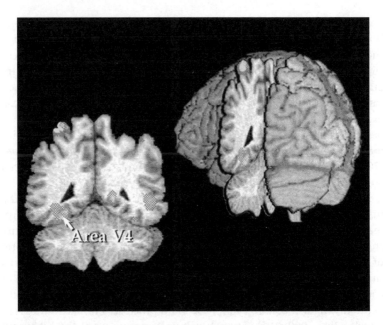

Figure 3.1   Area V4 of the brain. Photo courtesy of Professor Semir Zeki. From the Laboratory of Neurobiology at UCL, www.vislab.ucl.ac.uk

Ramachandran, 'synesthesia is more common among artists, poets and novelists than the general population.' However for Jamie Ward, synaesthesia may affect us all to a certain extent since 'beneath the surface we all have mechanisms that link together sound and vision and the mechanisms seem to be pretty much the same in both synaesthetes and other members of the population' (Ward 2004).[7] There is also an apparent link between synaesthesia and the development of language, as Ramachandran asserts 'we have several types of interactions in place' that 'enhance each other's results in a whole avalanche that we call language' (Ramachandran 2004).

Synaesthesia is important in an analysis of many digital practices such as *Blue Bloodshot Flowers* (2001) and *The Matrix* trilogy (1999–2003), where the interaction of the physical and virtual creates inclusive, jarring metaphors. This mixture of wide metaphor produces an aesthetic effect caused by the interplay of various mental sense-impressions, which unsettle the audience by frustrating their expectations of any simple interpretation, and in so doing create a new kind of synaesthetic effect that is analogous to the perceptual experience caused by the above cross-activation of discrete areas of the brain.

While damage to the primary visual cortex V1 (the visual gateway) generally results in total blindness, occasionally an interesting phenomenon known as 'blindsight' occurs, where individuals although being completely blind can point to and differentiate between objects whilst at the same time denying they can see them. One supposition is that the brain instead of using the primary cortical visual pathway in response to visual stimuli diverts the incoming signal, and makes use of a much more primitive visual pathway which travels via the superior colliculos (nerve cells located at the apex of the brain stem whose function is primarily related to eye movement) directly to higher brain centres such as the parietal lobes (Ramachandran and Blakeslee 1999, 76).

The implication of this is that only the newer visual pathway is capable of conscious awareness whereas the more primitive pathway can use visual input for all kinds of behaviour without any conscious awareness of what is happening.[8] A further assumption has been that some cells in V1 have remained intact following damage and remain capable of producing effects in this region. Whatever the reason, visual information is received and acted upon by a blindsighted person and yet at the same time that visual input is denied.

Moreover, a new form of blindsight has been noted where invisible graphemes can induce synaesthetic colours. It occurs when a grapheme is crowded out by other graphemes and therefore not consciously detectable yet evokes in the viewer the colour that correlates to the missing grapheme. This again implies that colour is evoked at an earlier sensory level rather than a higher cognitive level (Ramachandran and Hubbard 2001, 8). In other words the brain is responding to visual stimuli without this response producing any conscious awareness (Crick 1994, 173).

Art and perception

In relating the visual apparatus to the perception of art, surprisingly, there are neurological differences between viewing naturally coloured objects that have definite shapes, such as trees, plants, cars and buildings and colour in the abstract – that is, colours that have no reference to any particular objects or scenes, such as found in the abstract paintings of Mondrian. Viewing naturally coloured objects activates not only V1, V2 and the V4 complex but also various other areas in the brain including the hippocampus (memory and learning) and the inferior frontal area of the right hemisphere (thinking and planning). In contrast, when viewing abstractly coloured objects with no recognizable form, the activity in the brain is restricted largely to the visual areas of

V1, V2 and V4. However, when viewing artwork where the form is representational but the colour is unnatural, such as in the work of the Fauvists, V1, V2 and V4 are again activated, together with a different frontal cortical area – the middle frontal temporal region but not the hippocampus. This indicates that the V4 complex is only concerned with constructing colours in an abstract way without relating those colours to any particular object. The larger implication is that when viewing colour in the abstract, 'automatic computation' takes place in certain areas of the brain. However, when viewing naturally coloured objects, additional factors are used by the colour system, such as memory, learning and judgement. A further and more important implication for digital practices is that activation of the middle-frontal convolution[9] of the frontal lobe, when viewing non-representational colour, may not mean that this region is exclusively devoted to non-representational colour perception but rather it responds to different elements of the unusual in general (Zeki 1999, 197–203).

When viewing objects in motion, a specific area of the brain is activated – V5, and damage to this area of the visual cortex causes akinetopsia, that is, individuals with this condition are unable to view objects in motion. Although this region of the brain may not be the only area that is implicated when viewing kinetic art, V5 is necessary to view motion at all. Again when motion is meaningful V5 together with an area anterior to it is activated. However, when motion is abstract activation is restricted to V5 (206).

Form, also in abstract, activates fewer areas of the brain than when that form becomes figurative and representational. Therefore, when viewing representational art, recognizable forms activate areas beyond the fusiform gyrus, whereas when viewing more abstract works activation is mainly restricted to the fusiform gyrus. The inference of this is that all non-representational works of art activate fewer areas of the brain than representational and narrative art. However, all works of art that conflict with our prior experience of visual reality or, in other words, frustrate our expectations of any clear resolution, such as the art of the Fauvists and the Surrealists – and by implication digital practices, such as those of Palindrome and Troika Ranch, are likely to activate a specific area of the frontal lobe which appears to deal with the resolution of perceptual/experiential conflict (207–8).

This neurological examination of perception, to a certain extent, supports theorization from an aesthetic perspective; since when it comes to making aesthetic judgements every example must precede the rule and rules are created on each occasion, which can in no way be determined beforehand and no set judgement can exist. The sublime, which is unlimited and formless but nevertheless has 'purposiveness without purpose', is exemplary of this need to strive continually towards a judgement that can never be guaranteed (42–69). This of course has consequences for technologically informed and other experimental artworks and performances since aesthetic judgements need to be continually revised and by implication must involve conflict with prior experience, and may very well involve the middle region of the frontal lobe which seems to respond to elements of the unusual.

A further neurological perspective on art and perception comes from Ramachandran, who in the search for artistic universals proposes a phenomenon called the 'peak shift effect' that quintessentially explains caricatures and many other aspects of art (Ramachandran and Hirstein 1999, 15). The peak shift effect involves a system of reward that is linked with emotional pleasure – for example, if a rat is rewarded for distinguishing between a rectangle and a square, it will develop a preference for that shape over the square but paradoxically will also respond even more vigorously to a caricature of that shape than to the original rectangular prototype. The supposition is that the rat learns the rule of rectangularity rather than a particular example of that rule and the visual system is continually searching for 'the rule' (Ramachandran and Blakeslee 1999, 288). It is suggested that during human and primate evolutionary development many of the visual areas that are specifically concerned with extracting correlations and rules, and attaching visual attributes (colour, motion, form, shading, and so on) along different dimensions such as 'form space' or 'motion space' have become directly linked to the emotional limbic structures that in turn produce pleasure sensations, and in doing so enhance survival of the species (Ramachandran and Hirstein 1999, 22). The mechanism for this process with its limbic association is more prominent in the right hemisphere of the brain.

Accordingly, exaggerating a particular rule and eliminating excess detail proves even more pleasing. For instance, when applied to art, the aesthetic pleasure of viewing a Van Gogh or a Monet may be due to a 'caricature' of 'colour space', and in a similar way when applied to digital performance, the representationally abstract dancing avatars of Cunningham's *BIPED* may be one of form. Similarly, a painting may be far more evocative than a photograph since 'the photograph's details may actually *mask* the underlying rule' (Ramachandran and Blakeslee 1999, 288). Although what is being caricatured is not always obvious it seems that certain art forms, such as Cubism, tap into innate 'form primitives' of the brain which are not as yet fully understood (Ramachandran and Hirstein 1999, 22).

Again this can be seen to be analogous to the aesthetic sensation of the sublime 'negative pleasure' generated by some digital practices, such as those discussed within this book where arguably the digital/virtual interface of the artworks taps into form primitives. Yet, since the search for rules is continually frustrated, pleasure can never be completely unequivocal.

Consciousness and the digital

> There is nothing that we know more intimately than conscious experience, but there is nothing that is harder to explain.
>
> (Chalmers 1998, 9)

The exploration of consciousness may well be the final frontier of our very human need to both understand and to be meaningful; in short, to make sense of ourselves and by implication our world or what we perceive that world to be. A perspective on consciousness is proffered by Crick, who clearly prioritizes a scientific approach over the philosophical, and whose primary question relates to the correlation between consciousness and active neuronal processes (Crick 1994, 207). The 'neuronal correlate of consciousness' is usually referred to as the NCC and indicates the neural basis of conscious experience together with the structure and physiology which gives rise to that conscious experience. Its location is as yet unknown. Neural correlate generally refers to the correlation between neuronal activity and the sensation, thought, or action that relates to that mental activity.

De Menezes in her work, *Functional Portraits* (2002b), used functional magnetic resonance imaging (fMRI) to create artworks from the real time visualizations of brain activity in order to realize 'who/how the person is'. She has created portraits (including her own) of individuals involved in various activities whilst at the same time undergoing brain imaging, the resulting art being created 'simply by thought' (2002a).

Crick and Koch have speculated that certain 35–75 hertz neural oscillations[10] in the cerebral cortex might be the basis of consciousness (1995a, 121–3). These oscillations consist of a widespread network of neurons that stand out from the background of regular neuronal firing for at least 100–200 milliseconds at any given moment in time (Zeman 2002, 289). They appear to be correlated with awareness in a number of varying modalities. Crick and Koch have also suggested that a synchrony of these oscillations is central to the process of binding information where various aspects of separate representations of an object are brought together and later integrated into a unified perception (see below). A further hypothesis relates to the activation of the mechanisms of working memory and by implication other kinds of memory (Crick and Koch 1990, 263–75).

Underlying the notion of the NCC is the assumption that all aspects of consciousness employ a basic mechanism or a few basic mechanisms and if one aspect is known then it should be possible to discover the rest. For whilst some neuronal processes appear to correlate with consciousness others do not. So what is the difference? For instance, are neurons that correlate to consciousness of any particular type? What (if anything) is special about them (Crick 1994, 207)?

The argument is that consciousness, a highly evolved system and one of the most crucial properties of the human brain, must have a useful function. For instance, the function of visual consciousness is to provide the best interpretation of a visual scene and to be able to make sense of that scene experientially. This is in contrast to systems that can generate stereotypical behaviour but bypass consciousness (Crick and Koch 2001, 193). Central to the NCC has been the suggestion that consciousness occurs as a result of an emergent property of several interacting cortical neurons (Libet 1995). A further hypothesis is that within the cortex there are specific sets of 'consciousness' neurons, whose subsets give rise to appropriate conscious experience (Crick and Koch 1995a, 121–3). These particular neurons would perhaps consist of distinctive physiological and structural characteristics and demonstrate specific behaviour or as Crick and Koch claim, they 'would, most likely, be characterized by a unique combination of molecular, biophysical, pharmacological and anatomical traits' (2001, 194).[11]

There is yet another possibility that all cortical neuronal cells are capable of participating in representing conscious experience at different times and in a variety of ways, also known as 'binding by neural synchrony', and it describes an activity pattern that temporarily occurs within a subset of nerve cells (Crick and Koch 2001, 193–4). For instance, when we perceive an object more than one set of neurons will fire in various regions of the cortex as we take in the colour, form and motion of that object. As already mentioned, colour is perceived before form that in turn is perceived before motion, yet all visual attributes are combined to provide us with an integrated experience. This experience of perceptual unity suggests that the brain binds together neurons that are responding to different aspects of a perceived object in a 'mutually coherent way' (Crick 1994, 208).

According to Crick, there appear to be several methods of neural binding. For instance, there are neurons, probably as a result of genetic determination and development, which in responding to a short line can be regarded as binding together a set of points. There are again other neurons that bind together strongly as a result of a frequently repeated experience or overlearning, as in the recognition of familiar objects, such as letters of the alphabet. However, the form of binding that occurs neither as a result of genetics nor of overlearning, but instead responds to a new experience of perception has attracted the most interest. It follows the experiencing of objects whose combination of features may be quite new and unusual (208–9). An example of this would be in viewing digital practices such as *Blue Bloodshot Flowers*, those of Stelarc, Optik, Troika Ranch, Eduardo Kac and many more with their often unique juxtaposition of various elements.

This particular binding arises rapidly and is transitory and capable of an almost infinite range of possibilities, though possibly only being sustained for a few combinations at any one time. Moreover, if the same stimulus is repeated frequently, transient binding would become the overlearned type of binding, since its experience is repeatedly reinforced and thus becomes no longer different. It is not as yet known exactly how the brain expresses this transient binding and what neural activity correlates to it (202), although it has been suggested by Wolf Singer and Charles Gray[12] that it may arise as a result of a synchronous firing of the various neurons that represent all the different attributes (colour, form and so on) of an object (Crick 1994, 244–5). Thus, for Crick and Koch, a function of consciousness is to:

> Present the result of various underlying computations and ... this involves an attentional mechanism that temporarily binds the relevant neurons together by synchronizing their spikes in 40 Hz oscillations.
>
> (1990, 272)

David Chalmers, on the other hand, offers a philosophical perspective believing that 'consciousness is an ambiguous term', which refers to many different phenomena that can be divided into 'hard' and 'easy' problems. The easy problems are those that respond to the usual cognitive scientific methodology and fundamentally relate to awareness, which can be explained in terms of 'computational or neural mechanisms', such as the above notion of the 'neuronal correlate of consciousness' proffered by Crick and Koch. The hard problems are those that appear to resist that methodology. The most difficult being the 'problem of *experience*', in other words, the *subjective* response to what we perceive and sense (Chalmers 1998, 9–10). For Chalmers, although such a theory as the NCC is valuable, it does not explain 'why oscillations give rise to experience' (14) and although Crick and Koch hypothesize that there is a suggested link between binding and experience they fail to explain that association (Crick and Koch 1995b, 84–5). However, as Crick reminds us, 'our customary usages of words may not accurately describe the actual activities in our brains' (Crick 1994, 247).

There are several collective terms that refer to subjective experience, including 'phenomenal consciousness', 'conscious experience' and *qualia*. Qualia, a word that is particularly expressive, is the plural term of the Latin *quale*, and is an essential philosophical property that indicates the subjective quality of mental experience, such as the redness of red, 'the smell of freshly ground coffee or the taste of pineapple ... which we have all experienced but which, it seems, is very difficult to explain.'[13]

According to Ramachandran and Blakeslee, for qualia to exist at all, there is a need for an irrevocable short-term memory representation, for instance, the colour 'yellow', together with the choice over potentially limitless implications, 'yellow banana, yellow teeth, the yellow skin of jaundice and so on' (1999, 238). Qualia are associated with the intermediate stages in perceptual processing, where stable perceptual representations that have meaning are created, in other words, where the best course of action can be chosen from an infinite range of possibilities. These processes occur in the temporal lobe and the associated limbic system; the emotion centre of the brain (245).

The problem with qualia for most people is how subjective perceptual experiences can be explained in terms of the firing of neurons. Central to this is the question of reconciling first-person and third-person accounts of the world. To describe the perceptual sensation of the redness of red in the first person ('I experience red') is not the same as an objective account of red as being merely the result of an encounter with certain wavelengths of light that is made sense of by the human visual system. However, this seeming irreconcilability between the private and the third-person account is not necessarily a contradictory problem, rather it has been suggested that it arises as a result of a mistranslation from one language to another; from a language of nerve impulses, 'the spatio patterns of neuronal activity that allow us to see red,' to a language that allows us to communicate what we have seen, to others (231). The problem is that although it is possible to communicate what is seen by means of spoken language, the 'experience' of that subjective perception is forever lost in translation.

This notion of mistranslation supports my argument for an inter-semiotic significatory practice that is one that includes but also goes beyond language. Traditional ways of interpreting performance and other art practices have been dominated by the transference of the linguistic to the non-linguistic, making the body a secondary phenomenon. It is my belief that unless the immediacy of the physical (virtual) body is made the focus of interpretation, such heterosemiotic performances as the digital cannot be fully experienced or appreciated.[14]

Furthermore, if it is accepted that two mutually irreconcilable languages can describe perception, then the problem of qualia becomes merely one of mistranslation, rather than being irrefutable further proof of a mind-body division. Instead of a division between qualia and neurons (mind and matter), there are only barriers to translation (Ramachandran and Blakeslee 1999, 232).

Another perspective on consciousness and experience is offered by bioartist Kac, whose key investigative concerns are the investigation of interaction (including interspecies), issues of identity and the very possibility of communication. Therefore, it is not surprising that he should focus on 'the social dimension of consciousness' and 'the complexity of animal minds' since each individual is 'unique' (2003, 100), culminating in his recent transgenic event, *Alba the GFP Bunny* (2000). This raises interesting questions in relation to interspecies interaction. For instance, what would qualia mean to a rabbit? Would it be able to think in first person and experience the subjective quality of a mental experience? For Kac, in exploring intersubjectivity between various species, questions like this need to be taken into account, in order to fully appreciate each individual life form.

Qualia also have a lot to do with the 'self', since subjective experiences need to be experienced by something and the self as an entity needs experiences and memories to be a self. For Ramachandran and Blakeslee, there are several defining characteristics of the self. There is the *'mneunomic self'*, where there is a sense of continuity, that is, a sense of the past, present and future, a continuous personality; the *'unified self'*, an impression of coherence where varied sensory experiences, memories, beliefs and ideas are experienced as a unified whole; the *'embodied self'*, with its sense of embodiment or ownership, where the self is attached to the body; the *'passionate self'*, since emotions are an essential part of the self; and the *'executive self'*, a belief in free will, a sense of agency, of being in control of destiny (247–52). According to this analysis, the self is comprised of many different phenomena that together give it a sense of unison. However, as has been repeatedly demonstrated, this sense of coherence can easily be disrupted by disease or injury to the brain.

Benjamin Libet has posed an intriguing dilemma concerning consciousness and the concept of free will. According to Libet, 'one of the mysteries in the mind–brain relationship is expressed in the question: How does a voluntary act arise in relation to the cerebral processes that mediate it? The discovery of the 'readiness potential' (RP) opened up possibilities for experimentally addressing a crucial feature of this question' (1985, 529). The brain wave or 'readiness potential', as it is commonly known, appears on an electroencephalograph (EEG) approximately one second or more before a voluntary movement is realized. Importantly, the willingness to physically accomplish a movement occurs at the time of the actual movement, yet the readiness potential is evident prior to both the intention and the action. In fact, 'the brain decides to initiate or at least prepares to initiate the act before there is any reportable subjective awareness that such a decision has taken place' (534). Moreover, the readiness potential only occurs in voluntary movements not in involuntary ones.

According to Libet, the above findings should not be taken as 'being antagonistic to free will but rather as affecting the view of how free will might operate', since although the intention to act may arise unconsciously, there may still be 'conscious veto or blockade' over the motor action itself (538–9). Nevertheless, the discovery of the readiness potential not only problematizes the accepted notion of free will, but also ultimately our concept of causality. For, if a voluntary movement is voluntary (has cause and effect), why is the apparent sensation of that movement delayed; if it is not voluntary (has no cause and effect), what is the purpose of free will in evolutionary terms? As Ramachandran suggests, perhaps 'our very notion of causation requires a radical revision' (2003). This destabilization of accepted concepts of causality and determinism is reflected in the indeterminacy of many experimental art practices such as digital practices. For instance, Neo's opposition to a deterministic future in *The Matrix*, demonstrates the executive self, which is a belief in free will and a sense of agency. However, the discovery of the readiness potential not only problematizes this notion of free will, but also ultimately the concept of causality itself.

Finally, the embodied self is central to digital practices, particularly in such works as those of Cunningham, Stelarc, Palindrome, Troika Ranch and Optik, where notions of the corporeal are prioritized. However, boundaries of this embodied self are not as fixed as we would like to believe. The self as well as being embodied is also emotional, and the primary function of the amygdala together with the rest of the limbic system is to monitor perceptual representation and in a given situation decide what, if any, is the most appropriate response. Emotional responses include anger, love, fear, in fact, all the basic feelings that we as humans easily recognize and share. An emotional response can be measured by a device that monitors the galvanic skin response (GSR), which is fundamentally the change in skin resistance caused by perspiration. This primary 'fight or flight' mechanism causes changes to the blood circulation. It increases the heart rate and the blood supply to meet the perceived challenge, and perspiration dissipates the resultant heat (Ramachandran and Blakeslee 1999, 61).

Emotion, in keeping with consciousness itself, is essentially an evolutionary device that ensures our survival. It allows us to respond appropriately to a given situation and also to decide what that response should be. Surprisingly, our GSR does not only respond to events that directly affect us and our bodies, though of course there is a strong reaction when we are directly stimulated. It has been demonstrated that it also responds to events that affect objects that we have appropriated as being part of our body.[15] This may well go some way to explaining the mechanism of love where another identity is appropriated by our own and as such becomes literally part of our body (250).

Certain digital practices add a further dimension to this appropriation since the motions of a performer's body, captured technologically, results in a modified extension of that physical body. Likewise in the audience interaction with Jeremiah in *Blue Bloodshot Flowers*, the avatar is clearly emotionally appropriated, being viewed as an extension and modification of a human being. The implication for digital practices is that the embodied self as any other aspect of the conscious self, is primary yet transitory, heterogeneous, indeterminate, self-reflexive, fragmented and has a certain shift-shape property, all traits that are reflected in the following performances.

Notes

1. One of the earliest mappings of the human brain relied on a model called the *homunculus* (little man), which was discovered by Wilder Penfield during various neurosurgical operations in the 1940s and 1950s. During these operations he experimentally stimulated, with an electrode, various regions of the brains, of locally anaesthetized patients, who could report the resultant bodily sensations. Thus, the map was drawn from real human brains and its

representation shows a grossly deformed body mapped onto the brain. The genitals, for instance, are located beneath the feet (Penfield and Rasmussen 1950). There is now technology available that can perform the same task of mapping the brain without the need for invasive surgery. One of these is called magneto encephalography (MEG), which is a modern neuroimaging technique that again relies on reaction and response. The map of the imaged body closely corresponds to that of Penfield's homunculus.

2. In August 2003, I presented a performance entitled *Dead East/Dead West* at the Institute of Contemporary Arts in London. As well as locating 'liminal' spaces between virtual and physical performers, in this work I also suggest that such spaces are located on the threshold of race and colour, and as a result tensions exist. This project involved a collaboration with Jeffrey Longstaff, a choreographer from the Laban Centre, London; Martin Dupras, Jez Hattosh-Nemeth and Paul Verity Smith, digital interactive artists from the University of the West of England and 3-D film-maker Brian McClave.

3. Beneath each square millimetre of the cortical surface of V1 lie approximately 250,000 neurons. V1 and the area surrounding it, V2, discriminately distribute visual signals to the other visual areas. A large area of V1 is dedicated to signals received from the fovea of the eye, which has the highest density of receptors and is concerned with detailed vision. In contrast, the peripheral region of the retina is underrepresented and thus the retinal map of the cortex rather than being a simple translation of a visual scene is a map that emphasizes a particular field of view (Zeki 1999, 17). This abnormal scale is known as the 'magnification factor' (Crick 1994, 147).

4. A gyrus is the apex of the prominence on the surface of the folded cerebral cortex.

5. James Clerk Maxwell (1872, 260–9), quoted by Zeki (1999, 186).

6. According to Ramachandran and Hubbard, the number/colour or grapheme colour type of synesthesia, the most common form of this condition, is most likely due to cross-activation or cross-wiring of both the colour and visual number regions within the fusiform gyrus in genetically predisposed individuals (9). Interestingly enough, in these individuals, Roman numerals, unlike Arabic numerals, do not on the whole invoke colour, which implies that the visual appearance of numbers is represented in this area rather than the abstract concept of ordinality or sequence (11). The concept of number is thought to lie within the angular gyrus located in the left hemisphere of the brain. There is yet another form of synaesthesia where colour is evoked in relation to an abstract concept of sequence or ordinality and for these individuals, days of the week or months of the year induce a colour. This 'higher' synaesthesia (being located higher in the brain) is again thought to be the result of cross-wiring, this time between the angular gyrus and the colour centre – V4 (14).

7. Jamie Ward is a neuro-psychologist from University College, London.

8. However, there is some dispute regarding this since studies have shown that the cones in the retina of these individuals still react to wavelengths of light; this in turn makes the colliculos unlikely to be the only pathway used since no colour-sensitive neurons have been found in that area (Crick 1994, 172).

9. One of the convex folds of the surface of the brain.

10. Also known as 'gamma' and sometimes '40-Hz' Oscillations (Crick 1994, 276).

11. Crick has posited that 'bursty' pyramidal cells in layer 5 of the cortical visual areas may play an important role since they are the only neurons that project out of the cerebral system and thus may be able to send out the results of neural computations to the rest of the brain (1994, 235).
12. See Gray and Singer (1989), for a more detailed discussion of binding by neural synchrony.
13. David Lodge (2002, 8), quoting from *The Oxford Companion to the Mind*.
14. In contrast to formal semantics, which is homosemiotic, where meaning is determined by fixed stipulated rules (for example, mathematics), non-formal semantics is heterosemiotic, its meaning is constituted from interpretive approximations where various kinds of nonlinguistic readings are reconciled by the principle of linguistic expression (see Ruthrof 1997, 46–7).
15. See Ramachandran and Blakeslee (1999, 61–2) for an account of research methodologies and outcomes.

4
Live Performance and the Digital

In live performance and the digital, the delimited body and intelligent interactive technologies are prioritized. Additional features are an emphasis on hybridization and a rejection of the notion of an integrated personality in favour of the deconstructed, post-human subject. These performance practices blur the boundaries between the physical and virtual and what is seen as conventional art practices and innovative technical experimentation. They also share certain aesthetic traits, such as innovation, indeterminacy, marginality and an emphasis on the intersemiotic.

Intelligence, interaction, reaction and performance: The Jeremiah project

It is within ... tension filled liminal spaces of physical and virtual interface that opportunities arise for new experimental forms and practices.
(Broadhurst 2002, 162)

Blue Bloodshot Flowers was the first of a series of practice-led research projects entitled 'Intelligence, Interaction, Reaction and Performance'. These performances consist of various physical/virtual interactions using a diverse range of technologies including motion capture, artificial intelligence and/or 3-D animation. *Blue Bloodshot Flowers*, which I directed was a collaboration with Richard Bowden, a systems engineer from the University of Surrey. It had its public presentation at the 291 Gallery in London in 2001. The work focuses on a performance space that allows a physical performer to interact directly and in real time with an 'avatar' or data projected image.[1]

Blue Bloodshot Flowers, a development of a previous performance, was an attempt 'to exceed everything that can be presented' (Lyotard 1988a, 166). The initial production was a text and movement-based piece that was performed at Brunel University in 2000. It was written by a colleague, Phil Stanier, and involves the remembrance of a love affair.[2] There is some ambiguity regarding whether the affair is between two adults, or an adult and a child or if the narrator is dead; the ex-lover is obviously long gone. The performer, Elodie Berland, was French and we used a French voiceover as a memory device with good effect. There was some music used intermittently throughout provided by David Bessell from the London College of Music.

The project involved a collaboration with Bowden. who researches methods that allow both humans and objects to be located and tracked seamlessly and in real time. The applications of this technology range from visual surveillance to virtual reality. When I decided to combine this original piece with interactive technology, I initially wanted a female avatar and perhaps a child to represent the child of the love

Figure 4.1   Elodie and Jeremiah from *Blue Bloodshot Flowers* (2001). Director: Sue Broadhurst; Technology: Richard Bowden. Image: Terence Tiernan

affair or the inner child. However, this all seemed too literal and when I saw the avatar Jeremiah, I immediately wanted him in the performance and decided to leave it to the audience to interpret this virtual presence–though, of course, most people would assume it was the image of the departed lover.

Blue Bloodshot Flowers was both a pilot scheme for future projects and a feasibility study. It is our intention, since the public performance proved so successful, to develop the technology further. We have discussed introducing speech and hearing to an avatar. With this in mind, we developed Saul, an avatar capable of speaking; and Rachel, who can morph between male and female. Both Saul and Rachel are, like Jeremiah, heads only, but our next collaboration will contain a full-bodied avatar. Despite this, Bowden, Berland and I are very reluctant to lose Jeremiah.

Jeremiah is a computer-generated animated head based on Geoface technology (DECface), consisting of a simple mesh representing the face with an underlying bone structure that allows the mesh to be deformed.[3] He (It) has a simple bone structure that allows him to express himself and emotions, such as anger, sadness or happiness. He was developed from surveillance technology–therefore, his eyes can see. During the performance a video camera fitted with a wide-angle lens was used to capture movement, which was relayed to Jeremiah's 'emotion' engine. The camera was located above the backdrop. Although we could have used more than one camera, one proved sufficient.

Jeremiah's emotion engine determines the current state of his apparent emotions from simple parameters extracted from objects of interest within his visual field. This simple set of rules allows chaotic behaviour in a similar fashion. For instance, Jeremiah likes visual stimulus: high rates of movement make him 'happy'. He likes company: a lack of stimulus makes him 'sad'. He does not like to be startled: high rates of change in the size of objects surprise him. Similarly, Jeremiah does not like to be ignored. If objects exist but do not move, he assumes he is being ignored and gets 'angry'. Also, if Jeremiah experiences too much 'pleasure' due to too much of any particular stimulus, he will reduce the stimulus' influence on him and grow 'bored'.

Jeremiah is capable of not only interacting but also reacting. In fact he possesses artificial intelligence to the degree that he can demonstrate several emotions simultaneously as a reaction to visual stimulus. Jeremiah is unique in that he embodies intelligence that is in no way prescriptive. Therefore, the performance is a direct and real-time interaction between performer, audience and avatar (technology).

Figure 4.2 Elodie and Jeremiah from *Blue Bloodshot Flowers*. Image by Sally Trussler and Richard Bowden

One of the most interesting aspects of the Jeremiah Project is how much the performer/spectator projects onto the avatar. This is not so surprising since, as already mentioned, a substantial area of the human brain is devoted to face recognition. The ability of humans to recognize facial expressions is so sophisticated that even very slight differences are noticed and made meaningful. In this performance, it was remarkable just how much information could be gleaned by the spectators from Jeremiah's facial expressions on very little evidence, leading to a variety of emotions being projected by them onto the avatar.

Jeremiah consists of computerized artificial intelligence with the ability to track humans, objects and other stimuli and to react to what's going on near him directly and in real time. However, interacting with Jeremiah is anything but objective, in fact, it is quite emotional. Most people, when they first see Jeremiah, find him 'spooky'. Then, after the initial contact leads to a degree of familiarity, people tend to treat him as they would a small child or a family pet. They usually try to make him smile and generally to please him. For instance, his face demonstrates sadness when he is left alone, so much so that many people find it difficult to walk away. As has been demonstrated by Ramachandran and Blakeslee, embodied emotional response is not only due to direct events that affect the self but can also be due to the stimulation of external objects that have been appropriated by the body (1999, 61–2). Arguably, an avatar, such as Jeremiah, is emotionally appropriated by the audience and perceived as an extension and modification of a human being.

Moreover, although Jeremiah is programmed to react to certain stimuli with specific facial emotional expressions, he can also demonstrate random behaviour that can be disruptive during a performance. This unpredictability adds a further 'real life' dimension to working with a virtual being. This aspect of the performance questions orthodox notions of origin and identity since Jeremiah's identity is in no way fixed and his origins are not easy to specify beyond listing some technical specifications. In addition to questioning conventions of authorship, the digital technology that created Jeremiah subverts assumptions of reproduction and representation because in every performance Jeremiah is original, just as an improvising artist is original. Jeremiah is literally 'reproduced again' and not 'represented'.

Blue Bloodshot Flowers is divided into two sections. The first part consists of a scripted movement-based interactive piece with the human performer (Berland), while the second part involves spectators who are invited to interact directly with Jeremiah and to explore his supporting technology. Surprisingly enough, in the first part of the performance, although initial interest and curiosity was directed towards Jeremiah, the spectators' attention was mainly focused on Berland. However, the spectators' focus shifted to Jeremiah when he decided to display fairly inappropriate behaviour, such as demonstrating happiness at an intense moment in the performance. We had no way of controlling his behaviour, which he learnt as he went along. We could, of course, turn him off but we were very reluctant to do this. Jeremiah was the focus of the performance during the second part when he directly interacted with the spectators. Because I had decided not to restrict when people could enter the 291 Gallery, audience members arrived right up until the very end of the scripted performance. I allowed unrestricted entrance for the very reason that Jeremiah would interact with any new arrivals he

Figure 4.3   Jeremiah and Director, *Blue Bloodshot Flowers*. Image by Terence Tiernan

spotted. And of course he did, which amused everyone, except possibly the late arrivals.

From a technological perspective, Jeremiah is based around two subsystems: a graphics system, which constitutes the head, and a vision system that allows him to see. The vision system surveys the scene and sends information to the head model, which then reacts. So Jeremiah is both the vision system and the head model. He also contains a simple emotion engine that allows him to respond to visual stimuli via expressions of emotions. The entire system is capable of running on a single PC, but for speed of operation each subsystem ran on its own dedicated PC connected via a network crossover. The whole system is self-standing and, with the construction of a flight case, truly portable.

Jeremiah's head contains a simple Newtonian model of motion with random elements of movement, blinking and ambient motion (Bowden, Kaewtrakulpong and Lewin 2002, 127). The Geoface-articulated bone model, DECface, provides a lifelike facial avatar that can be animated to produce various facial expressions. The software was custom written and produced by Bowden who 'prescribed' what Jeremiah's expressions would actually look like. Four basic pre-scripted expressions for key emotions are used within the system: happiness, sadness, anger and surprise (125). Jeremiah's vision system is based on a Gaussian mixture model of colour distributions (statistical order of the colour of each pixel within an image) that uses expectation maximization within the Grimson motion-tracker framework.[4] This allows Jeremiah to probabilistically differentiate between the foreground and background pixels of a new image. Jeremiah's visual system additionally suppresses shadow and removes noise, allowing static background scenes to be learnt dynamically and at the same time prioritizing foreground objects (125–6). Jeremiah's attention is randomly distributed between these objects, weighted by their size and motion. Therefore, objects closer to Jeremiah appear larger and capture his attention more than objects further away, thus leading him to interact with the foreground objects in real time via expressions of emotions.

Blue Bloodshot Flowers as a performance is hybridized and intertextual. It demonstrates such aesthetic features as heterogeneity, indeterminacy, reflexivity, fragmentation, a certain 'shift-shape style' and a repetitiveness that produces not sameness but difference. A distinctive aesthetic trait central to this performance is the utilization of the latest digital technology.

The employment of wide, jarring metaphors is a central characteristic of *Blue Bloodshot Flowers*. The colourful and figurative use of language and the juxtaposition of metaphors evoke surreal images of sex, violence and death. The interaction of the physical and virtual also creates inclusive, jarring metaphors. This mixture produces an aesthetic effect caused by the interplay of various mental sense impressions, which unsettle the audience by frustrating their expectations of any simple interpretation and in turn produce a new type of synaesthetic effect that can be likened to the experience caused by cross-wiring or cross-activation of discrete areas of the brain in certain perceptual conditions (Ramachandran and Hubbard 2001, 9).

In *Blue Bloodshot Flowers*, due to the hybridization of the performance and the diversity of media employed, various intensities are at play. It is these imperceptible intensities, together with their ontological status, that give rise to new modes of perception and consciousness. According to Deleuze and Guattari, 'experimentation has replaced all interpretation (1999a, 162). Their view of art as 'sensation' as a 'force' that ruptures everyday opinions and perceptions, 'to make perceptible the imperceptible forces' (1999b, 182), provides a means of theorizing the unpresentable or sublime of this kind of performance.

Likewise, for Lyotard, instead of a conceptual interpretation of meaning, the 'figural', a territory of form, colour and the visual, indicates flows and drives of 'intensities' which continually displace the identity of the reader (or spectator). The aim is to eliminate oppositions in favour of intensities and it is useful in a description of such digital practices as *Blue Bloodshot Flowers* with its diverse elements that often escape meaningful interpretation.

Since the project is a science and art collaboration, there are very marked qualities in the research rationale and questions. For Bowden, the Turing test describes a system as artificially intelligent if a human user cannot distinguish the system from another human in conversation. He is attempting to test this concept of intelligence by providing an interactive human avatar with simple rules and chaotic behaviour. Bowden believes that the interactivity and human embodiment of Jeremiah is sufficient for people to accept him as a living entity. Therefore, Bowden's foremost question is, 'How real can Artificial Life become? How do we interact with A' Life? (Bowden and Broadhurst 2001).

My interest, on the other hand, is concerned with more arts-related questions. I want to explore and analyse the effect these new technologies have on the physical body in performance. Underpinning this is a series of specific research questions:

1. What are the effects of new technologies in the analysis of the performing body?
2. What are the theoretical implications of virtual performance for the body and space?
3. What are the implications of, and how do we theorize the resultant destabilization of identity and origin?
4. What is the potential for participation and interactivity, between and among performers and spectators, within this new art's practice?

Although much interest is directed towards new technologies, such as Jeremiah, it is my belief that technology's most important contribution to art is the enhancement and reconfiguration of an aesthetic creative potential which consists of interacting with and reacting to a physical body, not an abandonment of that body. Furthermore, it is my belief that despite or even due to new technologies there remains the need to articulate and analyse innovative performance in ways other than the linguistic. There is now more than ever the need for an intersemiotic significatory practice, that is, an analysis that includes but also goes beyond language.

In conclusion, this is an ongoing project – part of what is hoped will be a variety of performances that combine the physical and virtual in performance. *Blue Bloodshot Flowers* was performed at Brunel University in June 2001, and at the 291 Gallery, East London, in August of that year to quite a large audience. However, the rehearsal process proved extremely stimulating and may prove ultimately more beneficial for research than the finished product. Throughout, emphasis is placed more on the process of adaptation, how the performance develops and so on, than on the finished product. In this way, strategies are exposed and the apparent seamlessness of performance and technology is negated. Thus, my goal is to destroy theatrical illusion, while at the same time resisting closure from within a place that is not completely aesthetic but is nevertheless a performance (performative) space.

Digital dance, evolution and chance: Merce Cunningham's *BIPED*

> I thought for years that dance and technology, because technology is ninety percent visual, they are mated. Because you look at dancing and you look at the technology.
>
> (Cunningham 2000b)

> A man is a two-legged creature – more basically and more intimately than he is anything else.
>
> (Cunningham 1997b, 86)

The premiere of *BIPED* was performed at the Zellerbach Hall, University of California, Berkeley, in 1999.[5] In *BIPED*, an absolutely stunning if ultimately distancing performance, pre-captured dancing avatars are rear projected onto a translucent screen giving the effect of a direct interface between the physical and virtual bodies. Cunningham's use of motion capture, in collaboration with Eshkar and Kaiser, displaces the boundaries of physicality in a fairly radical way. Physical movement generates virtual bodies through the mediation of technology and the digital designers. Hand drawn abstract images and figures by Eshkar, animated by motion capture data provided by real dancers are seen together with live dancers on stage bringing into question notions of embodiment, identity and origin.

Figure 4.4   Merce Cunninghan Dance Company performs 'BIPED' at the Lincoln Center Festival (1999). Credit: © Stephanie Berger

This was not the first time that Cunningham had employed new tech-nologies in his work. He had been experimenting with the software program, 'LifeForms' (now known as 'DanceForms'), for many years as an aid to choreography, notation and performance. The software, a 3-D human animation program, was developed by Tom Calvert, a computer scientist and kinesiologist from the Simon Fraser University, Vancouver, in collaboration with choreographers, Thecla Shiphorst and Catherine Lee. LifeForms was first used by Cunningham in *Trackers* (1991). The title refers to the 'tracking' of the dancers with a camera and also to 'a button on the dance computer, called "Track"' (Cunningham quoted by Vaughan 1997, 256). According to Cunningham, although there is the potential to create an infinite possibility of physical movements with this technology, 'I much prefer working with the human body within its limits' (Cunningham 2000b).

Cunningham had also previously collaborated with Eshkar and Kaiser on *Hand-drawn Spaces* (1998), a digitally animated virtual installation. In that piece, 72 choreographed phases of movement were optically captured from two performers (Jeannie Steele and Jarad Philips), that is, reflective discs ('motion capture sensors') were placed on key joints of the performers' bodies and their dance movements were digitally mapped by a series of cameras linked to a computer. These dots were then digitally applied to skeletal animations, which could be further manipulated. The hand-drawn, partially humanoid figures sketched by Eshkar were choreographed with the help of the LifeForms computer program. The final virtual performance was projected onto large multiple screens.

One of the key influences on Cunningham's work is television with its effect on our 'modes of perception' (Reynolds 2000, 1). Cunningham has stated that, 'one thing must not necessarily follow another. Or rather anything can follow anything. We see it on television all the time. In the 20th century this new continuity is part of the life we live' (2). According to Cunningham, *BIPED* was about working with technology and also to do with the notion of television channel surfing, 'flicking through channels on TV' (Kaiser 2004a). This motif was evident in the presentation of the performance where 'movement phases are combined and recombined and scale and pacing are in constant flux' (Scarry 1999).

Roger Copeland takes issue with this analogy and believes that television viewing is in its rhythm a variety of flows that ultimately blur such essential distinctions as those between 'fact and fiction' and 'news and entertainment'. For Copeland, Cunningham's work does not go with the 'flow', since wholeness and unity together with the blurring of boundaries is rejected and the discreteness of the various elements is maintained (Copeland 2004, 283–4).

BIPED with its interface and interaction between physical and virtual bodies can be seen to displace fixed categories of identity. In the performance each carries a 'trace' of the other, given that the virtual performers are the digital reincarnation of the human bodies. For Derrida, the trace is 'the *pure* movement which produces difference' (1976, 62). The difference between two terms is perceived from the perspective of one of the terms, the term of plenitude from which the second term is held to derive (physical versus virtual). The problematic of the trace articulates the recognition of that privileged term in a difference of opposition that could not appear as such without the opposition that gives it form. Therefore, the trace explains why a concept of plenitude of presence can be thought only within binary conceptual structures. Differance, a term used by Derrida in order to provide a critique of the notion of differentiation, is not simply deferring but also implies difference. In other words it indicates both temporality and space. And space is seen as '*a movement*, a displacement that indicates an irreducible alterity' (Gasché 1986, 200). A process marked by its supposedly 'self sufficient present' and its 'becoming-time of space' (198), a condition necessary for the possibility of identity since 'any entity is what it is only by being divided by the Other to which it refers in order to constitute itself' (202).

Cunningham in his choreography rejects traditional notions of space, such as the proscenium centre stage viewed front on. For him, all space is equal and no point has priority. Moreover, it needs to be remembered that our cultural perspective on the world is constructed not given. From Alberti onwards, between the 'distance point' and the 'vanishing point', a new world was created by means of the artist's grid-like perspective applied to our perception of the world; 'the self as a spectator behind a window has become the world's measure by making the world a matter of its vision' (Romanyshyn 1989, 65). According to Cunningham, 'most stage work ... is based on a perspective, a [fixed] centre point from which everything radiates.' However, this perspective on the world is inaccurate not only 'in art, but in general' (Lesschaeve 1985, 172). Referring to a quote by Albert Einstein that refutes 'fixed points in space', Cunningham states that 'if there are no fixed points, then every point is equally interesting and equally changing.' This brings with it 'an enormous range of possibilities', including 'different movements in different rhythms' together with 'new ways of looking' (Cunningham with Lesschaeve 1999, 29–30). For Cunningham, movement is not a referent or a signified for some other meaning; rather, it is to do solely with the nature of the movement itself: 'I think movement is so fascinating. I never can understand why people think there should be something behind it. I understand that you can think that way to try and have a meaning or a reference point ... but for me it really is what it is,' (2001, 46) and 'I thought of as nonsense' the idea that a particular movement means something specific (Greskovic 1999, 72). Cunningham in his early career danced with Martha Graham's dance troupe and this comment was specifically aimed at one of her central tenets.

Movement has been a way for Cunningham to explore and discover new parameters of embodiment, and what it means to be 'human'. In his choreography, familiar relations of the human body are frequently dislocated in time and space, destabilizing notions of identity. He continually frustrates audience expectations by providing disparate elements that are juxtaposed together creating a distancing effect and causing the audience to actively participate in the activity of producing meaning. In many of his works, movement, lighting and sound, are developed independently, frequently being brought together only at the performance itself. There is also an emphasis on collage whose 'juxtaposition is separated by a gap of space and time', and unlike montage with its fusion of 'separate components into a single entity', which is 'imposed on the viewer', it is 'inherently less manipulative' (Copeland 2002, 20).

Similarly, Copeland argues that Cunningham's work demonstrates a 'polyvocal' approach to performance making rather than a univocal one. Polyvocal is a post-structuralist term indicating many disunified voices rather than one single voice. In Cunningham's work various artists do come together but remain autonomous in their creativity. In refuting the term of *Gesamtkunstwerk* to describe Cunningham's work, Copeland follows Adolphe Appia's belief that every element of this total performance should follow a single direction and director. 'Collage', as Copeland describes Cunningham's performances to be, resists such a '"centralized" control' (2004, 180). However, arguably this could be an overly reductive interpretation of the Wagnerian term, though there is no doubt Cunningham's performances do speak through many and varied voices.

Expressiveness is eschewed, as is narrative content and structure, that is, there is no sense of closure or resolution. In fact Cunningham's work can be seen to be anti-dramatic in the conventional sense of that term in his rejection of 'conflict and resolution, cause and effect, and climax and anti-climax' (Vaughan 1997, 7). Rather, the dramatic in his work results from the theatrical experience with its emphasis on the corporeal and kinetic. A major influence on Cunningham since the 1940s was his working and personal relationship with John Cage. The non-metrical structure of Cage's music enabled Cunningham to escape from conventional dramatic and choreographic structures. Writing of 'events' that 'led to large discoveries in my work', Cunningham states that

> The first came with my initial work with John Cage ... when we began to separate the music and the dance. Using at that time what Cage called a 'rhythmic structure' ... This allowed the music and the dance to have an independence between the structure points ... working in this manner gave me a feeling of freedom for the dance, not a dependence upon the note-by-note procedure with which I had been used to working.
>
> (1997a, 276)

One of the key procedures in Cunningham's work process has been his use of 'chance' principles, in particular, his reliance on *I Ching* also known as the *Book of Changes*. Cage was influential in introducing this element into Cunningham's creative process in the early 1950s.[6] The performance of *Sixteen Dancers for Soloist and Company of Three* (1951), a collaboration with Cage, was the first time it was used in Cunningham's choreographic process (Vaughan 1997, 58). *I Ching* is an ancient Chinese method of divination and prophecy. It is also the source of Confucian and Taoist philosophy. Questions are answered and advice is given by referring to the text, which accompanies one of 64 hexagrams that are selected at random. Traditionally, this was done by means of various numerical combinations of yarrow sticks. However, for Cunningham, answers are sought by means of the toss of coins or the throw of a dice, 'when I choreograph a piece by tossing pennies – by chance, that is … I am in touch with natural resources far greater than my own personal inventiveness could ever be' (Cunningham 1997b, 86).

Chance procedures initially influenced the choreographic elements of Cunningham's performances. For instance, 'what phrases follows what phrase, how timewise and rhythmically the particular movement operates', how many dancers are to be used, and how the space is to be divided (1997a, 276). However, various other elements of Cunningham's performances, for example, sound, set design and costumes, have also arisen from this chance method of devising. For a recent project, *Split Sides* (2004),[7] commissioned by BITE: 04 Barbican, London, and the Brooklyn Academy of Music, New York, he exaggerated his use of chance procedure to the limit by allowing the piece to evolve from strategies of randomness and risk. The order of the choreographic elements rested on the throw of a dice as did that of the actual performance itself, since another of Cunningham's works accompanied the piece and it was only decided at the beginning of the evening's performance which work would lead. Similarly, the design elements: mise-en-scène, lighting and costumes, together with the sound, all rested on chance. There were two separate choreographic sections from Cunningham and different backdrops provided by 2002 Turner Prize-nominee Catherine Yass and American photographer Robert Heishman, two costume designs from James Hall, and the digital sound was supplied by the British alternative rock band, Radiohead and the Icelandic experimental rock band, Sigur Rós. Out of a possible 32 combinations of these various elements, it was determined nightly when and what the audience would see by the roll of a dice.

Emphasizing the similarities between technology and the chance procedures of his choreographic process, Cunningham has for several years, since the late 1960s, used computer terminology to describe his performances. In referring to his piece, *Walkaround Time* (1968), he writes, 'the title comes from computer language. You feed the computer information then you have to wait while it digests. There's some argument as to whether the computer is walking around or those who are waiting' (1968, n.p.). However, in *BIPED*, technology and chance are intertwined in the actual performance itself culminating in astonishing visual effects. According to Kaiser, the order of the various sequences of animation in *BIPED* was decided by 'chance operations'. Cunningham, after being given a list of sequence titles and durations by Eshkar and Kaiser, rolled the dice to establish their order and timing, which was then fixed. Kaiser describes how as a result of such a chance operation, 'one of the first dancers on stage (Jeannie Steele) was haloed in a projection of her own motion capture, as if I were dancing inside myself, she said afterwards' (Kaiser 2004a). Using similar chance procedures Eshkar and Kaiser went on to motion capture Cunningham's hands for the production of *Loops* (2001) in order to create a 'digital portrait' of him.[8] Kaiser claims that since Cage and Cunningham left many of their creative decisions to chance – 'to the roll of the dice', their works became truly autonomous. According to Kaiser, in *Loops*, 'these radical notions of realism and autonomy' were extended (Kaiser 2004b). However, although *Loops* was a remarkable demonstration of the use of technology in performance, it lacked *BIPED's* visual impact.

According to Kaiser, the name *BIPED* had a special significance, since '"Biped" had been the working title for the alpha and beta releases of Character Studio', the figure-animation software created by Michael Girard and Susan Amkraut of Unreal Pictures, and used to choreograph the virtual dance of *Hand-drawn Spaces*. Kaiser suggests that together with the technological there is also an anatomical connotation since Cunningham has had a lifelong interest in investigating 'all that a body on two legs can do' (Kaiser 2004a) For Copeland, the title of the work 'evokes an evolutionary landmark', that separates humans from most other primates (2004, 219). Referring to Erwin Strauss's argument about 'the gaze of upright posture' which infers the 'cultivation of various varieties of "distance"' (for example, distance from the ground and from each other) and also the voluntary repression of '"automatic" responses and instinctual "drives"' (217), he posits that Cunningham's *BIPED* implies the next evolutionary stage, 'the transcendence of the "grounded" body' (219). The development of new technologies which potentate such virtual bodies as those of *BIPED*, may indeed suggest a desire and potential need for humans to eventually not only exchange their physical bodies for those of the prosthetic and cybernetic, but also their earthly space for that of the extraterrestrial.

For *BIPED*, Kaiser and Eshkar created approximately 25 minutes of animation for the 45-minute-long performance. These were discontinuous sequences, ranging in length from about 15 seconds to four minutes (Kaiser 2004a). *BIPED* was developed over a two-year period from the captured dance phrases initially used in *Hand-drawn Spaces*. The motion-captured phrases were optically recorded by digital-video cameras and the resultant data transferred to 'Biped', an animated 3-D figure, using the software program, Character Studio. In short, corporeal movements are transmitted from live dancers to a computer. According to Cunningham, dance and technology are made for each other since they are 'about a way of looking' (Vaughan 2000, 61), and for Kaiser, *BIPED* 'is a simulated wire frame of a body, but a body with a good deal of computer intelligence' (Kaiser 2000). However, for Ann Dils

> Motion capture and animation technologies make it possible to create portraits of people that consist primarily of human motion, replacing identifiable bodies with more generic forms. Do these images work as portraits? What is the impact of leaving the body behind?
>
> (Dils 2002, 94)

Motion capture and animation techniques may provide an example of the phenomenon known as the 'peak shift effect', which explains caricatures and many other aspects of art. It has been suggested that during evolutionary development, visual areas of the brain specifically concerned with extracting correlations and rules, and attaching visual attributes along different dimensions such as 'form space' or 'motion space', become directly linked to emotional limbic structures that in turn produce pleasure sensations (Ramachandran and Hirstein 1999, 22). Accordingly, exaggerating a particular rule and eliminating excess detail, as demonstrated by *BIPED's* representationally abstract dancing avatars proves to be even more pleasing.

For *BIPED*, unlike *Hand-drawn Spaces*, Kaiser's and Eshkar's animations were intended to furnish the mise-en-scène of a live dance performance where virtual and live dancers would seemingly interact in the same performance space. According to Kaiser, five minutes of motion captured from *BIPED* animated the figures more freely and went far beyond *Hand-drawn Spaces*:

> We had dot bodies (from the dots seen in motion capture), stick bodies (inspired by the yarrow sticks cast by I Ching practitioners like

Cunningham and Cage), and cubist/chronophotograph bodies (our nod towards Marey and Duchamp).

(Kaiser 2004a)

These animated figures together with patterns of vertical and horizontal lines, were projected onto a scrim (gauze curtain) at the front of the stage. The live performers danced behind. Cunningham has claimed that 'the relationship between the dance and music is one of co-existence, that is being related simply because they exist at the same time' (1968, n.pag). For *BIPED*, composer Gavin Bryers was given no instructions for the concept or structure but was told only the duration of the performance and he also played the score, which was a blend of electronic and acoustic sound, live at the performance in London. Suzanne Gallo, known for using unusual materials, designed the costumes, which were made out of a metallic material that shimmered with reflected light.

The performance presented a sublime interaction between physical and virtual bodies with some truly haunting moments. The huge animated virtual bodies were astonishingly beautiful appearing predominantly as colourful abstract humanoid representations that morphed and demorphed into a variety of patterns and shapes. They seemed to dance alongside the physical dancers though above, suggesting a deified presence. The avatars appeared and disappeared randomly at various points of the space and cast moving reflections in the vertical lines at the back of the space. According to Eshkar, 'we conceived of it as a forest, a forest of poles, and at any point in this three-dimensional forest of poles a figure could emerge, but clipped in a 2-D way, as though it had just come out of nowhere' (Eshkar 2000). The physical dancers too at times mysteriously materialized and dematerialized, approaching from the back of the stage and leaving the same way.

The live as opposed to virtual choreography of *BIPED* was also devised with the assistance of DanceForms software, the dancer's bodies reflecting the slightly disjointed gestures of much of Cunningham's recent works. However, in contrast to many of his other pieces, there were no moments of stillness. The physical dancers were in constant flux; their movements sometimes conflicting with the slower movements of the projected virtual bodies. Each dancer's movements were individualistic and followed their own timing through similar gestures and sequences. There was an emphasis on the repetitiveness of certain gestures, such as the elevation of the right arm, evoking ritualistic connotations. The live performers were frequently seen without the projected images, whereas the avatars appeared as if to counter the complex rhythmic patterns of the live choreography. According to Kaiser, 'the dance is successful if your perception of the dance has been affected by the projections, even when they aren't present on the screen' (Kaiser 2000).

Finally, art does not 'actualize the virtual event', rather, it embodies the event or gives it 'a body, a life, a universe' that is neither 'virtual' nor 'actual' but 'possible' (Deleuze and Guattari 1999b, 177). This potential embodiment is central to Cunningham's *BIPED*, where both physical and virtual bodies continually become-other and where various imperceptible intensities exist that give rise to new modes of perception.

Deleuze and Guattari's notion of a body without organs which is an 'intense and intensive body' can also be useful in an analysis of potential embodiment. No longer is there a '"Self" ... an organism that functions but a BwO that is constructed' (Deleuze and Guattari 1999a, 162). The body does not have organs but (liminal) 'thresholds or levels' (Deleuze 2003, 45) as do the avatars from *BIPED*. It is produced by desiring-machines and these machines work best at the moment 'they break down' (Deleuze and Guattari 1984, 8). This metaphor of 'machine' denotes a shift away from the organic and human towards a timeless entity with no identity, intent or even end. In short, a model of pure machinic production, always in the process of becoming and making new connections. As Cunningham writes:

> With the dance computer, I am aware once more of new possibilities with which to work. My work has always been in process.
>
> (Cunningham, 1997a, 276)

Virtuality, cybernetics and the post-human: Stelarc's obsolete body

> When I talk about the obsolete body I don't mean that we should discard bodies altogether, but rather that a body with this form and these functions cannot operate effectively in the technological terrain that it has created.
>
> (Stelarc 2002b, 122)

> Of all the possible implications that first-wave cybernetics conveyed, perhaps none was more disturbing and potentially revolutionary than the idea that the boundaries of the human subject are constructed rather than given.
>
> (Hayles 1999, 84)

For several years, the controversial and somewhat sensationalist performances of the Australian artist Stelarc have served as an interdisciplinary forum for cultural and social theory, art, science and science fiction, translating concepts of the 'posthuman' into performative actualizations of physical and technological interface. Stelarc advocates a 'planetary escape velocity' for the human body, which he sees as an 'obsolete body' that cannot operate in the technological terrain it has created. To this end he has used medical instruments, prosthetics, robotics, virtual reality systems and the Internet to explore alternate, intimate and involuntary interfaces with the body.

Stelarc has been suspended from on high by hooks penetrating his flesh (1976–88). He has performed with a *Virtual Arm* (1992–3), a *Third Hand* (1976–81), an *Extended Arm* (2000), a *Stomach Sculpture* (1993), an *Exoskeleton* (1998) and *Hexapod*, a six-legged walking robot, now developed into the *Muscle Machine* (2003a). Stelarc's *Fractal Flesh*, *Ping Body* and *ParaSite* performances (1995–8) have explored involuntary, remote and Internet choreography of the body through electrical stimulation of his muscles. His *Movatar* (2000) is an inverse motion capture system which allows an avatar to perform in the physical world by accessing and actuating a host body. Stelarc's *Prosthetic Head* (2003d) involves an embodied conversational agent, an avatar that speaks to any person who interrogates it, and he has attempted to surgically attach a 'soft' prosthesis in the form of an *Extra Ear* (2004c) to his body (His attempt to incorporate such a prosthesis had partial success in 2006). For Stelarc

> The prosthetic is viewed not as a sign of lack but rather as a symptom of excess. So as technology proliferates more, technology is more excessive. As technology becomes more microminiaturized and bio-compatible it becomes more suitable to be incorporated as a component within the fabric of the human body.
>
> (2003c)

In contrast to the increasing emphasis placed by theorists on historical and cultural contextualization, Stelarc insists on isolating his performances within an aesthetic localized framework, which as Ross Farnell notes, rejects both 'its own ideological basis' together with the sociocultural 'consequences that must inevitably arise from such posthuman strategies' (Stelarc 1999, 130). The 'posthuman' describes the transformation of bodies modified or *polluted* by technology. Human identities are mutated by the impact of various information technologies, which at the same time identify that impact. The post-human body is thus inscribed and reconfigured by its own mediatized and mediated narrative, 'by the very technology that determines it' (Clarke 2002, 33). For Stelarc, 'to be posthuman is to take up a strategy where one needs to shed one's skin and consider other more deeper and more complex interfaces and interconnections with the technologies that we've generated' (1999, 131).

Stelarc is viewed by many as being a strong advocate for an optimistic post-human future, whilst others have very real misgivings regarding his seemingly naïve and undertheorized approach to technology (Dery 1996, 151–69). However, this apparent naivety can be seen as a critical deconstructive practice. For whilst appearing to be complicit with dominant means of digital representation, Stelarc's performance attempts at the same time to destabilize those structures by identifying concerns that affect us all.

Stelarc makes it clear that for him technology does not necessarily mean '"hardware" or "state-of-the-art"' technology, since the roots of technology come from 'the word "*techné*" meaning skills'. Therefore, technologies are contemporary bits of hardware that allow 'alternate strategies'. Neither is he 'naively utopian' since his work is grounded in 'experience', 'constrained by the limitations' of his body, the 'determinations of the hardware' and 'what interfaces are possible' (Stelarc 1999, 138). According to Stelarc

> What I am really interested in is when disruptions and transgressions occur ... none of my writings have been anything more than poetic speculation ... I don't use extensive citations. That doesn't mean that I haven't read Virilio, Baudrillard, Lyotard and Derrida and a lot of other theorists ... But these ideas can only be authenticated through the performances that I do and they only have meaning when generated by these performances.
>
> (2002b, 118)

Moreover, 'what's interesting for me is simply not going more and more virtual but rather exploring the interface between the actual and the virtual' (116). As with all digital practices, tensions exist within the liminal spaces created by this interface of body and technology. It is within these tension filled spaces that opportunities arise for new experimental forms and practices.

One of the central elements in Stelarc's work has been the exploration and utilization of cybernetics, particularly the 'cyborg'. This reflects his preoccupation with the 'human/machine interface – hybridizing of the body with its technologies' (Stelarc 1995, 46) and 'the body as both an anatomical and evolutionary structure' (Stelarc 2003d, 11); the 'notion of post evolution being one of choice' (Stelarc 1999, 145). Writing on the human evolutionary structure, Stelarc claims:

> Apparently, the explosive growth of the cortex occurs after bipedialism. All of a sudden two limbs become manipulators, producing artifacts and instruments and the whole relationship with the world changed. These minor anatomical changes produced a radical new orientation in the world.
>
> (1995, 46)

Therefore, 'if we are really caring about life in general and intelligence in particular', we should allow the development of 'any form of life that can perpetuate these values in a more durable or a more pervasive form' (49).

The term 'cyborg', first noted in the *Journal of Astronautics* (1960), was used by NASA researchers, Manfred Clynes and Nathan Kline, to define an entity that 'deliberately incorporates exogenous components extending the self-regulatory control function of the organism in order to adapt it to new environments' (1995, 31). The term is derived from the merging of 'cybernetics'[9] with 'organism', the human as cyborg becoming a hybrid of machine and organism. NASA's focus on the cyborg was concerned with techniques for adapting and modifying certain behavioural patterns, for example, overcoming negative psychological responses to adverse sensory stimulation. In short, the mechanical adaptation of an organic life form to ensure its most efficient performativity. In contrast to this prescriptive behaviourist model, the notion of the cyborg, from an artistic and cultural perspective and certainly in its use by Stelarc, is more concerned with 'developing circuitry and feedback loops linking human and machine in a continuous sequence of action, always with the effect of confusing which is the controller and which the controlled' and 'far from being simply a macho "control freak", Stelarc minutely explores the phenomenon of control as reversible and even, ultimately, delusory' (Goodall 1999, 163).

Cyborgism now covers a range of cultural and technological phenomena – from simple computer and videogames interactions and the Internet, to the more sophisticated example of bionic interface in the artworks of Stelarc, or the virtual/physical interface of Jeremiah in *Blue Bloodshot Flowers*, particularly when the technology involved is felt to have some kind of agency. The cyborg is also central to the cyber fiction genre where new genetic hybrids are created, which couple humans to bionic components, whether to prolong life or to allow existence in alien environments, or to allow access into virtual worlds where humans are 'jacked in' and interface their brains with cyberspace as in the cyberfictions of William Gibson, and more recently the Wachowskis' *Matrix*.

In Donna Harraway's seminal work, 'A Cyborg Manifesto' (1991), 'an ironic dream' of mediated hybridity 'for women in the integrated circuit', the cyborg is 'a creature of social reality as well as a creature of fiction' (149), where high-tech culture challenges the dominant Western dualisms 'in intriguing ways' (177) and 'is a dream of not a common language, but of a powerful heteroglossia' (181). However, for Stelarc, the cyborg is not the collectivist entity theorized by Harraway. It is rather an individual who is technologically enhanced: 'I am not talking about redesigning the species' (Stelarc 1999, 145). And Lyotard, somewhat tongue-in-cheek, in questioning 'Can Thought Go On Without A Body?' (1988/89), writes of the body as 'hardware' whilst 'the material ensemble called man is endowed with a very sophisticated software.' Following the sun's demise in 4.5 billion years, this 'hardware will be consumed in the solar explosion taking philosophical thought along with it (along with all other thought) as it goes up in flames' (78–9). So the problem for Lyotard is how to provide 'this software with a hardware that is independent of life on earth.' Since perception is always already embodied, 'it isn't enough for these machines to simulate the results of vision or writing fairly well', it is rather a matter of '"giving body" to the artificial thought of which they are capable' (82). However, this 'analogizing power' which belongs to the body and mind mutually 'is inconsequential compared to an irreparable transcendence inscribed on the body by gender difference.' Thus, 'thought is inseparable from the phenomenological body: although the gendered body is separated from thought' and for this inevitable futuristic separation of mind and body with all its complexities 'post solar thought' needs to be fully prepared (87).

According to Stelarc, 'there are some gender distinctions [between the ways males and females utilize technologies], but ... gender becomes a blur of lots of shades of subtle distinctions rather than a male and female, a heterosexual or gay, polarization' (1999, 142–3). In referring to his body as '*the body*' (138), Stelarc has been accused by some critics including Anne Marsh (1993), as rejecting embodiment and even of '"somatophobia": fear of the body' (Fleming 2002, 97), which points to the inevitable dualism of mind/body opposition. However, instead of the Cartesian cogito, Stelarc shows that 'to be a body is to be tied to a certain world' (Merleau-Ponty 1962, 148). And perception is always already embodied within a specific context or situation.[10] As Chris Fleming states, 'in contrast to Descartes' epistemology, Stelarc's work is preoccupied with the possibilities of the body, at the same time that it makes its boundaries, and hence its identity, ambiguous,' (2002, 96). According to Goodall, 'Stelarc's art is reliant on multi-dimensional knowledge's of the body, all of which are experiential as well as theoretical' (1999, 162). For Stelarc, thought is not localized or interior: 'What's meaningful is what is possible ... not to deny theory, but rather ... to manifest theory in an action.' As a result 'the body' is 'seen without the entrapments of ... a Cartesian "split" between mind and body', as 'a structure rather than as a psyche' (1999, 138–9).

In writing on *How We Became Posthuman* (1999), Katherine Hayles claims that, 'conceptualizing control, communication, and information, as an integrated system, cybernetics radically changes how boundaries were conceived' (84). For Hayles, the discovery of constructed boundaries around the human subject has far reaching implications since a view of the self as 'autonomous' and 'independent of the environment' leads to the fear that if boundaries are breached, that self will dissolve. In contrast 'when a human is seen as part of a distributed system', human capability can be seen 'to *depend* on the splice rather than being imperiled by it' (290). Stelarc's work exaggerates markedly this disruption and destabilization of self, by blurring the boundaries of his own body. As Goodall mentions, 'Stelarc explores the possibilities of connectivity to a point where he can claim that the body linked up with electronic circuitry has ceased to function as a delimited entity' (1999, 151).

Fractal Flesh: Split Body: Voltage in/Voltage Out (1996),[11] a performance that I attended in Perth, Western Australia, consists of Stelarc's body being stimulated by members of the audience who can view and control his movements by means of a touch screen web interface located in the gallery space. At the same time, Stelarc controls his robotic *Third Arm* by stimulation from his abdominal and right leg muscles. His body is split into two, the left side activated by the web interface, the resultant movements being involuntary, whilst he retains control of the right side of his body, which in turn controls the robotic prosthesis. According to Stelarc, 'the body acts as a more complex entity with a split physiology, interfaced and engaged with a multiplicity of tasks. It structures the performance initially through its hardwiring, and of course, it's aware of what's going on' (Stelarc 1998, 193–4). This performance had been presented the previous year (1995), where audiences in Amsterdam, Helsinki and Paris, used a similar device to activate muscles of Stelarc's body whilst he was located physically in Luxemburg. As a performance the resultant images were striking but at the same time disturbing, given that one side of Stelarc's naked body jerked involuntarily in response to the electrical stimulation of his muscles, whilst the other side moved voluntarily as it in turn controlled the *Third Arm*. The involuntary interface provides Stelarc, with what can only be seen as an extra neural circuitry, at the same time it blurs notions of body and agency in the resultant destabilization of identity. It also presents a literal and lived example of the consequences of global connectivity.

In later performances, such as *Ping Body* (1995–8), the notion of agency becomes even more blurred as all human intervention is replaced by Internet activity – Stelarc's gestures becoming a reproduction of the Internet itself. *Ping Body* involves sending global signals, the process of 'pinging' being the measurement in milliseconds of the time it takes for receipt of those signals to be acknowledged. Numbers resulting from these measurements are used as inputs to randomly control Stelerc's movements. So, 'instead of collective bodies determining the operation of Internet, the usual interface of the body to the Net. Internet activity moves the body' (Stelarc 1999, 146). Accompanying the *Ping Body* are the *ParaSite* performances where the body-as-parasite is added to the Internet. It 'is not about master-slave control but feedback-loops of alternate awareness, agency and split physiologies' (146). The notion of parasite is presented as being reversible where the body is invaded but also becomes a parasite, motivated by 'an extended, external and virtual nervous system'(Stelarc quoted in Goodall 1999, 164). According to Stelarc, 'what you have here is an obsolete body that seems to have evolved as an absent body and has now been invaded by technology, a body that is hollow, that now performs involuntarily for remote people over the internet' (2002b, 115).

The term 'hollow' is frequently used by Stelarc to describe 'the body'. It refers to a body without organs or BwO as an 'intense and intensive body' (Deleuze 2003, 44), which by extension and assemblage can become a post-human body, a model of pure machinic production, always in the process of becoming, neither 'virtual' nor 'actual' but a 'possible' body (Deleuze 1999b, 177), as that of *Fractal Flesh* and *Ping Body*. It can appropriate new technologies into itself, sometimes literally, as in Stelarc's *Stomach Sculpture* where an artwork is inserted into his 'hollow' stomach and filmed by means of endoscopic equipment, invading 'the body not as a prosthetic replacement, but as an aesthetic adornment' (Stelarc 2004b), or potentially in the form of nanotechnology, as 'SPECK-SIZED ROBOTS [that] ARE EASILY SWALLOWED, AND MAY NOT EVEN BE SENSED' (Stelarc 1997, 248–9).

The 'virus' is another metaphor commonly employed by Stelarc; it describes his view of technology. However, unlike McLuhan whose use of the term indicates catastrophe, Stelarc employs the term in a positive sense 'since technology hasn't been inside the body long enough ... so the body doesn't have any evolutionary raison d'etre to reject it' (1999, 140) and 'it is time to recolonize the body with MICROMINIATURISED ROBOTS to augment our bacterial population ... At a nanotechnology level, machines will inhabit cellular spaces and manipulate molecular structures' (1997, 248–9). In Stelarc's performance *Movator*,[12] the virus, becomes an actuality as 'an inverse motion capture system' motivated by the interface of a physical body and the Internet. *Movatar* consists of a motion prosthesis, a pneumatically operated device with 'only three degrees of freedom for each arm' allowing '64 possible combinations' of movement (Stelarc 2002a, 75), that is wrapped around the upper torso and arms of a physical host enabling precise and fast movements, splitting the body not from left to right but from top to bottom. The intention is that an avatar, imbued with some AI, possesses a physical body via the *Movatar* prosthesis in order to perform in the real world, thus further blurring the distinctions between the virtual and actual. According to Stelarc, the avatar can be thought of as 'a kind of viral life form' or agent that lies dormant except when it is connected to a physical body. It then becomes activated and in turn reactivates the host body. Therefore, the body shares its agency with an artificial entity that has the ability to learn to a limited extent, developing its behaviour within the duration of a performance (2002a, 76).

The *Muscle Machine* (2003a) developed from the *Hexapod* was a further attempt by Stelarc to construct an interactive and operational system,[13] this time, in the form of a walking robot.[14] It is a system, which couples the biological body with machine architecture, combining muscles with mechanism. Rubber muscles are inflated with air; as one set of muscles lengthens the other shortens in order to produce movement, at the same time translating human bipedal gait into a six-legged insect-like motion. Optical senses are located below the chassis where the physical body (Stelarc) sits, ensuring that the robot will only travel in whichever direction that body is facing. When the physical body sits, the robot lowers, and when it stands the robot lifts. At the performance I attended, there were some problems with weight distribution and Stelarc was unable to sit. Instead, he had to stand with his feet on the floor, as a result of which the machine's ability to walk was compromised. However, the coupling of the physical body with the mechanical was nevertheless striking.

Figure 4.5   MUSCLE MACHINE. Gallery 291, London (2003). Photographer: Mark Bennett. STELARC

For Merleau-Ponty, instrumentation and technology are mutually implicated with the body in an epistemological sense. The body adapts and extends itself through external instruments. Therefore, to have experience, to get used to an instrument, is to incorporate that instrument into the body (1962, 143). In Stelarc's performances, the body is coupled with a variety of instrumental and technological devices that instead of being separate from the body become part of that body, at the same time altering and recreating its experience in the world.

Other examples of prosthetic possibilities are provided by Stelarc's *Extra Ear* (2004c) and *Prosthetic Head* (2003d) projects. The former is a soft prosthesis provided by Oron Catts and Ionat Zurr from their 'Tissue Culture & Art Project', based within SymbioticA: the Art & Science Collaborative Research Laboratory, School of Anatomy and Human Biology, University of Western Australia, where they explore the use of tissue technologies as a medium for artistic expression; 'we refer to this kind of experiential work as "getting one's hands wet" with life manipulation' (Zurr and Catts 2003).

Stelarc has been collaborating with the School of Anatomy and Human Biology, UWA, since 1997 on this project (Stelarc 2004c), eventually meeting and working with artists Catts and Zurr in 2002. For them, 'bioart raises a profound array of ethical considerations', relating to the exploitation of other species that results from the perception that humans are a 'separated and privileged life form'. Consequently, 'as artists', their 'role is to reveal inconsistencies in regard to our current attitudes to life and focus attention on the discrepancies between our Western cultural perceptions and the new techno scientific understanding about life' (Catts and Zurr 2003). However, as with other bioartists, by manipulating life forms, there is always the risk of them being seen to be complicit with the same biotechnological knowledge and techniques that they seek to expose.

In contrast to many such artists who concentrate on the consequences of genetic engineering in their art, Catts and Zurr focus instead on 'another level of the biological system – that of the cell and communities of cells: tissues' (Catts and Zurr 2002, 365). Their art centres on the manipulation, growth and 'three-dimensional formation of tissue' on specially constructed 'scaffolding'. Although they often use genetically modified cells, their work is 'conceptually closer to cybernetics ...

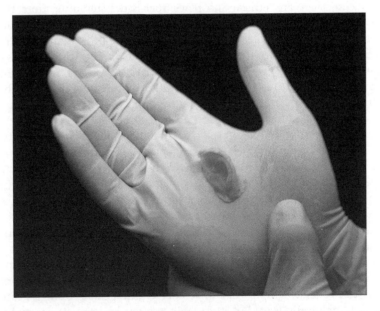

Figure 4.6 Extra Ear – ¼ Scale (2003). The Tissue Culture & Art (Oron Catts & Ionat Zurr) in collaboration with Stelarc. Biodegradable polymer and human chondrocytes cells, 3cm × 1.5cm × 1.5cm. Photography by Ionat Zurr

and the effects of technologies on complex biological systems, than to molecular biology-based art' (365). These tissue-engineering techniques are used for the creation of semi-living entities, which are parts of complex organisms that are sustained alive and proliferate outside the body thereby creating a living 'artistic palette'. They can be coerced to grow in predetermined shapes. For this project a quarter-scale replica of Stelarc's ear was grown using human cells and cultured in a rotating micro-gravity bioreactor, which allowed the cells to grow in three dimensions (Catts and Zurr 2004). *Extra Ear ¼ Scale* has been presented several times and in several types of venues including the Kapelica Gallery, Ljubljana, Slovenia; the National Gallery of Victoria, Australia; the Power House of the Midland Railway Workshops, Perth, Western Australia; and as part of the Art of the Biotech Era, 2004 Adelaide Festival, Australia (Catts and Zurr 2003).

According to Catts and Zurr, the project relates to 'two collaborative concerns'. It represents a recognizable human body part that is intended to be eventually attached to the body as a 'soft prosthesis', thus problematizing the concept of a unified body. It can also be seen to be a 'partial life-form', partly constructed and partly grown. For Catts and Zurr, there are 'ethical and perceptual issues stemming from the realization that living tissue can be sustained, grown and is able to function outside of the body' (2003). Stelarc, on the other hand, is ultimately concerned with the attachment of the ear to his (the) body as a soft prosthesis. However, due to the potential risks to the host body, he has up until very recently had difficulties in this attempt since the attachment as 'an issue of excess' goes beyond 'cosmetic surgery', and is a problem also of 'medical ethics' (Stelarc 2002b, 126).

Stelarc's *Prosthetic Head*, on the other hand, is not a biological entity; it is rather an extended operational system. The performance at the ICA, London, consisted of a huge interactive head projected in a darkened space.[15] The head is an embodied conversational agent with real-time lip-syncing and facial expressions. Its eyes, teeth and tongue are separate moving elements. It is automated and animated, and speaks to the person who questions it. It has a database on a server in Philadelphia and as a conversational system requires a human user. The head is only as intelligent as the person who interrogates it and as well as answering personal, professional and philosophical questions, it has algorithms that can generate simple 'Haiku-like poetry' and it can also sing. It cannot automatically learn but it does log the conversations it has and it demonstrates a certain conversational strategy together with a limited memory; its database being modified and personalized by Stelarc's own life experiences. It is intended that by initiating conversation, the head will not only gain experientially but will also expose performative aspects of conversation (Stelarc 2003d, 13). Interacting with the head proved initially to be somewhat unnerving since it dominates the performance space. As with Jeremiah from *Blue Bloodshot Flowers*, it also demonstrates random disruptive behaviour, adding a further 'real life' dimension to working with a virtual being. However, the head, although having some autonomous agency, is somewhat limited in its ability to communicate since all discussion needs to be keyed in via a keyboard. The result is that the head, which closely resembles Stelarc in appearance, becomes emotionally appropriated by the spectator as a recognizable extension and modification of a human being rather than being perceived as an autonomous virtual agent.

Finally, it has been demonstrated that not only does the body respond to events that directly affect us, but also to events that affect objects that we have appropriated as being part of our body (Ramachandran and Blakeslee 1999, 61–2). Certain digital practices, such as Stelarc's performances, add a further dimension to this appropriation since the mechanical and virtual prostheses used by Stelarc result in a modified extension of that physical body. The implication for digital practices is that the embodied self is delimited, hybridized and indeterminate.

Notes

1. Video clips and notes relating to the performance and the technology used can be found at Jeremiah's website (Bowden and Broadhurst 2001).
2. See Phil Stanier (2001).
3. See Keith Waters (1987, 1999–2004) and Waters et al. (1998).
4. Jeremiah's vision depends on a background segmentation approach developed from an intelligent visual surveillance system based upon the work of Chris Stauffer and Eric Grimson. For more information please see Richard Bowden et al. (2002, 125).
5. The performance I attended was at the Barbican Centre in London (2000a)
6. Cage had already been using chance procedures for his musical composition when the composer Christian Wolff introduced him to *I Ching*. Cage found he could use the book as a basis for his own creative process (Vaughan 1997, 58).
7. *Split Sides* premiered in New York, towards the end of 2003. I attended a performance of this work at the Barbican Centre, London, 6 October 2004.
8. *Loops* was commissioned by the M.I.T. Media Lab for the 'ID/Entity' show. It was curated by Christina Yang of the Kitchen and premiered at the Media Lab, MIT. The performance I attended was at the ICA Media Centre, London, in September 2002.
9. Cybernetics is concerned with the control systems of electrical and mechanical devices that can usefully be compared with man-made or biological systems.

10. For Merleau-Ponty, 'to perceive is to render oneself present to something through the body ... But such formulas are just so many enigmas unless we relate them to the concrete developments which they summarize' (1974b, 226).

11. I attended a performance of *Fractal Flesh* at the Perth Institute of Contemporary Arts, courtesy of the Cyberminds Conference hosted by the School of Design, Curtin University, Western Australia, 28 November 1996.

12. The full system has only been implemented once at Casula Powerhouse Arts Centre, 19 September 2000. However, the avatar has the potential to be located as a VRML entity on a website, and theoretically anyone, anywhere would be able to access it (Stelarc 2002a, 76).

13. Stelarc, in private correspondence, kindly provided the following in-depth description of the *Muscle Machine*: 'The Muscle Machine is a six-legged walking robot, five meters in diameter. It is a hybrid human-machine system, pneumatically powered using fluidic muscle actuators. The rubber muscles contract when inflated, and extend when exhausted. This results in a more flexible and compliant mechanism, using a more reliable and robust engineering design. The fluidic muscle actuators eliminate problems of friction and fatigue that was a problem in the previous mechanical system of the Hexapod prototype robot. The body stands on the ground within the chassis of the machine, which incorporates a lower body exoskeleton connecting it to the robot. Encoders at the hip joints provide the data that allow the human controller to move and direct the machine as well as vary the speed at which it will travel. The action of the human operator lifting a leg lifts the three alternate machine legs and swings them forward. By turning its torso, the body makes the machine walk in the direction it is facing. Thus the interface and interaction is more direct, allowing intuitive human–machine choreography. The walking system, with attached accelerometer sensors provide the data that generates computer-structured sounds augmenting the acoustical pneumatics and operation of the machine. The sounds register and amplify the movements and functions of the system. The operator composes the sounds by choreographing the movements of the machine. Once the machine is in motion, it is no longer applicable to ask whether the human or machine is in control as they become fully integrated and move as one. The six-legged robot both extends the body and transforms its bipedal gait into a six-legged insect-like movement. The appearance and movement of the machine legs are both limb-like and wing-like motion'.

14. The premiere of this performance, which I attended, was at the 291 Gallery, East London, 1 July 2003. Stelarc was also interviewed and this performance documented by Iranian film-maker Mostafa Yarmahmoudi (2003c).

15. I attended a performance of the *Prosthetic Head* at the ICA, London, 12 March 2003.

5
Digital Sound, New Media and Interactive Performance

In recent years, there has been a proliferation of performances that utilize electronic sound technology for real-time interaction. One of the reasons for this is the development of musical instrument data interface (MIDI) and more recently Open Sound Control (OSC) together with real-time programming environments, such as Max that have the special advantage of being interactive with visual and network technologies.

Optik: Contact, impulse and electro-acoustic sound

> Certain modern musicians oppose the transcendent plan(e) of organization, which is said to dominate all of Western classical music, to the immanent sound plane ... Or rather it is a question of a freeing of time ... an electronic music in which forms are replaced by pure modifications of speed ... which affirms a process against all structure and genesis, a floating time against pulsed time or tempos, experimentation against any kind of interpretation, and in which silence as sonorous rest also marks the absolute state of movement.
>
> (Deleuze and Guattari 1999a, 287)

> The development of real-time electronic composing was the key breakthrough for Optik in terms of sound.
>
> (Edwards and Jarlett 2003, 49)

Optik is an independent company based in London that has developed a distinctive style of performance practice. The company was formed in 1981 by director Barry Edwards who brought together musicians, visual artists and actors to create an innovative style of physical and visual theatre. Today, the company's work ranges from minimal performance

Figure 5.1   Optik perform *Xstasis* (2003), Montreal, Canada. Photo: Alain Décarie

centring on simple physical movements, to an eclectic mix of sound, live music, video, theatre and dance. Optik tours to many different performance venues and also makes site-specific work in non-theatre spaces and locations. Early works such as *One Spectacle* (1981), *A Short Tour of Ancient Sites* (1984) and *Stranded* (1985–6) toured the United Kingdom. More recent productions such as *Tropic* (1993–5), *In the Presence of People* (2000) and *Xstasis* (2003) have been collaborations with international partner venues, festivals and organizations. Optik has worked with Tacheles Berlin, Roxy Klub Prague, Amorph Festival Helsinki and many more. The company's international touring has taken it to, amongst other places, Warsaw, Alexandria, Sofia, Sao Paulo and Montreal.

Optik's key precept is a compositional practice that is performer-centred. It engages three primary creative elements: live action (body, space and time); live and digital sound; and live video. The group concentrates on a performer technique that enables performers to improvise within a structure organized by specific conditions of body, space and time. The precise conditions are determined by what is present at each event. For Optik, the term improvisation refers not to the notion of verbal improvisation as in the theatrical sense, but rather working with key human actions with no pre-planned spatial or temporal score given in advance.

Optik has continually evolved over the years in their approach to performance, though retaining what Edwards refers to as 'performing presence', that is, 'the engagement with physical live performance without pre-planned notions of significance, meaning or the desire to communicate' (1999, 191), they have also adapted to new technological advancements where opportunities have arisen for new experimental forms and practices in performance. One key element in Optik's performance practice is to allow each performer an independent decision-making process, which for Edwards is a way into the 'exploration of consciousness' (1999, 193).

Consciousness is always already 'embodied', just as perception is already interpreted or 'stylized' by a horizon of human undertakings that extrapolates meaning. This pre-reflective stance is guided by an 'operative intentionality' that prioritizes gesture, sexuality and even silence. Consciousness cannot be fully explained by an autonomous intrinsic or *a priori* condition for abstract cognition. Without the complex 'intertwining' (Entrelacs) and 'chiasm' (chiasme) between pre-theoretical, lived experience and conceptual judgement; there would always be the inevitable dualism of mind/body opposition (Merleau-Ponty 2000, 130–55).

Sound has always been a crucial element in Optik's performance practice but in their early performances it came from specific acoustic sources, mainly percussion such as, drums, cymbals, marimba and so on. Ambient sound also played an important role, for example, footsteps, breathing, laughter and general sound from the performance space. From their inception through to 2000, the company used no electronically generated sound except for one exception which was *Tropik* (1993), performed in Poland, where Optik sampled a soprano voice and wired different pitches of this voice, sung in long notes, to a set of electronic drum pads. Each pad produced a particular pitch and length of the note. With six pads to play on, the drummer was able to produce a stunning mix of harmonic and rhythmic sound, often leading to multitextures of choral dimension. This particular performance was part of a tour of Poland and Germany. However, the sound system was used only in the first performance at the Rotunda, Krakow, and immediately abandoned.

For Edwards, the problem with this system was that sound was produced in advance of the performance and the imported sampled voice did not work because the original sound source was not present; 'the sound of the source in Optik is always diegetic (to use a cinematic term). That is, the source of the term is always present, not imported' (2005). Diegetic sound in cinema is sound whose source is visible on the screen or whose source is implied to be present by the action of the film.[1] It includes voices of characters, sounds made by objects in the story and music represented as coming from instruments within the story space. This is opposed to non-diegetic sound, that is, sound whose source is neither visible nor has been implied to be present in the action. For example, the narrator's commentary and sound affects which are added for dramatic and mood effect. Therefore, non-diegetic sound is represented as coming from a source outside the story space. However, given that sound which appears to come from a source within the action of the story or performance space may be contrived, whilst non-diegetic sound may actually emit from a source within this space, this apparent duality becomes somewhat blurred. Since in any rigorous analysis all 'origin' is merely difference, diegetic sound just like non-diegetic sound is only another signifier in an endless chain of signification and 'dissemination' (Derrida, 1981a, 25).

According to Edwards, 'sound, when produced acoustically is able to improvise in the same actional sequencing as the actors, that is, working with durational and complex, rather than linear compositional strategies – serial technique (to use a musical term), rather than linear' (2005). However, since 2000 Optik have again incorporated electronically generated sound into their performances. This largely resulted from a new addition to the Optik Company in the form of sound technician, Ben Jarlett. The challenge was to integrate electronic sound into this performance environment without losing the high levels of intuitive and often unpredictable responses within the performance. The first sound experiment of this collaboration, *In the Presence of People*, took place simultaneously in London and Sao Paulo, on 26 October 2000, and it involved a telepresence linkup of live sound from one location – a drama studio in Brunel University (London) and a live physical performance whose images were streamed from both inside and outside performance spaces in Sao Paulo; the Karman – Kompanhia Teatro Multimedia and the Placa da Se Sao Paulo. In short, live sound created by Simon Edgoose, a percussionist in London, was relayed over to the performance spaces in Brazil and at the same time images from the live performers, Clare Allsop, Simon Humm and Hannah Seaton, were sent over to the drama studio in London.

The public performance was scheduled to start in Sao Paulo at the Karman Teatro at 9 P.M. and in London at 11P.M. (2 hours ahead of Sao Paulo). Two weeks prior to this, there had been a workshop performance at Brunel, where Edgoose had installed a drum and percussion kit in one studio whilst in another studio, across the corridor in the School of Arts building, were the three performers. This experiment was open to the public and lasted approximately 50 minutes. This was a performance I attended, and real-time images of the performers were projected onto the walls of both studio spaces. At the same time the performers interacted with the sound that was relayed to the studio where they were located and Edgoose in his studio in turn responded to their real-time virtual images with his sound. This performance was striking in its imagery and movement and the real-interaction worked very well.

However, when the experiment was repeated with an attempt to link the distance between London and Sao Paulo, rather than across a corridor in the same university building, it did not work nearly as well. Communication was difficult since the phone line to the theatre had to be brought down to the performance space and when the company went on line, the company had to resort to using a mobile phone to establish contact with the technical team in London. Eventually an image of the London audience was transmitted which received great applause from the audience in Brazil. The camera in Sao Paulo was in turn focused on a small group of spectators and this image was in turn received in London, where I was again among the audience. However, the transmission was extremely slow with approximately one image being received every two minutes, thus removing all of the movement quality found in the prior workshop performance. The technical team in the Sao Paulo theatre removed the visual signal coming from London in an attempt to send a faster signal. This was moderately successful with London receiving approximately one frame every 30 seconds. Sound, although generally not a problem with Edgoose's drumming being heard clearly and in real-time, disappeared for about 15 minutes during the performance in Brazil. In fact, Edgoose had been playing a cymbal quietly that was not picked up and it was thought that the signal had been lost. In Brazil, the web camera also failed to pick up the audience and performers who had moved to the far end of the space and everyone in London thought the performance had either ended or the signal had been lost. According to Edwards, this apparent feeling of two separate events was shattered by the voices of the technicians from both locations which were also relayed over the loud speakers. The performance event ended in Sao Paul at about 10.30 P.M. local time, but Edgoose carried on playing until 1 A.M. local time in London. For Edwards, 'there was no linked up sense of resolution or ending, which led to a strange separation at the final moment – the link was turned off. It had an emotional impact, especially on the performers' (2001).

In this performance, each performer engaged in a mutually exclusive set of action rules. These included: standing, walking, running, lying and rolling on the floor. No two actions could be undertaken at the same time and there was no pre-planned order in which these actions could be taken; there was no strategy for relating or responding to other performers. Neither was there any intended resolution or closure. Each performer needed to continually make decisions on which action to engage with and for what period of time. According to Edwards, 'this allows the performer (and the spectator) to explore deeper emotional resonances linked to the body in space and time' (2001). In the performance, there was an interesting link between much of the action-based decision making (do this or do that) and the action of the virtual image. For instance, when a live performer was walking in real space in real time, they could stop or continue whenever they wanted. The virtual image could also stop or continue at any time, when it did so, a frame of the performer was 'frozen'. Consequently, when the digital image resumed its movements, there were fleeting moments when a walking live performer met two digital images of themselves, the virtual performer, still frozen and the virtual performer moving.

The technology used in this performance consisted of two PCs fitted with videoconferencing codec, one of which was used for the Sao Paulo link up. The video output from a camcorder was connected to the codec on each of the two PCs. Two camcorders were used for the Sao Paulo link connected to the codec via a production mixer. This offered a view of the audience as well as the performers in Brazil. To project the received image, a Super Video Graphics Array (SVGA) resolution data was used in each of the performance areas. Four condenser microphones were used to pick up the sound of the percussion which were plugged into four of the mixer's input channels. The audio out from the codec was mixed with a signal from a talkback microphone and sent out to a hi-fi where Edgoose was able to provide audio feedback.[2] According to Edwards and Jarlett, the random delay and manipulation of the sound reaching Sao Paulo from London added a key texture to the performance; 'the system of transmission became another player in the interface between musician, instrument, cable lines, speakers, performers and audience' (2003, 50).

A 'live' image digitally broadcast on a television or as *In the Presence of People,* relayed to another monitor in a different location, can never be uncontaminated by its 'censor, frame, filter' since what is produced 'live' by this technology is *'produced before being transmitted'*. And no matter how immediate or direct it 'technically' might appear, it is the result of various kinds of intervention; the live or direct is never intact. However, knowing or believing that the 'live or direct' is possible, is enough to transform 'the field of perception and experience in general' (Derrida and Steigler 2002, 40).

Following this performance, Optik decided to build on the idea of electronically manipulated sound. Since Edwards wanted to keep the core compositional structure intact, any electronically generated sound needed to be sourced in real time and space, that is, sound composed during the moment of performance. It was felt that pre-recorded or edited sound would destroy the *'raison d'etre* of the performance' (Edwards and Jarlett 2005, 50).

The search for such a system began in March 2001, when Jarlett was asked to investigate possibilities for real-time sound interaction and he came up with the idea of 'granular synthesis'. The first experiment took place in the dance studio of the Rambert School in Twickenham, London. Jarlett brought along a simple microphone and two tiny speakers together with his computer. He recorded ambient sounds, footsteps and so on and some vocal sounds, such as laughter and breathing. According to Edwards, the group was astounded by the results. While the performers were still moving a sound score could be heard that had been recorded moments earlier from the actual sounds of the performers themselves. The performers could then respond to this sound and Jarlett could respond back – nothing was fixed. This meant that there was now an improvisational dialogue between electronic sound and the actional sequences, which is what Optik had been searching for. After that Optik moved on quickly to reintroduce acoustic music, for instance, voice, viola and wind instruments. However, the basic principle had been discovered, namely that they could have a responsive electronic sound score, composed moment by moment, which used only 'diegetic' (present) sound sources. Edwards describes this as a 'crucial break-through' for Optik's compositional practice (2005).

This system was trialed publicly in *Taking Breath*, performed at the SKC Belgrade, Serbia, in October 2001, which was a site-specific piece for three performers and incorporated live electronic sound and web cam projection. The performers included Allsop, Humm and Jennifer Lewin. In this performance only ambient sound was used and the process worked very successfully, the performance structure was not only maintained but grew in complexity. Texturally, the sound was per-cussive, moody or tense. However, it became difficult to move away from tension to lighter texture, which ultimately led Jarlett to further develop his interactive electronic sound system.

Granular synthesis is the process of taking digital audio, slicing it into pieces of definable length and then playing them back at definable times with definable pitches enabling the creation of rich textures from almost any sound input. Jarlett developed a performance system consisting of a PC, a copy of Granulab and Wavelab, a 16 slider MIDI controller, mixer and reverberator (reverb) unit. Reverb units are designed to re-create the sonic properties of a 'real-world' (or invented) space and make the music sound as if it were created in that environment. Whether recording in a studio or attempting to manipulate the natural sonic properties of a real-world space, a reverb unit affects the overall ambience of the sound. In the Optik performance, the reverb was used to smooth out some of the harsher textures produced, though it was not involved in the actual improvisation.

It was found that two microphones placed on the floor of the performance space were adequate to capture the sound of the performers breathing, walking and running. The addition of voice and instruments required separate close microphones so that their sound could be amplified and routed to a computer. The mixer was set up so that the microphones recording the ambient sound did not have a direct route to the PA system. This was important since the Optik does not perform in regular spaces where the audience is facing a stage; rather, the audience is in the same space as the performers making audio feedback difficult. A MIDI controller is important to this system since it turns the computer into an instrument allowing the operator to respond instantly to influences coming from the performance space. MIDI is an interface that allows a synthesizer or other electronic instrument to be controlled by a computer or another electronic instrument. The main benefit for Jarlett was the ability to access several controller devices at any one time (only one is possible using a mouse); in short, an increased ability to create multiple media effects.

Established in the early 1980s by a group of leading musical instrument manufacturers as an agreed universal standard method for sending and receiving musical controller information digitally, the application of the basic MIDI interface has developed and expanded leading 'to dramatically improved techniques for composition' (Winkler 1999, 14). Not only does it eliminate the need for digital synthesizers to have keyboards, it also provides a standardized interface for a wide variety of control devices, such as breath controllers, drum pads and devices that measure gestures. Its codes have also been adapted to control a variety of non-musical devices such as audio mixing panels, theatrical lighting controllers and audio processing devices such as reverberators and via SMPTE/EBU and other timecodes to coordinate with video and graphics devices.[3] The development of MIDI has had a strong impact on the accessibility and variety of interactions that can be utilized in performance. Also the limited amount of data transferred by MIDI has added to this accessibility by enabling home computer users to handle music processing in real time.

However, while computer-processing speeds have increased, the MIDI protocol is still restricted to the 7-bit 1980s standard. This restriction of data also means that important musical information, for instance timbre and pitch, are not as accurately defined as is theoretically possible. Similarly, the processing methods used by MIDI are restrictive for real-time interaction, being particularly weak at handling continuously changing data.[4] This in turn has led to the proliferation of numerous highly programmable interactive systems, using MIDI inputs that can offer immediate feedback, Max being the most widely used program for this purpose. It has also led to the development of OSC,[5] which is a protocol that allows the real-time control of computer-synthesis processes from gestural devices as does MIDI. Although OSC does not include MIDI messages, MIDI messages can be mapped into OSC, making OSC commands part of the MIDI protocol. According to Mark Ballora, 'OSC offers increased resolution and definition of gestures and synthesis parameters, as well as more accurate time control,' and since it is transmitted over networks, it is also suitable for broadcasting performances of computers and performers interacting with each other from different locations (2004).

For Jarlett, improvements were necessary to the existing granular interactive system since the amount of time and concentration required to capture a sound and start it playing in a stream needed to be reduced. He began working with Max/MSP, a similar interactive system to granulab that also includes capture and editing within the program as well as the addition of equalization and reverb. All of which enabled him to have more time to concentrate on the performance (rather than the operation of the computer), and also reduced the amount of equipment needed to no more than a laptop and MIDI controller, thus making the technology much more mobile.

Though still retaining granulab, Max/MSP was first trialed by Jarlett in the performance of *Stream* (2002), which was presented at the Institute of Contemporary Arts, London. This was also where live-video processing was first introduced into the Optik performance space. The performance was a collaboration with Billy Currie, a well know musician playing the viola and Howie Bailey who provided the live video. The real-time video-processing images of the performers, Allsop, Humm and Lewin proved spectacular. With this latter interactive system not only was the sound instantly manipulable but so was the visual imagery creating a stunning *Gesamtkunstwerk* of movement, sound and vision.

For Optik's more recent performances, *Xstasis* (2004) and *Space* (2004), Max/MSP was fully utilized. *Xstasis* was conceived as both a training and production project and was commissioned by Canadian based director Kate Bligh. In addition to the core of regular Optik artists (director Edwards; performers Allsop and Humm; sound artist Jarlett; and now video artist Howey Bailey), there were 16 participants on the project

Figure 5.2   Optik perform *Xstasis* (2003), Montreal, Canada. Photo: Alain Décarie

drawn from Montreal-based professional and student dancers, actors and musicians. Work on *Xstasis* took place over an intensive two-week development period hosted by Concordia University Music and Theatre Departments. The project culminated in three site-specific perform-ances during Montreal's Festival of Theatre of the Americas. *Xstasis* integrated live action with video and electro-acoustic sound. In keeping with Optik's main tenet, the performances were constructed around each artist's engagement and openness to encounters with the body and emotion, as well as the technology.

Space (2004) was a culmination of this process, performed in The Camden Centre, London – a large ornate 1930s civic hall. This per-formance again was improvisatory, relying on the performers' reactions and interactions; it utilized all the aural and visual imagery of *Xstasis*. Again, the performance was intriguing in its use of the performance space, providing striking moments of physical contact and emotional impulse. In this performance, live-voice recording was also introduced by one of the performers and Jarlett using Max/MSP was able to put it out into the sound score instantly, 'something that wouldn't have been possible with granular synthesis' (Edwards 2005).

Max was developed at the Institute de Recherche et Coordination Acousstique/Mustique (IRCAM) in Paris in 1986. The principal author was Miller Puckette. Over the years, Max has grown into a versatile graphical programming language central to the real-time control of MIDI devices which are vital to interactive performance. In 1990, Max developed along two different lines. One was the development and extension of a commercially available version by David Zicarelli that was released in 1991 by Opcode Systems, Inc. as a Macintosh programming environment. According to Todd Winkler, 'because of its ease of use and availability, Max has been adopted by a large number of composers' (1999, 18). At the same time IRCAM developed new hardware systems as a response to increased demands for interactive real-time signal processing, one of which was the IRCAM Signal Processing Workstation (ISPW), which was a powerful hardware environment without the need for MIDI devices. Puckette adapted Max, adding a collection of signal-processing objects for this environment. However, the ISPW was out of the price range of many and it also relied on the NeXT computer to run, whose production unfortunately ceased fairly soon after the workstation's introduction. The main software used for signal processing and synthesis on the ISPW was 'faster than sound' (FST).

Since leaving IRCAM, Puckette has now developed a new software system Pure Data (Pd) that provides the main features of Max/MSP and FST whilst redressing some of the shortcomings. Pd is an open-source, free software system and like Max/MSP provides a real-time programming environment for the live performance of music and multimedia. It allows a programmer to create a series of patches for a specific purpose; rather, than depending on an existing programme which carries large computing overloads. Therefore, making the computer's response as fast as possible. It operates with Graphics Environment for Multimedia (GEM), a sub-program purpose written by Mark Danks that runs under Pd and provides real-time image manipulation. According to Winkler, 'by taking advantage of faster processing speeds, Pd is able to integrate audio synthesis and signal processing with video processing and 3-D graphics in a single real-time software environment' (1999, 19).[6] Pd is now emerging as one of the primary software systems for real-time interaction in performance.[7] However, for Puckette, 'many problems remain open and improvements are constantly sought in our existing repertoire of techniques' (2005, 155).

Finally, as well as investigating notions of ownership and intertexuality, the digital technology that creates Optik's electro-acoustic sound subverts assumptions of reproduction and representation because in every performance the interactive sound is original, just as is the improvising performer/s and performance. Therefore, sound is 'reproduced again' and not 'represented'. Thus, challenging fundamental dualisms in relation to performance including those of original and reproduction and live and recorded.

Palindrome: 'Intermedia', collaboration and interaction

> Unique and largely unexplored problems face composers and choreographers as they collaborate on interactive performance works, not least of which is settling on schemes for mapping the various parameters of human movement to those possible in sound.
>
> (Rovan, Wechsler and Weiss 2001)

Common interests from a diverse range of disciplines and creative art practices have converged in recent times leading to new interdisciplinary research and the formation of conceptual models influenced by computer processing capabilities and the global expanse of the Internet. Palindrome, based in Nürnberg, Germany, is one of an expanding group of pioneering performance companies that investigate the use of 'intermedia' and utilize new technologies in their performance practice.[8]

From their inception in 1982, they have been leaders in the field of interactive technology, prioritizing the interface between digitally manipulated sound and visual imagery. Their performance, *Seine hohle Form*, is exemplary of their work and premiered in November 2000.[9] The title words signify the challenge of creating a musical work that only exists when a dancer moves. The choreography is influenced by the live production of sound through the use of sensors and real-time synthesis, and these movements in turn shape the resulting music. There are no musical cues for the dancers, since without their movements the music is either non-existent or missing key elements (Rovan, Wechsler and Weiss 2001).

Palindrome has grown from a small ensemble of choreographers, performers and media artists experimenting with computer-assisted work into a growing network of international practitioners and artists who work on collaborative projects and enterprises, which create and propagate new technological performance and art discourses. The company was founded in New York by Robert Wechsler, artistic director and choreographer. Wechsler had been collaborating with Frieder Weiss, a free lance computer engineer based in Germany, and moved the company to Nürnberg in 1990.

Since 1995, Wechsler and Weiss (now co-director) have been working on developing interactive methods of performance that utilize new technologies, primarily focusing on the interface and interaction between virtual sound and the physical body. Their work centres on performances and installations that use physical bodies to control sound, light or projected images, creating real-time interaction (Wechsler and Weiss 2004b). As well as working in performance, Palindrome have also designed and created interactive software and hardware, such as EyeCon – a camera-based motion-sensing system,[10] and much of their time is dedicated to teaching practitioners how to use technology more creatively and efficiently. Weiss, an interactive-systems designer who authored EyeCon, has also created miniaturized, portable technologies that allow individual movements of performers to control other media, for instance, one such device allows a performer's heartbeat to control media in a variety of ways, such as in the tempo of the accompanying music.

According to Wechsler, Palindrome's primary aim is to combine 'art and science', since 'they are not combined very often in the world and yet there is a lot to learn from combining them and a lot to inspire' (2004). Unlike Merce Cunningham, whom Wechsler has studied with and who also uses specialized software such as Danceform to both choreograph the movements of dancers and to create computer-generated images, Palindrome concentrates on real-time interaction between technology and physical performers, which Cunningham does not. For instance, the movements of the virtual performers in Cunningham's *BIPED* do not affect the performance in any way, unlike the interactive technologies of Palindrome that do have a drastic effect on the performance.

For Palindrome, media accompanying a performance is not already devised. Instead, the performer has a crucial role in creating the media, so that media is actually literally part of a live performance. When the body alone cannot reach the meaning aimed at, it builds its own instruments and projects around itself a mediated world (Merleau-Ponty 1962, 146). Instead of being separate from the body, technology becomes part of that body, at the same time altering and recreating the body's experience in the world.

Palindrome use sensors to track performers' positions and movements. That data is then used to create simultaneously performed artistic media. Biosensors, such as electrode systems are sometimes used. Electrodes are small electronically conductive pads that are attached to the skin and allow surplus electronic signals from various biological processes, such as heart and brain activity, to be recorded. With appropriate technology, which includes amplifiers and so on, they can be used to generate a visual or aural representation of what is happening inside a performer's body.

Three different kinds of electrode systems have been developed by Palindrome: 'EMG (for skeletal muscles), ECG (for the heart muscle) and EEG (for Brainwaves)' (Wechsler and Weiss 2004b). All the systems are wireless to allow a performer unimpeded movement, and the EMG and ECG systems are also miniaturized. In performance terms, systems such as these can be used to provide an intermedia performance event, such as the conversion of the electronic signal from a performer's heart beat by means of specially modified software into a different sound, simultaneously accompanied by the visual projection of that heart beat.

However, Palindrome, in their work, predominantly rely on their video-based system – EyeCon, to track performers and create real-time media interaction. The system permits movement of visual events that are viewed by a video camera to potentate media effects. Although there are several other systems that allow this real-time interaction, such as Max/MSP, EyeCon is a simple interface that can be used by performers and practitioners who may not be skilled technologists. In other words, it offers a way to create interactive video environments without requiring the skills needed to undertake graphical or script-based programming. Importantly, it has been designed specifically for performance practice.

EyeCon is designed to create a virtual 'architecture' (Wechsler and Weiss 2004a, 1). Visual elements, such as 'lines' and 'fields', can be drawn on the top of a video image. These are then 'mapped' to media events so that if, for instance, a performer crosses a line, a sound or image is activated.[11] Fields can also be applied that can detect movement or other formal qualities such as size, shape and direction of motion. This in turn controls various media events, such as sound volume or video-clip speed. Moreover, EyeCon can track individual performers within the camera area by using video sequence analysis algorithms, even when the performers overlap within the field, by making intelligent assumptions about their probable location (1). However, for Wechsler and Weiss, the 'dramatic effectiveness' of a performance depend on a variety of factors, including movement dynamics, movement in space, direction, muscle tension, use of weight and so on. And although sensors can detect most of these movement parameters, the artistic decision then is which ones to apply to a given setting, and which music parameters should be applied. This application is a key element of Palindrome's enterprise, since the problem for them is that 'interaction may not occur at all', in the sense that the audience would not be aware of the interaction.

Figure 5.3 Demonstration of EyeCon System. Palindrome IMPG (2000), Dancer: Aleksandra Janeva. Photo: Jürgen Henkel

Whether actual interaction relies on an audience being aware is debatable. However, Palindrome's primary aim is 'to design a degree of transparency' into their collaborative performance projects (Rovan, Wechsler and Weiss 2001, 2).

Seine holhe Form was a collaborative performance between Wechsler and Weiss from Palindrome and Joseph Butch Rovan from the Centre for Experimental Music and Intermedia at the University of North Texas. The project's sound and movement were conceived interactively with Rovan composing the music and implementing the interactive system, and Wechsler together with Helena Zwiauer (also from Palindrome) realizing the dance. The choreography is affected by the live generation of sound and the movements form the resulting music. Therefore, without movement there is no sound. As a result this method of working, to a certain extent, necessarily becomes a forced improvisation. It also causes a sharing of artistic roles in the process with 'dancer' becoming 'musician' and 'composer' becoming 'choreographer' (Wechsler and Weiss 2004b). The performance is striking with its emphasis on exaggerated corporeal gestures that in turn create sound.

The stark imagery of the grey-clad performers and the intermittent, somewhat eerie, sound provides a fragmented landscape of a bleak futuristic world.

Palindrome in their work, explore issues of perception and movement, concentrating on a notion of 'gestural coherence', which for them is 'the perceptual coherence between sound and the movement that generates it'. Underpinning this is the premise that 'an emergent integrity arises when the relationship between the dance and music is "believable"' and that believability relies on gestural coherence, which is brought about through a system of mapping that mediates the music and movement (Rovan, Wechsler and Weiss 2001, 3). Moreover, the perception of movement or sound can differ substantially from the visual or aural information present, that is, the video camera and computer perceives these elements differently than humans, as a result of which certain modifications may be necessary to either the choreography or composition (Rovan, Wechsler and Weiss 2001, 2).

Figure 5.4 This image shows a real-time video effect linked to a technology that responds to the touch of two dancers. From the Palindrome opera *Blinde Liebe*, (2005). Dancers: Aimar Perez Gali, Helena Zwiauer

A variant use of EyeCon involved Palindrome's 'shadow' performances, where by using an infrared light source and infrared-sensitive camera, a performer's shadow is projected in different colours, together with varying time delay, position and orientation shifts. One such piece was done in collaboration with Phase-7, a Berlin-based performance company, and was performed in Duisburg (2003) in the Landschaftspark, a former steel mill. The piece was performed by Emily Fernandez and consisted of the use of EyeCon together with a Miburi bend-sensing body suit. The stage and screen were vast, the stage being approximately 66 feet wide, all of which needed to be lit, adding further to the technical challenge of the performance. The imagery was stunning with the multicoloured projected shadows appearing to take on a life of their own. Another shadow performance, again featuring Emily Fernandez, was *Solo4>Three* (2003) that was equally striking. Both works applied the traditional theatre technique of the 'shadow play', combined with digital technology, particularly, motion sensing and real-time audio-image signal processing. According to Palindrome, such shadow performances are intended to be 'a reminder of the organic connection between body-image and body-reality', the theme being 'the shifting border between body and mediated virtual body image' (Dowling, Wechsler and Weiss, 2004, 78).

The shadow effect is achieved by placing a light source in one corner of the performance space that throws a shadow image onto a large screen. However, because all visible light has been filtered out only infrared light reaches the screen. A special infrared camera captures the projected shadow image and inputs the digitized image into a computer where it is processed. The processed image is made visible by a connected video projector which projects onto the same screen where the invisible shadow is located. The digital processing includes variable delays, multiply transposition, colouring, reversing, accelerating/decelerating and freezing and dissolving, all which produce bizarre effects in performance as the shadow either splits, multiplies, freezes, dissolves and so on. According to Dowling et al., 'our brain is constantly trying to sync our different senses, making predictions about what is most likely to happen and then making the whole into a perception we call now' (Dowling, Wechsler and Weiss 2004, 78).

However, when looking at objects in performance, colour is perceived before form, which in turn is perceived before motion (Zeki 1999, 66). The consequence of this is that the brain over very short periods of time is unable to combine what happens in real time; instead, it unifies the results of its own processing systems though not in real time. Nevertheless all visual attributes are combined to provide us with an

Figure 5.5   Solo4>Three (2003). Dance and Choreography: Emily Fernandez. Interactive video system: Frieder Weiss. Photo credit: Ralf Denke

integrated experience. Palindrome's shadow performances, as a result of their multilayered, distorted and delayed effects, challenge the notion of an 'integrated experience' by making perceptible this sequential variation, at the same time they ensure the audience's active participation in the production of meaning. The shadows shift seamlessly between what is '*known*' and what is '*surprising*' making 'the piece fascinating to watch' (Dowling, Wechsler and Weiss 2004, 78).

When viewing objects in motion a specific area of the brain is activated – V5, and although this region of the brain may not be the only area that is implicated when viewing kinetic art, if motion is to be viewed at all. Non-representational works of art activate fewer areas of the brain than representational and narrative art. However, all works of art that conflict with our prior experience of visual reality or in other words frustrate our expectations of any clear resolution – such as, the performances of Palindrome, are likely to activate a specific area of the frontal lobe which appears to deal with the resolution of perceptual/ experiential conflict (207–8).

Central to Palindrome, as other digital practices, are the unusual and diverse range of media codes present in their performances. Any interpretation of these works can never be conclusive since their multiple signals require habits different from ordinary habits of reading. This thinking makes little distinction between the referent and meaning, or for that matter, between 'reality' and representation. In the perception of these works there is a need for the brain to attempt to find essentials and stability in order to make sense of the images before it. However, due to the multilayered nature of these performances, a certain defamiliarization effect is produced leading to the audience being continually frustrated by the inherent lack of closure.

Finally, the intertwining of body, technology and world is central in an analysis of such works as those of Palindrome. And rather than the body being dominated by the use of technology in performance, technology extends that body by altering and recreating its embodied experience. As Wechsler remarks:

> Just as my words form sentences from ideas in the mind, the computer is a tool for manipulating information, a tool for connecting one kind of information with another, so our work involves taking the image of the dancer's motion, digitizing it, turning it into zeros and ones in the computer's chips and memory and then reforming it in sound and light.
>
> (2004)

Troika Ranch: An electronic disturbance

> As a dancer, I inherently understand the realm of the body. I had no idea that technology would enter into that understanding until I chose to entwine myself with the machine. I was altered and so was my body as it expanded to include sound, light and image.
>
> (Stoppiello 2003)

Based in New York, Troika Ranch are leaders in the field of interactive performance. They transcend traditional music composition in dance performance by using computer technology. In common with Palindrome, their mission is to create live performances that hybridize sound, dance, theatre and interactive digital media and to share information about their techniques with others. The company was founded in 1994 and the Artistic Co-Directors of the company, composer and media artist Mark Coniglio and choreographer Dawn Stoppiello, who began collaborating whilst undergraduates at the Californian Institute of Arts, have been widely recognized as being innovators in the field of live performance and interactive media. In June 2005, they were awarded an 'Eddy' Award at the 13th Annual Entertainment Design Awards, which is the US annual celebration of the best in design and technology for live events. The theme of the award was 'Bridging the Gap between the Artist and the Technology'. David Johnson, the editorial director and associate publisher of *Entertainment Design/Lighting Dimensions/SRO*, announced the award. As Johnson notes, 'Troika Ranch, which incorporates interactive video technology with live dancers, takes the relationship of man and machine to an entirely new level'.[12]

According to Stoppiello, *troika* (Russian for 'three') indicates the three core elements of the group's focus, which are digital media, dance and theatre. Coniglio who is originally from Nebraska, sees the term 'ranch' as being analogical to ensemble or 'group' and symbolizes the collaboration among its members.[13] Coniglio and Stoppiello encourage all in the company to share ideas, techniques and processes, in order to create aesthetically rich, multilayered, real-time interactive performance works. Their overall aim is to fully integrate their core elements into a live and mediated *Gestamtkunstwerk* (total artwork).

Like many artists, Troika Ranch utilize digital software tools to construct the visual and aural materials so central to their work, and also as a means of allowing individual performers to express themselves through performance. However, for Troika Ranch, interactive media and technology is an essential component in the '*performance*' of their 'work' (Coniglio and Stoppiello 2005). Usually, sensory devices are used to allow the movements or vocalizations of a performer to manipulate in real time some aspect of the performance's media, such as sound, video or light. As dancer Michou Szabo notes, 'working with the sensor device adds a whole other layer to the performance experience. You're asked to be suddenly more than a dancer. You're a musician' (Thompson 2003, 12–13).

Believing that most media technology is 'dead', in the sense that it is exactly the same each time it is presented, Troika Ranch want the media elements of their work to have the same sense of vitality, dynamism and 'liveness' as the physical performers it accompanies. To this end, the human body is imposed on the media in an attempt to bring it back to life (Coniglio and Stoppiello 2005). According to

Coniglio, 'in addition, this linkage of body and technology highlights the uneasy relationship between the organic and electronic – a central theme of our work' (Jorgl 2003).

Troika Ranch generally have three components in their interactive system. First, there is an input device that 'watches' what the performer is doing and converts that information into digital signals. Then there is intermediary software that gathers and analyses sensory information, interprets it in a predefined way and sends signals to various media to achieve a desired effect. Finally, the media devices present the media as instructed by the intermediary software.

Troika Ranch utilize a variety of input devices; for instance, MidiDancer which is wireless and measures the flexion of joints; LaserWeb that senses interruption of light beams; Piezo Sensors which sense impact; and Wireless Cameras that are used directly but also for live manipulation. MidiDance is the primary input device used by Troika Ranch and grew out of the necessity for allowing performers greater freedom of movement, together with increased flexibility in manipulating media devices. It is a wireless sensory system that tracks a performer's movements and converts that information into digital signals. Sensors are worn on the performer's body and can measure the flexion of up to eight joints and then transmit their location to a computer, which can interpret that information and use it to control a variety of media, including video, audio, lights, robotic set pieces and various other devices. The MidiDancer consists of two small boxes and eight sensors. One of the boxes, an encoder/transmitter, is a single-chip microcomputer and radio transmitter and is worn by the performer, usually on their back underneath their costume. It is connected to the flex sensors, which are positioned on the performer's body at locations, such as the elbows, wrists and hips. The thin wires that connect the sensors to the encoder are usually also worn underneath the performer's costume to allow free movement. Thirty times a second the microcomputer converts analog voltages from the flex sensors into a digital number that varies continuously between zero and one hundred depending on whether the sensor is straight or fully bent. These values are then passed on to the transmitter which broadcasts them over a 300 foot range. The broadcast is received by the second small box, which consists of a radio receiver and another single chip microcomputer. The received data is checked for errors by the microcomputer. Any corrupted data is ignored and only valid data is converted into a stream of MIDI messages that represents the position and acceleration of the performer's limbs. The output from this second box can then be connected to any personal computer with a MIDI interface and routed to the various interactive media devices which are pre-programmed to react.

According to Coniglio and Stoppiello, 'the technological elements are only one part of the equation'. Linking movement to media is analogous to creating a traditional musical instrument, since the MidiDancer allows the gesture of a performer to be 'amplified and translated' into an alternative medium, 'as does an instrument like the violin' (Coniglio and Stoppiello 2005). However, the performer's body gestures provide a multiplicity of intersemiotic signals which the audience will attempt to interpret unlike the playing of a violin which is limited in its semiotic signification. Another difference is that the functionality of a violin is fixed, whereas there is variety of ways in which the MidiDancer can convert movement into media control. However, in doing so, there is of course, the concern that the audience cannot perceive the control element, and thus the real-time interaction between the performer and the media effects. Although for some this may not be an issue, for Troika Ranch, the 'liveness' of the technology is central to their project. Coniglio presents a further analogy between the MidiDancer and a musical model when he writes of the improvised performance of a jazz pianist where the audience may not perceive that some level of improvisation is occurring since they may have little prior understanding of the instrument (piano) with which the performer controls that manipulation (Coniglio 2004, 8–10). There is an even greater lack of experiential perception from an audience viewing the MidiDance manipulation of media devices within a performance due to the audience having no prior understanding of this interactive device.

To have experience, to get used to an instrument is to incorporate that instrument into the body. Habit is neither intellectual nor an involuntary action, but the body as 'mediator of a world' (Merleau-Ponty 1962, 143). Technology, such as the MidiDancer, then would imply a reconfiguration of our embodied experience. According to Stoppiello, 'my choreography has changed in response to my close contact with computers and computer-controlled devices'. In describing her experience of working on *In Plane* (1994), she notes that

> The piece was to be a competition between the corpus and the electronic doppelganger; a body that bleeds, sweats, gets tired and feels pain versus a body made of light, which is not bound by time, space or gravity ... The beauty of using the MidiDancer system was that the notion of a duet with the video was much more than conceptual idea, but was in fact the result of a tangible physical relationship: body-sensor-video.
>
> (Stoppiello 2003)

The second component in Troika Ranch's interactive system is an intermediary software called Interactor LPT. Created by Coniglio and Morton Subotnick, it is a graphic media-programming language used as an authoring tool and it allows performers to realize real-time interactive performances by means of MIDI messaging. In Troika Ranch's own performances, it functions as 'the master software "brain"' of any interaction between performance and technology. It controls media devices by means of data from movement information via the MidiDancer and/or musically generated events from MIDI controllers, such as keyboards and piezo sensors.

Isadora, a graphic programming environment created by Coniglio, exemplifies Troika Ranch's media presentation, the final component in their system. Its primary function is as an authoring tool intended to provide performers with a means of designing and directing input from a variety of sources. Isadora provides interactive control over digital media with a special emphasis on real-time manipulation of digital video. It functions as an engine that drives the visually manipulated components of performance by linking together graphically represented building blocks, each of which performs a special function such as playing or manipulating digital video, capturing live video, searching for MIDI input or controlling a digital camera. These basic building blocks are called 'actors' and there are over 70 available within the Isadora environment that perform varying functions from simply searching for a MIDI signal to the more complicated manipulation of live video. By linking the various modules together, complex interactive relationships are established allowing information to travel from one source to another, both within the computer and outwards to external interfaces. Therefore, in connecting several operations together, a performer can determine the level and type of interactivity within a performance.

The program is accessible to individuals who may not have sophisticated programming skills, since its visual display on a computer monitor or screen allows performers to effortlessly view the various data. According to Coniglio and Stoppiello, Isadora assists the performer 'as both a compositional tool and as a collaborative partner in live performance' (Farley 2002). In effect, the MidiDancer and Isadora work together, by firstly tracking a performer's gestures by means of the MidiDancer, and then transmitting that information to Isadora, which interprets the sensory information in a predefined way, and signals are sent to the media devices being controlled in order to achieve the desired effect. As Kathryn Farley points out, 'artistically ... the immediate reaction of the computer (to both *Isadora* programming commands and *MidiDancer* signals from a dancer's body) allow for expressive possibilities that may be impossible to achieve by any other means' (2002). Troika Ranch's performance of *Surfacing*, which premiered in 2004 at Danspace Project, New York City, is 'a fluid world of video and movement ... a dreamily violent piece of beauty, danced well' (Batson 2004). Interestingly, it is a fairly low-tech performance in contrast to their other works, even being referred to as 'Troika Unplugged'. According to Troika Ranch, this performance is highly personal as it reflects the relationship between key members of the group.[14] The starting point for the performance came from the word 'surface' leading to an exploration of the term both from a physical sense, the surface of skin, the surfaces of architecture and so on, to an exploration of imaginary surfaces, the tensions between the private and personal, what is shown to the world and what is kept hidden; suggesting other 'related dialectic relationships: tenderness versus aggression, the desire for solitude versus the need for community'. And rather than being an 'exposé of cutting-edge technology, it was more a reflection on introspection and quiet solitude'.[15]

The piece was choreographed by Stoppiello, and unlike other Troika Ranch performances, she did not perform in it. The performers, Danielle Goldman, Patrick Mueller, Sandra Tillett and Michou Szabo appeared to materialize and dematerialize in the performance space at varying times and speeds. The very simple mise-en-scène was composed of four tipable wedge-like rectangular sculptures on whose surfaces, captured live or pre-recorded images would freeze, fragment, speed up, slow down or warp in a shimmering effect – all by means of Isadora. Another wooden sculpture served as a platform for live video capture. The opening scene consisted of captured bodies that appeared to rise and shimmer as they were projected onto the sculptures. The sculptures were placed in various positions in the space, mainly upright, providing a fragmented background where the performers appeared to walk or run or simply melt into their own virtual image as they went behind the sculptures. In fact, at times it was difficult to identify which were physical and which were virtual bodies. When tipped over, the sculptures lay horizontal on the floor, the captured images giving the appearance of bodies walking on their side. Added to this were dreamlike images projected to the rear of the space, images that had been slowed right down to provide an almost serial freeze effect in a halo of ephemeral light. The images were from a pre-recorded film that had been shot using exaggerated delay techniques in a special effects studio. *Surfacing* with its ritualistic sound akin to a form of Gregorian chant became at times a cathedral of ethereal imagery. The juxtaposition of private and public, solitude and community, tenderness and

Figure 5.6   Danielle Goldman in *Surfacing* (2004). Photo: Richard Termine

aggression were reflected in the lighting and imagery, which sometimes appeared cold and distancing and then, warm and alive, the space seemingly on fire with red light.

In contrast with *Surfacing*, *The Future of Memory* (2003)[16] made full use of a wide variety of Troika Ranch's interactive technology. Using 'Isadora in tandem with MidiDancer', the performers, Stoppiello, Goldman, Szabo and Tillett, manipulate sounds and images in real time; 'floating in a chaotic world of movement video and sound, the four characters ... swirl in and out of reality as they attempt to regain the memories that define who they really are' (Coniglio and Stoppiello 2005). Stoppiello's choreography seamlessly incorporated media control, at the same time leaving room for the performers to add onto the original structure, allowing the piece to be transformed from performance to performance.

Aptly titled, *The Future of Memory* explored memory and the act of remembering – 'how memories are created, stored, romanticized, repressed and lost' – by means of a multilayered collage of imagery and sound; the technology acting as a 'metaphor for memory' itself (Coniglio and Stoppiello 2005).

Historically, metaphor has been identified with the Freudian notion of 'condensation', and metonymy with 'displacement' (Lyotard 1989e).

Figure 5.7 The Company in *Future of Memory* (2003). Photo: Richard Termine

However, Lyotard, in his writings on metaphor takes a different stance. For Lyotard, there is a certain futility in bringing everything back to the linguistic 'as the model for all semiology', when it is 'clear that language, at least in its poetic usage, is possessed ... by the figure' (30). The figural for Lyotard is not the figuration of representational art but is instead that of creativity and elusiveness; it is important since it mirrors many digital practices such as *The Future of Memory*, placing the performance firmly within the context of a libidinal economy.

In this performance, the performers created electronic soundscapes that enhanced the live music performed by Alica Lagger (violin), Leigh Stuart (cello) and Julian Molitz (marimba). The flexion of the performers' limbs were used to trigger musical notes or phrases and to manipulate their timbre. At the same time their bodily movements influenced the playback speed and intensity of visual effects, which were presented as fragmented periodic images of stunning seascapes; waves washing over feet dripping with blood; a lighted match from a birthday party; a shimmering droplet of water; and live captured close-ups of faces; imagery which sped up, slowed down, froze or dissolved and was projected onto 20 individual screens, each approximately the size of a human body. Each screen displayed an individual image or at times, a single image was displayed over all the screens. However, in this performance, even a single image was never whole since it was fragmented by the spaces in between the screens. Central to *The Future of Memory* is Troika Ranch's principal strategy of mapping the organic and chaotic nature of the human body onto the fixed nature of digital media.

The *Chemical Wedding of Christian Rosenkreutz* (2000)[17] is another work that is exemplary of this process, especially in its theme of transformation where humans evolve into machines. It takes its title from an anonymous source, a seventeenth-century alchemical allegory that focuses on how alchemy is used to transform a human soul by means of a 'chemical wedding'. The performance explored and examined the process of technological transformation from the perspective of a human living 500 years in the past and another one living 50 years in the future. It was also influenced by a writing from Ray Kurzweill, which predicted that due to the present growth of technology it would be possible 'to download a human mind into a working silicon replacement by the year 2050' (Coniglio and Stoppiello 2005). The narrative from the past was told mainly through choreography, music and surrealist imagery. However, the narrative from the future, from the human about to download his mind, is heavily influenced by the fear of transformation and what that will ultimately mean for the soul. The 'future' character is 'shadowed' by a dancer that embodies his emotions through movement whilst he addresses the audience through a multimedia voice that combines live sound, mediated recordings and projected text. The performers seemingly attempting 'to unearth the richness gained from transitory moments and the sadness and confusion resulting from letting go' (Farley 2003).

The performance was complex and rich, demonstrating a variety of organic and electronic elements. The technology provided an eclectic mix of pre-recorded and live aural and visual imagery, whilst a live musician performed a cello accompaniment throughout. The media was manipulated in a variety of ways including algorithmically edited video imagery, electronic music and sound and digitally controlled lighting. Stoppiello as the Angel that visits Rosenkreutz (Coniglio) was at once frightening and surreal, as she glided, crawled and soared, triggering explosions of light and sound as she crossed laser beams located within the space, at the same time her movements activated a video image of multiple eyes. As Steve Dixon notes, *The Chemical Wedding* 'is spiritual in tone and choreographic style, which makes use of numerous dance lifts and other symbolic ascents, as well as secretive gestures ... The projected imagery fuses surrealism with mysticism' (2004, 24).

Another performance from Troika Ranch that demonstrates this linkage between technology and the body is *The Electronic Disturbance* (1996), inspired by the book of the same name from the Critical Art Ensemble. Here the human body is shown in flux, a body where contacts are made not physically but electronically with digital high-speed telephone lines. At the same time a simultaneous performance was presented via the Internet at The Kitchen (New York), The Electronic Café (Los Angeles) and Studio X (Santa Fe).

The recent work of *16 [R]evolutions* (2005) is a performance where cutting-edge choreography and multimedia effects explore the similarities and differences between human and animal and the evolutions that

Figure 5.8 Motion tracking leaves three-dimensional traces of the performers' movements in Troika Ranch's *16 [R]evolutions* (2005). Performers: Johanna Levy & Lucia Tong. Photo: Richard Termine

both go through in a single lifetime; the body literally writing itself in performance.

According to Beliz Demircioglu from *The Dance Insider*:

> Troika Ranch's new '16 [R]evolutions' ... is an immersive journey that travels through a matrix of imagination, reality and time ... The performance evoked a journey through experiences, sometimes in a very realistic form and sometimes in a more 'dream-like' or abstracted one ... '16 [R]evolutions' is a journey that makes you laugh, think, realize and get confused.
>
> (2006)

Reflected to a certain extent in Troika Ranch's use of electronic technology is Deleuze and Guattari's concept of a 'machine'. Originally appropriated from a Lacanian term, the machine denotes a shift away from the organic and human towards a timeless entity with no identity, intent or even end; a model of pure machinic production, always in the

Figure 5.9 Colour and multiplicity are introduced to imply evolutionary change in *16 [R]evolutions* (Performers: Johanna Levy & Daniel Suominen – photo A.T. Schaeffer)

process of becoming and making new connections. Central to becoming and making new connections is the body without organs or BwO. It is 'the field of immanence of desire' (Deleuze and Guattari 1999a, 191) and an 'intense and intensive body' (Deleuze 2003, 44). Desiring machines and the body without organs can be seen as two sides of the same coin, or 'two states of the same "thing", a functioning multiplicity one moment, a pure, unextended zero-intensity the next' (Bogue 1989, 93). Similarly in *The Future of Memory, The Chemical Wedding of Christian Rosenkreutz, The Electronic Disturbance, 16 [R]evolutions* and, to a lesser extent, *Surfacing*, the ebb and flow between the organic and electronic is in a continual process of becoming and making new connections.

For Coniglio, 'live performance is perhaps the most inefficient of contemporary art, because you cannot do with it what you can with digitally stored artworks', that is, mass-produce it inexpensively. Moreover, for Coniglio, it is the 'ineffable quality of liveness' that leads him to create and attend performances. Also by having a live audience and using new technologies, his performers are able to create work that is 'absolutely unrepeatable' (2004, 12). However, it is my belief that digital technology also challenges fundamental dualisms in its relation to performance, including those of original and reproduction, and live and recorded, since in cases where a performance has been electronically stored, the 'recording' can be made either before or after the 'original' performance using *MIDI* technology. What is actually recorded through the MIDI cable is a set of instructions for recreating the original performance rather than a transcription of that performance. The recording is therefore an original performance; the same binary information that is produced in performance is entered onto the recording. When the stored information is subsequently decoded to produce sound or visual imagery, it is literally 'reproduced again' not 'represented' just as is a 'live' improvised performance. Although, of course a live performance is capable of improvisation and spontaneity, whereas a MIDI file is not, both are reproduced again and not represented. This aspect of the digital deconstructs the valued distinction between 'live' and 'recorded' performance, as well as that between 'original' and 'reproduction'. Not surprisingly, as Coniglio points out, the cultural commodity market depends precisely on such distinctions together with the concurrent maintenance of these dualisms for its existence. This privileging, which entails an idealization of the performer as the author of an authentic work, the source of the original style and a reification of the performer's presence is challenged and subverted by the practices of digital technology.

Finally, Troika Ranch explore and investigate essentially what it is to be human in a time of rapid technological change and increasing physical alienation. Their innovative use of digital technologies and unique sensor systems has led them to be widely recognized as creative leaders in the field of digital practices. As Coniglio notes, 'our purpose' was

> To create dynamic, challenging artworks that fused traditional elements of dance, music and theatre with interactive digital media ... by directly linking the actions of a performer to the sound and imagery that accompanied them, we would be led to new modes of creation and performance and, eventually, to a new form of live art work.
>
> (2004, 5)

Notes

1. Diegesis is a Greek word for 'recounted story'.
2. For more technical details of *In the Presence of People*, see (Edwards 2001).
3. SMPTE timecodes are a set of cooperating standards to label individual frames of video or film with a timecode defined by the Society of Motion Picture and Television Engineers. Timecodes are added to provide a time reference for editing, synchronization and identification. The need for timecode was based around the problem of synchronizing mechanical motor-based playback systems. Even a variance of 0.5% in the motor speeds of different devices meant that synchronization could be lost within a few seconds. The time code numbers imprinted on tapes and a flexible motor system meant that a 'master' tape could be established and all the other devices would 'chase' it, remaining continuously synchronized. Early analogue videotape was difficult to edit, as cutting created signal drop-off on the control track that led to distracting jerks and flashes on cuts. The invention of timecode made modern videotape editing possible and led eventually to the creation of non-linear editing systems.
4. For a more detailed account of MIDI technology see Rossing, Moore and Wheeler (2002, 677–9).
5. Open Sound Control was created by the Centre for New Media and Audio Technologies (CNMAT) at the University of California, Berkeley, in the 1990s.
6. MSP provides the signal processing in Max and the more recent Max extension Jitter provides real-time video processing and 3-D graphics.
7. In my performance *Dead East, Dead West* (2003), Pd was very successfully used as a real-time interactive environment by Martin Dupras, one of the performance's digital interactive artists.
8. According to Palindrome, they are an 'intermedia' performance group. With the help of technology, they combine art forms in new ways. Their aim is not to create 'multi-media', where many things happen at once. Instead, they are interested in live interaction between media, artists and audience. According to Rebecca Schneider, '"intermedia" was introduced into the arts

lexicon by Dick Higgins in 1965', to describe 'artworks at the interfaces of established media and the interstices between art and life' (2000, 130 n. 5).

9. *Seine Hohle Form* premiered at the CEMI – Centre for Experimental Music and Intermedia, University of North Texas.

10. A similar easy-to-use video tracking system, VNS (Very Nervous System), was developed by the Canadian sound and video installation artist David Rokeby as early as 1986, and is still used by many composers and artists.

11. Mapping is the process of connecting one data port to another. However for Palindrome, this term relates specifically to the application of a given gestural data derived from a sensor system, to control a given sound or video synthesis parameter (Dowling, Wechsler and Weiss 2004, 1).

12. See *Entertainment Design* (30 March 2005).

13. Discussion with Troika Ranch following a performance of *Surfacing*, Chancellor Hall, Chelmsford, Essex, UK, 12 May 2005.

14. Discussion with Troika Ranch following the performance of *Surfacing*, Essex, 2005.

15. Troika Ranch UK Residency publicity leaflet, released by Essexdance, 2005.

16. The *Future of Memory* premiered at The Duke, 42nd Street, New York, February 2003.

17. *The Chemical Wedding of Christian Rosenkreutz* premiered at HERE Art Centre, New York, June 2000.

6
Digital Film

> With the cinema, it is the world which becomes its
> own image, and not an image which becomes world.
>
> (Deleuze 1986, 57)

In digital film, there is an emphasis on the use of new technologies that can produce a plethora of visual and aural special effects. *The Matrix* trilogy and *Star Wars* prequels, with their utilization of paint box, animation and 3-D modelling, and much more, epitomize this digital practice. Although not experimental in the sense of other practices analysed, that is, being instances of mainstream popular entertainment as opposed to marginal and mainly localized practices, digital film is essential in any analysis of the digital since much cutting-edge technology in live performance is first utilized in the film world where studios such as George Lucas's Industrial Light & Magic have the necessary resources to undertake the initial research, design and development of this technology.

The *Matrix* trilogy and the *Star Wars* prequels exhibit many similarities, not least of which is the absolute centrality of digital technology, together with narratives that focus on the search for a 'Chosen One'. However, although the first Matrix gained much praise in comparison to it sequels, it was the final episode of the *Star Wars* prequels that proved the most successful for critics and audience alike. Nevertheless, regardless of how both trilogies were received they have been exemplary in their emphasis on new technologies with *Star Wars* being regarded as somewhat of a point of reference for science fiction films in general, and also being arguably the first film franchise to extend its 'sci-fi' culture far beyond the films themselves.

The Matrix trilogy: 'Bullet time', simulation and virtual cinema

> The more a system nears perfection, the more it approaches a total accident. It is a form of objective irony stipulating that nothing ever happened. September 11th participated in this. Terrorism is not an alternative power, it is nothing except the metaphor of this almost suicidal return of Western power on itself ... But it is not about being nihilistic or pessimistic in the face of all that. The system, the virtual, the *matrix* – all of these will perhaps return to the dustbin of history. For reversibility, challenge and seduction are indestructible.
>
> (Baudrillard 2004, italics mine)

> Bullet time is a stylistic way of showing that you're in a constructed reality – and that time and space are the same as, you know, us today living our lives. It is slowing down to such an extent that you really see everything around you as clearly as you possibly could ... Everything begins with the simulation ... it works backwards from there.
>
> (Gaeta 1999)

> Humans are crazy enough not only to build machines with an overall intelligence greater than our own, but to defer to them and give them power that matters ... Linking people via chip implants directly to those machines seems a natural progression, a potential way of harnessing machine intelligence by, essentially, creating superhumans.
>
> (Warwick 2000)

The *Matrix* trilogy completed in 2003, offered a multiplicity of special technical effects including 'bullet time', computer-generated images and virtual cinema, producing a stunning spectacle of the future as a machinic dominated world, which creates a simulated reality that masks the apocalyptic 'real'. Humans or 'coppertops' are enslaved, becoming literally batteries that provide power in order to sustain this technological world. The first of the trilogy was *The Matrix* (1999), which was ground breaking at that time in its use of technology, gaining four Academy Awards for Best Visual Effects, Best Sound, Best Film Editing and Best Sound Effects Editing. This was followed by *The Matrix Reloaded* and *The Matrix Revolutions*, both released in 2003. The sequels, which were filmed at the same time, were in fact seen as being two sections of a larger film. According to producer Joel Silver: 'it's one enormous movie that's being cut in half and shown in two halves' (Wells 2002, 75); whereas, the first *Matrix* although an introduction to the latter was also more of a stand-alone project.

The films which were written and directed by Andy and Larry Wachowski abound with chthonic symbols, iconic imagery and mythological beings. They provide a visual cacophony of dreamscapes and primordial worlds where violence, terrorism, passion, tragedy and human affirmation through love, all take place. Powerful religious and cultural archetypes are invoked, including references to the Holy Trinity, a ritualistic rebirthing, a link to the Merovingians, reputed to be the protectors of the Holy Grail, through to Baudrillard's *Simulcra and Simulations*,[1] and even to the white rabbit from Lewis Carroll's *Alice in Wonderland*,[2] who signposts the way for both characters and spectators. The term 'matrix' was previously used by William Gibson in *Neuromancer*, where it was defined as 'a consensual hallucination experienced daily by billions' (1984, 51).

The Matrix' fictional world fundamentally creates an illusion that no longer exists – a representation of a twentieth-century location in time and space that is merely a dream world for humans at the end of the twenty-second century – approximately, we are told in the year 2199. This illusion is fed into the brains of humans as they sleep in their womb-like cocoons. In this 'virtual reality' humans believe they are going about the normal business of living and loving in all its physical actuality but instead they are merely living virtually within their own minds whilst machines dominate the world. Humans are needed to provide power for this computer system becoming literally the electrical energy needed to sustain the machinic world.

After the birth of 'Artificial Intelligence' (AI), 'a singular consciousness that spawned an entire race of machines,' the 'real' world was destroyed by humans who 'scorched the sky' in an attempt to destroy the machines (Wachowski and Wachowski 1999). It was believed that this would prevent the machines from functioning but they swiftly adapted to the environment by enslaving humans, in order to literally replace solar energy by organic means. Needing only a small charge to cause an electrical reaction, the machines found an ever ready supply in human bodies.

The 'matrix' would seem to be a combination of hardware and software with a mainframe somewhere external to the system that develops and maintains the programs, which support this virtual world. Human beings becoming no more than electrical signals converted into specific output, in order to both support the machinic world and make sense of the virtual one. Interestingly, this is not so different from our own actuality where consciousness is also constructed by means of the brain's electrical signals which gathers information and converts it into sensations and signification, in order for us to both make sense of and to make our world meaningful.

The Matrix trilogy's use of virtual reality technology can be seen as a literal depiction of human consciousness transcending the body and becoming no more than an instance of data within the circuits of a computer. In doing so, it reflects 'a defining characteristic of the present cultural moment' within Katherine Hayles's post-human analysis. Here, there are 'no essential differences or demarcations between bodily existence and computer simulation' and there is a privileging 'of informational pattern over material instantiation' (1999, 1–3). Hayles suggests that the notion of the embodied human has been replaced by a new ideal of the cybernetic where 'posthuman boundaries of the human subject are constructed rather than given' (84). Similarly, there exists 'the belief that information can circulate unchanged among different material substrates' independent from the actual world (1). Human beings are essentially information that is contingently embodied and thus able to be 'uploaded' into 'super-intelligent' communication systems that are infinite in time and space (16).

The story line of *The Matrix* centres around a computer programmer, Thomas Anderson (Keanu Reeves), who by day is an office drone but by night is a notorious hacker known as Neo, and is first seen asleep in the technological surroundings of his apartment. Neo supplies illegal virtual environments, keeping his 'supplies' hidden appropriately in a hollowed-out copy of Baudrillard's *Simulacra and Simulation*. The action is set in an illusionary Western city that could be anywhere in the world at the end of the twentieth century. A stunning action sequence opens the film with a leather clad Trinity (Carrie-Ann Moss) attempting to evade 'sentients' led by Agent Smith (Hugo Weaving). The 'Agents' within the Matrix are sentient programs, that is, artificially intelligent programs that think for themselves. They serve as spooks and law-maintenance officers for the machine world having the ability to morph into the virtual body of any human being. In order to escape the agents, Trinity reaches a ringing telephone just before its booth is destroyed by a truck, seemingly disappearing into the receiver and down the telephone wire.

Trinity contacts Neo with a proposition for him to meet the rebel leader and terrorist Morpheus (Laurence Fishbourne). However, the rebels unbeknown to them have been betrayed by Cypher (Joe Pantoliano). As agents come to arrest him, Neo has to choose whether or not to escape by clambering around a narrow window ledge. He decides to surrender and finds himself arrested and interrogated by Agent Smith. On being refused his customary phone call, he gives Smith the finger, a gesture that 'encapsulates a violence embedded in the very structure of human sexuality' that is both 'contraceptive' and 'conceptive' (Kimball 2002, 89). As a result Neo enters into a 'fuzzy' world where accepted laws of physics appear to have no place. Here anything can and does happen including the removal of Neo's mouth and the penetration and implantation of an insect tracker bug into his abdomen. However, this is only the beginning of Neo's journey into a world where the boundaries between the virtual and the 'real' are more blurred and unstable than he could have ever dreamt of.

Neo is debugged by Trinity after being repenetrated by an extraction device that anticipates his birthing into the 'real' world. He eventually meets Morpheus, whose life has been dedicated to finding 'the One', the saviour who is prophesized to lead humans out of their enslavement and defeat the machines. On meeting Morpheus, Neo asks, 'What is the Matrix?' and is told that 'the Matrix is everywhere. It is all around us, even now in this very room ... It is the world that has been pulled over your eyes to blind you from the truth' (Wachowski and Wachowski 1999). Morpheus offers Neo the choice between two alternate realities, one leading to amnesia and the other to the 'truth':

> Unfortunately, no one can be told what the Matrix is. You have to see it for yourself. This is your last chance. After this there is no turning back. You take the blue pill, the story ends, you wake up in your bed and believe whatever you want to believe. You take the red pill, you stay in Wonderland, and I show you how deep the rabbit hole goes – remember all I am offering is the truth, nothing more.
>
> (Wachowski and Wachowski 1999)

Neo chooses the red pill and enters the world of actuality, of truth, of physicality, in short, the world as it is in 2199. This is a post-apocalyptic world of perpetual darkness, where the descendants of the survivors of the holocaust who managed to escape the machines live deep below ground in the city of Zion. The humans and their descendents who did not escape are harvested in huge power plants. They are kept in womb-like pods where they are sustained by means of feeding on other dead humans and where their energy is continually drained in order to support the machinic world whilst simultaneously they live their virtual lives in 1999. Morpheus quoting Baudrillard welcomes Neo to 'the desert of the real'. For Baudrillard:

> Today abstraction is no longer that of the map, the double, the mirror, or the concept. Simulation is no longer that of a territory, a referential being or a substance. It is the generation by models of a real without origin or reality: a hyperreal. The territory no longer precedes the map, nor does it survive it. It is nevertheless the map that precedes the territory – *the precession of simulacra* – that engenders the territory ... It is the real, not the map, whose vestiges persist here and there in the deserts that are no longer those of the Empire, but ours. *The desert of the real itself.*
>
> (Baudrillard 1994, 1)

The Wackowskis, influenced by their reading of Baudrillard, suggest in *The Matrix* that there is no longer a reality to which we can return because the map of the landscape (the simulacra) has replaced most of the original territory. All that remains of it is a barren and forsaken desert. For Baudrillard, simulation is universalized both historically and socially and implicitly in a historical process where each order of value is superseded and absorbed as illusion by the next. In Baudrillard's schema, the image draws increasingly away from reality until it bears no relation to reality whatsoever. As he writes,

> This would be the successive phases of the image:
> – it is the reflection of a basic reality
> – it masks and perverts a basic reality
> – it bears no relation to any reality whatever: it is its own pure simulation.
>
> (1983, 11)

This last development is where the image loses its referent altogether and where production is superseded by simulation, 'every century throws the reality principle into question as it closes but it's over today, finished, done' (Baudrillard 1990, 183).

Although the Wachowskis have been keen to cite Baurillard's writing, he has been less willing to comment on the *The Matrix*. In an interview for *La Nouvel Observateur* (2003), Baudrillard mentions that misinterpretations have arisen from the taking of 'the hypothesis of the virtual for an irrefutable fact and transforming it into a visible phantasm' (2004).

For Baurillard, 'it is precisely that we can no longer employ categories of the real in order to discuss the characteristics of the virtual'. According to Baudrillard, the *Matrix'* actors are either 'in the digitized system of things' or 'they are radically outside it, such as in Zion'. For him, the interest would be to show what happens when 'these two worlds collide'. He claims that 'the most embarrassing part of the film is that the new problem posed by simulation is confused with its classical, Platonic treatment'. He continues that what has been invented within the *Matrix* is a simulated real:

> A virtual universe from which everything dangerous and negative has been expelled … The *Matrix* is surely the film about the matrix that the matrix would have been able to produce.
>
> (Baudrillard 2004)

However, despite Baudrillard's protestations, *The Matrix* has managed to gain a certain cultural acumen by incorporating the ideas of a well known cultural and media theorist within its plot, even if based on a misunderstanding.

In stating that the 'matrix is everywhere', although we are 'blind' to it, Morpheus not only refutes any outside of the matrix but at the same time places AI firmly at its centre. The inside and the outside of a text, what is included and excluded, is a critical assumption posited by Derrida. He writes, '*there is nothing outside of the text* [*there is no outside-text; il n'y a pas de hors-texte*]' (1976, 156). In other words, text in a broad sense and including the non-linguistic is all there is.[3] This has often been read as indicating a defence of the interiority of the text to the exclusion of the outside, indicating a lack of political or social concern. However, for Derrida and also for Morpheus, the text (matrix) does not open to the outside because the outside is not completely outside (Derrida 1981a, 35–6). Similarly, in placing AI at its centre *The Matrix* demonstrates literally that there can never be presence without absence since the difference between two terms is perceived from the perspective of one of the terms, the term of plenitude from which the second is held to derive (1976, 62). In *The Matrix*, AI is initially prioritized over human intelligence yet the AI was created by humans. As the plotline continues, the organic in the form of Neo – 'the One' – subverts and replaces the centre (AI), at the same time remaining contaminated by its technology. Neo becomes literally part of the AI system, being able to move around freely in the virtual space without needing to be jacked or plugged into the system. In fact, the first *Matrix* ends with a clear indication of a new beginning, with Neo calling up the matrix main-frame on a hardwire phone to pronounce:

> You're afraid of change. I don't know the future. I didn't come here to tell you how this is going to end. I came here to tell how it is going to begin.
>
> (Wachowski and Wachowski 1999)

The 'Architect' (Helmut Bakaitis) in *Reloaded* claims that the matrix has been recreated several times since its original inception, each incarnation bringing with it a new reality with the seeming potential for 'an immanent power of creation'. In short, a virtual instantiation of the Nietzschean 'will to power'. The matrix can also be seen as 'a sphere of the virtual', where 'logic can only show ... without logic ever being able to grasp it in propositions or relate it to a reference' (Deleuze and Guattari 1999b, 140). According to A. Samuel Kimball: the Matrix represents 'a kind of parthenogenic – which is to say autochthonous – mother', a way of reproducing life without the need for sexual intercourse; analogical to the various myths and fables that relate to humans arising from the earth instead of being born (Kimball 2001, 191–4). Within *The Matrix* humans are not from the earth, but are reproduced by means of cloning technologies (matrix is derived from the Latin root *mater*, which means literally mother). For Kimball, the film both affirms and denies its 'autochthonous motifs', since it 'violently resists the myth of autochthony', whilst at the same time, by means of 'its imagery and techniques', recreates it (2001, 176).

Imagery of birthing occurs throughout *The Matrix*. For instance, Neo is shown within the harvest 'fields' where humans are suspended in red womb-like pods, each hanging from a stalk. After being unplugged and seized by the pincers of one of the AI machines and then discarded, Neo is able to free himself from his liquid 'womb'. Climbing out of his pod he is flushed or aborted into what appears to be a huge waste-disposal unit, where he is picked up by the crew in their hover ship.

After undergoing a rehabilitation period, Neo begins training under the mentorship of Morpheus, developing a variety of seemingly impossible martial arts techniques (with the help of Yuen Wo Ping who developed the device of 'wire-fighting' and who was brought in specially to choreograph the fight scenes within all three films) and gains various knowledge and skills, both practical and almost Zen-like, in order to overcome the artificial life forms, developing a love interest, on the way, in the form of Trinity.

The film is replete with references to Christianity as well as to other mythological forms. For instance, the trio of Neo, Morpheus and Trinity, strongly reference the Holy Family or Trinity of the New Testament with Morpheus as the father figure, Neo as Christ, the prophesised saviour, and Trinity taking on the role of the Holy Ghost. The names of characters and objects throughout the Matrix, similarly, carry some form of mythological and religious connotation. Neo is an anagram of the 'One'; Morpheus is named after the Greek God of dreams and is the captain of the Nebuchadnezzar, a ship whose name is derived from an Old Testament King and means 'to defend the boundaries'; and Zion is the name of the last human city located deep below the ground and was the promised land of the Israelites. Other characters that appear at various times are Cypher who betrays the crew, his name is short for cryptograph, a system of concealing a message using symbols (Lawrence 2004, 201); Deus Ex Machina (Latin for 'God in the Machine') that is, the composite face of the machines in *Revolutions*; Persephone who is the wife of Merovingian is named after a Greek goddess; Merovingian – her husband – who is a sentient program that keeps the 'Keyholder' prisoner in *Reloaded*, is named after the French aristocratic family that claim to be the direct descendents of Jesus Christ and Mary Magdalene and protectors of the Holy Grail (Brown 2003, 579); and the Oracle, the principal sentient program has the ability to see the future, prophesising the return of the 'One'. The Oracle (played by Gloria Foster in the first two films and by Mary Alice in *Revolutions*) reflects the famous Oracle of Delphi from Greek Mythology and also evokes the beliefs of Tibetan Buddhism in her (its) search for the reincarnated messiah.

Since the Oracle can see into the future there is the inference that everything is deterministic and that there can be no free will. Neo ineffectually attempts to exert his freedom from this teleological destiny, revealing his exasperation in the following dialogue:

Neo: You already know if I am going to take it.
Oracle: Wouldn't be much of an Oracle if I didn't.
Neo: If you already know, how can I make a choice?
(Wachowski and Wachowski 1999)

Neo later knocks over a vase after being told by the Oracle, 'and don't worry about the vase':

Oracle: What's really going to bake your noodle later is, would you still have broken it if I hadn't said anything.
(Wachowski and Wachowski 1999)

Neo's opposition to a deterministic future demonstrates one of Ramachandran and Blakeslee's defining characteristics of the self, namely the *'executive self'*, which is a belief in free will, a sense of agency, of being in control of ones destiny (1999, 247–52). However, Libet's discovery of the 'readiness potential', where an electrical reaction in the brain is produced before any conscious decision has been formulated to realize a voluntary movement (1985, 529–34), not only problematizes our (and Neo's) accepted notion of free will, but also ultimately the concept of causality itself.

Within *The Matrix* there are three distinct 'worlds' where the filmed action supposedly takes place: 'the virtual world of the Matrix, the real world, and the Train Station', which is a virtual reality program and though similar to the Matrix, it is not part of that program (Lawrence 2004, 10–11). Rather, it links the machine world to the matrix and it is where in *Revolutions*, Neo meets Sati (Tanveer K. Atwal), a program from the machine world appearing in the form of a young girl who is marked for deletion. Zion is part of the 'real world' and is a subterranean city where its inhabitants move around by means of hover ships, similar to the Nebuchadnezzar, as they negotiate the city's sewer systems. They wage war on the AI and free enslaved humans whenever they can. They are constantly under attack by the sentinels (also known as calamari due to their squid like appearance), which are sentient machines sent to destroy the Zionists and their city.

In contrast to Zion, where the chthonic is strongly referenced, a utopia beyond artificial intelligence, and where the organic reigns supreme, the virtual world of the matrix appears sterile and distancing. The exterior shots of the virtual world are digitally reworked, particularly the use of colours. For instance, the sky is depicted as being white instead of the brilliant blue of an Australian sky (where the film was shot). According to the director of photography Bill Pope, 'we didn't necessarily want the Matrix world to resemble our present world ... In Australia the sky is a brilliant blue virtually all the time, but we wanted bald white skies. All our TransLight backings were altered to have white skies, and on actual exterior shots in which we see a lot of sky, we digitally enhanced the skies to make them white' (Probst 1999, 36). There is also an overt use of green filters since again according to Pope, 'we wanted the Matrix reality to be unappealing' (36). This creates a defamiliarizing, distancing effect but at same time seduces the spectator with its highly self-referential stylistic features. Another factor in the films' lighting and colour approach was dictated by the use of a special slow-motion photographic technique dubbed 'bullet time'.

Paradoxically, *The Matrix* fetishizes technology whilst at the same time treating technology as the enemy. Of course, one main incongruity is that in the making of *The Matrix* films, far more technology is used to recreate the supposedly physical and actual domains of the 'present'. For example, the city of Zion, together with the post-apocalyptic earth landscape, the machine city, and the wars between the rebels and the sentient machines, are all created with the aid of virtual cinematography and computer imagery, whilst the supposedly simulated world of the *Matrix*, set in 1999, is far less dependent on technology and special effects for its representation. As the films progress from *The Matrix* through to *Reloaded* and *Revolutions*, far more sophisticated technology is introduced. However, the first *Matrix* did contain one stunning innovative technical effect – 'Bullet time' or 'Flo-Mo', which has the ability to capture both super-slow and high-speed motions at the same time on film – a technique needed to demonstrate Neo's increasingly skilful manipulation of virtual time and space, and that has since been copied by a variety of media productions in cinema and television.

According to visual effects supervisor John Gaeta of Manex Visual Effects (Alamedia, California), the Wachowskis wanted *The Matrix* to be 'about the complete manipulation of time and space in a simulated world' (Magrid 1999, 50). For the fight sequences, Gaeta was told to 'come up with a method of manipulating time so that the camera can be moving while all the high-speed stunt action is happening. They [the Wachowskis] just love using hyper-slow-motion' (50). In 1997, Gaeta developed '"Flo-Mo", which simulates the effect of a camera moving at very high speeds while shooting any desired frame rate up to 600fps' (Magrid 1999, 51). The Flo-Mo concept, dubbed 'bullet-time' by the Wachowskis, is not new and was used by Edward Muybridge in his very well-known 'Animal Locomotion Studies' during the 1880s, where he used the same principle to both explore motion and also achieve a sense of movement in still photography.

The Flo-Mo system can break down any camera movement, 'including 360-degree tracking shots and swooping crane shots', into specific increments. Individual Canon units were placed around a designated scene; 'one hundred and twenty cameras and two motion capture cameras' were used (Gaeta 1999). According to Gaeta, setting the intended shot was both difficult and time-consuming. Using an animated model as a stand-in for the actor, the team designed the camera pathway and calculated the placement of each camera, 'for example, we could shape the array into an elliptical path around our subject and then use adjustable rods to place the still camera up and down this path, which allowed us complete flexibility' (Gaeta quoted in Magrid 1999, 52). All the equipment was covered with green screen, except the camera lenses, to make it easier to digitally clean up shots later. The cameras, which could be triggered with as little as 1/1000th of a second between adjacent cameras, were controlled by a computer running Kaydara's Filmbox software (Montreal). The still images were then scanned into Kodak's Cineon software for compositing. In order to generate the motion between the still frames, Manex worked with Snell & Wilcox (UK) to produce new motion interpolation technology (Robertson 1999a, 54–5).

To place a background around the actor, Manex's George Borshukov helped develop an image-modelling technology called 'virtual cinematography' that converts 'a live-action location or set into a photo-realistic virtual set for generating any camera move' (Robertson 1999a, 54–5). Gaeta differentiates between 'virtual cinematography' and 'virtual cinema'. The former 'is the act of composing materials from components – humans, performances, background', whereas the latter is to do with 'a stand-alone scene sourced from the real world, and augmented and created into a whole new type of cinema'. According to Gaeta, virtual cinema will ultimately lead to 'dimensional filmmaking' ensuring a performance becomes immersive and interactive, in order to convince participants of 'the truthfulness of the space around them' (Gaeta 2003, 56).

Transforming the slowed down, choreographed action of the fight sequences from *The Matrix* into a series of still images required major previsualization (previz) techniques that involved the stunt coordinator, actors, the visual effects supervisor (Gaeta), the virtual cinematographer (Borshukov) and the previsualization animator (Dan Klem). The team working first with Yuen Wo Ping (the stunt coordinator), videoed his wire-rigged stunts from all perspectives in order to document the speed and trajectory of the actors' bodies that were then used to track the action in 3D. The frame rate was then selected. For Rodney Inwahina (Manex), 'previsualization was instrumental in the success of the Flo-Mo shots' (Magrid 1999, 53).

However, previsualization was not only used in the Flo-Mo scenes of *The Matrix* but later it was also used in many ways, across many scenes of the sequels, *Reloaded* and *Revolutions*. According to Gaeta 'for films that are as technically complex as *The Matrix* sequels are, it was mandatory to develop a method of orientating all types of film craftspeople toward a common objective. As such, previz was used extensively to create a centreline of intent and objectives' (Moltenbray 2004, 28). The 270-day film shoot of the *Matrix* sequels involved a variety of scenes and shots using extensive blue screen and green screen set-ups,[4] computer generated imagery (CGI) set extensions and integrated computer generated (CG) characters. Using previz, Gaeta could ascertain what action was taking place, what camera perspectives could be used and what objects could be digitally created. It was also used to determine what would be needed and the resultant cost for each frame. A more complex use of this technique was to determine what unique camera and lens styles to use in order to create spectacular shots. According to Gaeta, 'we did a number of virtual photography and Bullet Time shots that would have been impossible to do their full potential without visualizing them ahead of time in 3D' (Moltenbray 2004, 29).

Towards the conclusion of *Revolutions*, the Matrix' final sequel, Neo and Trinity pilot a ship through underground tunnels to reach the machine city. Above ground, they are attacked by sentinels and escape by soaring up through the dark chemically polluted clouds to the blue sky above. They crash back down again into the machine city where Neo meets Deus ex Machina.

A low-res 'master set' was built for this hundred-mile-wide city that could be viewed from multiple cameras. According to special effects lead Dan Rolinek: 'a huge area of the city needed to be encrusted with buildings and towers. So we didn't build real geometry. Instead we emitted particles that represented building parts' (Robertson 2003, 26). To create the atmospheric effects, Johnny Gibson, the CG supervisor, provided procedural shaders to create chemical clouds, fog and so on. For the attacks on Neo's ship, Rolinek again used particle systems to emulate the swarms of sentinels. The Machine God was modelled and animated from filmed footage of the Wachowskis' baby nephew with sentinel swarms making up the huge face, which in the film pulsated with expression, scattering the swarms with each emotional outburst (26–7).

One of the most sophisticated CG effects of the three films comes in the final sequence of *Revolutions*, when during the penultimate fight between Neo and Agent Smith, a punch from Neo targets Smith's face in extreme slow motion and super-high resolution. During this sequence Smith's resulting facial deformation and even the indentation of Neo's fingers can be clearly seen. According to Borshukov: 'finally, we could show in full screen all the techniques we've developed in the last three and half years for facial capture' (Robertson 2003, 27). In order to capture this shot, an array of cameras were synchronized to capture the actor's performance. Each individual pixel was tracked over time in each camera, and then combined with a scanned model of the actor's neutral expression. Animated colour maps were created by combining images taken from the multiple camera perspectives. Surface textures, such as pores and wrinkles were added using a 100-micron scan of the actor's face. One of the scans was then chosen that could be manipulated to emulate a maquette showing the facial damage caused by Neo's punch. Because Smith's face would be so close to the camera, the head needed to be remodelled at twice the resolution of the previous head. Borshukov continues:

> Every single pixel in that shot was computer-generated. The rendering ran almost a week because we had water drops in the air and on the surface of the skin, with reflections and refractions, and we had to have full-on three-dimensional depth of field so it was incredibly expensive.
>
> (Robertson 2003, 27)

Since human interaction and communication are largely dependent on face recognition it is not surprising that faces have such emotional impact. It is also not unexpected that a large area of the human brain is devoted to face recognition, the right non-dominant hemisphere taking a leading role in face perception (Zeman 2002, 216). So sophisticated is the ability of humans to recognize facial expressions that even very slight differences are perceived and made meaningful and that is why such a super high resolution mediated face as that of Agent Smith in *Revolutions* has such a powerful effect on the spectator.

The above scene also reflects the violence that pervades *The Matrix* films. According to Larry Wachowski (commenting on his film), 'there are many incredible and beautiful images in violence ... For example, what John Woo does with his sort of hyper-violence is brilliant. He pushes violent imagery to another level. We tried to do that with *The Matrix* as well' (Probst 1999, 34). Wide, jarring metaphors evoke surreal images of sex, violence and death.[5] This is accompanied by the interaction of the physical and virtual that also creates inclusive, jarring metaphors. The mixture of wide metaphor produces an aesthetic effect caused by the interplay of various mental sense-impressions, which unsettle the audience by frustrating their expectations of any simple interpretation, and in doing so create a new kind of synaesthetic effect that corresponds to the perceptual experience caused by the cross-activation or cross-wiring of discrete areas of the brain suggested in neuro-scientific studies of synaesthesia (Ramachandran and Hubbard 2001, 3–34).

To conclude, although the *Matrix* films are essentially concerned with humans overcoming technology; ironically, the Wachowskis have established a multi-million dollar franchise based on that same technology. In fact, the Digital Video Disc (DVD) home market was invented as a direct result of *The Matrix* (released by Warner Home Video, 1999). In the years prior to *The Matrix* previous attempts at upgrading home-video media for the digital age had failed. For instance, in 1998, DVD sales in the United Kingdom totalled 180,000 copies. However, by 1999, DVD sales of *The Matrix* in one month alone sold 200,000 copies (Clover 2004, 49). The attraction of the DVD was fundamentally due to its ability to store clips of special effects and key moments in the making of the film that could be replayed at will. One unique feature of the DVD, 'Follow the White Rabbit', is that the spectator, when interacting with an icon of a rabbit which appears at various intervals throughout the film, can access 'behind the scenes' footage for that particular portion of the film. The film's style and aesthetic traits bear many similarities to a huge video game and the DVD with its interactivity exaggerates this link. The DVD-Rom even features an interactive game called 'The One' that tests the viewer's knowledge of the film. In fact, *The Matrix* franchise has since produced its own video games on the back of the films.

A whole series of animated films, titled *The Animatrix*, have also been produced which are based on stories written by the Wachowskis. They were released in 2003 on DVD and VHS by Warner Home Video. According to Michael Arias, The Wachowskis 'wanted to expand on the Matrix theme in terms of storytelling, plus pay homage to anime and bring it to adult US audiences' (Doyle 2003, 18). As Joshua Clover remarks, 'like the Matrix, *The Matrix* is the movie that's everywhere, and was designed to be so' (2004, 49).

The use of digital technology is foregrounded in digital practices such as *The Matrix*, not only as an object of the technical but as a recognizable style. The digital's aesthetic features include: fragmentation, dehistoricization and repetition. Unsurprisingly, commodification finds support in its syntax that is, in its creation of desire, satisfaction of that desire, mobility, its local and locatable surfaces and its dehistoricization of history. However, although franchises like *The Matrix*, rather dubiously provide the link between commodification and digital creative practices, they also offer a multiplicity of aesthetic possibilities for visual and aural effects. Therefore, the real potential of the digital lies in the production of an ahistorical amnesia together with an infinity of new aesthetic styles, which demand active participation from its audience, thereby creating the potential for social performers to become non-'docile bodies' of non-performance (Foucault 1986, 135–69). As with all experimental performances, *The Matrix* as a digital practice is a site of aesthetic intervention and as such has an indirect effect on the political. Such practices reflect and are experimental extensions of our contemporary culture and times.

Star Wars prequels: The digital force of ILM in Phantom Menace, *Attack of the Clones* and *Revenge of the Sith*

> A long time ago in a galaxy far, far away ...
>
> (George Lucas, *Star Wars*)

> It took the modern cinema to re-read the whole of cinema as already made up of aberrant movements and false continuity shots. The direct time-image is the phantom which has always haunted the cinema, but it took modern cinema to give a body to this phantom. This image is virtual, in opposition to the actuality of the movement-image.
>
> (Deleuze 1989, 41)

> Sith happens ... The opening shot, which needs to top the beginning of *Star Wars* is a fully realised depiction of something that even a few years ago would have been inconceivable ... *Revenge of the Sith* is packed with equally astonishing, equally beautiful shots and sequences.
>
> (Newman 2005, 38)

The recent *Star Wars* prequels springing from the imagination of George Lucas have met with a mixed reception even from diehard Star Wars fans. The original 1970s/1980s *Star Wars* trilogy: *Star Wars* (1977) (now re-named *Star Wars: Episode IV – The New Hope*), *Episode V – The Empire Strikes Back* (1980) *and Episode VI – The Return of the Jedi* (1983), had a powerful impact on world audiences, quickly becoming a benchmark for science fiction films, even creating a 'Star Wars' culture that extended to other science-fiction films. As a result of this success Lucas arguably created the first film and media franchise with its resultant commodification and consumerism and infiltration into all aspects of the sociocultural realm.

The movie prequels: *Episode I – Phantom Menace* (1999), *Episode II – Attack of the Clones* (2002) and *Episode III – Revenge of The Sith* (2005a), add to and extend the *Star Wars* galaxy, being over 95 per cent digital with human actors mingling with digital characters and animatronic models as they wander through the computer-generated and digital matte-painted landscapes of cities and planets. Live performance is merged with 2-D and 3-D elements to create complex characters, such as the Gungan – Jar Jar Binks who is completely computer generated, and intricate environments. Notably, the garden planet of Naboo, which is the focus of much of the action, at least in the first two films, together with Coruscant, a polis of high-rise buildings and spaceports; Kamino, a storm-filled watery planet; Mustafar, a tumultuous volcanic world; and many more of the intergalactic settings that are assembled from live-action footage, miniature sets, digital models and background digital paint-box effects. These effects are created and woven together by Lucasfilm and the Lucas Digital's effects division, Industrial Light & Magic (ILM).

With the release of the prequels trilogy, the intention was to emulate the original success of the *Star Wars* conglomerate and further extend the Lucas media empire. *Star Wars: Episode III – Revenge of Sith* has indeed been voted the favourite movie and movie drama at the Thirty-Second Annual People's Choice Awards held at the Shrine Auditorium 10 January 2006. However, there has also been some extremely negative criticism from reviewers and film critics. For instance, according to Peter Travers from *Rolling Stone* writing on *Attack of the Clones*:

> The big problem, aside from the fact that *The Matrix* and *The Lord of the Rings* outclassed Lucas at his own game, is talk, talk, talk. Even with script help from Jonathan Hales, Lucas still can't write dialogue that doesn't induce projectile vomiting. And the film's visual snap (it was all shot digitally) leaves emotions at a chilly remove.
>
> (2002, 83)

And Kim Newman from *Sight and Sound* writing on *Revenge of the Sith*, remarks:

> It looks much better than it sounds ... Yet when the characters shut up and are in action (or even in tableau) *Revenge of the Sith* can claim to be the best looking *Star Wars* episode of all.
>
> (2005, 38–9)

Anthony Lane from *The New Yorker* writes:

> The general opinion of *Revenge of the Sith* seems to be that it marks a distinct improvement on the last two episodes, *The Phantom Menace*

and *Attack of the Clones*. True but only in the same way that dying from natural causes is preferable to crucifixion.

(2005, 94)

Of course one would wonder why a science-fiction film trilogy should warrant such extreme emotional response and accompanying acerbic comment from reviewers and, it must be said, some fans alike. Indeed, there is no denying that the dialogue and narrative content could be strengthened in these films. However, there are many more so-called Hollywood blockbusters that demonstrate the same deficiencies but escape with far less criticism. In my opinion, these strong responses stem from a misplaced nostalgia and belief in the organic primacy and egalitarianism of the original *Star Wars*, and a rebuttal of the new technologies that drive and give impetus to the prequels. It must be added that if the current technological possibilities existed at the time of the original *Star Wars*, they would most certainly have been utilized. Nevertheless, all this seems to me to miss the point of the magnification in creative possibilities which result from such a 'technological culture' as demonstrated by the *Star Wars* prequels, a potentiality which is highly relevant to digital practices and conversely understated in performance and theory. Furthermore, although the link between digitized technology and international commodification is undeniable and similarly reflected in the digital, I believe that such practices can nevertheless potentiate resistance strategies. For instance, their perceived complicity masks a critical deconstruction, and their promotion of a diverse range of 'perceptive strategies' can lead to a challenging of traditional institutions of authority.

According to Lucas, the films' writer and director, *Star Wars* is really one big film and is an archetypal story of the 'hero's journey', manifested in the character of Darth Vader:

Anakin is the chosen one. Even when Anakin turns into Darth Vader, he is still the chosen one ... the story is really about the villain trying to gain his humanity becomes really the story of Darth Vader's redemption.

(Lucas 2005b)

Lucas was directly influenced by Joseph Campbell's *The Hero With a Thousand Faces* (1968), on which he based most of the screenplay of *Star Wars: Episode IV – The New Hope* and he has often referred to Star Wars as a 'classic myth' (Lancashire 2000, 24). Lucas acknowledged using

Campbell's work and even considered him a mentor. Their close relationship was evidenced by him allowing the 1980s seminal television series, *Joseph Campbell and The Power of Myth*, to be filmed mainly at Skywalker Ranch, the film studio built by Lucas in California's Marin County. Indeed as Jonathan Young claims, 'the most successful film series in history was retelling the initiatory adventures that Campbell had so vividly described ... for Joseph Campbell, the study of myth was the exploration of the possibilities of consciousness. His lifetime of scholarship was nothing less than the search for the Holy Grail of radiant living' (2004). In an attempt to explain the universality of mythological themes or what Campbell terms 'the cultural monomyth of the cultures around the world' (Lancashire 2000, 24), he based his hero's journey on a model of 'initiatory elements in myth, religion literature, and ritual' (Young 2004). Campbell was also influenced by Arnold Van Gennep's writings on initiation rituals and further developed Van Gennep's template of 'departure', 'transformation' and 'return', pivotal stages in his *Rites of passage* (Van Gennep 1960).

Campbell's hero, a potential leader or 'chosen one' is called upon to fulfil a quest, going through a series of near-death or actual death experiences, and then is literally or symbolically redeemed leading to triumph for the hero and his followers. *The Hero With a Thousand Faces* presents the hero's rites of passage where there is the call to adventure, meeting with a mentor and the liminal (threshold) passage. The mentor can take many forms, for example, an elderly teacher, a wise enchantress or a mysterious magician. The mentor gives the hero something that is necessary for the quest. The challenge for the initiate involves finding allies and guides and resisting temptations, ultimately being required to face a supreme ordeal. The journey concludes with the 'return threshold passage, resurrection, celebration, accepting a role of service ... and finally merging two worlds' (Young 2004).

All six *Star Wars* films individually and collectively demonstrate this initiatory sequence and as a result their narrative is more plot-based than character-centred (Lancashire 2000, 26). In *Episode I: Phantom Menace*, Anakin Skywalker (Jake Lloyd), who will grow up to be Darth Vader, is shown as a young boy living on the desert planet of Tatooine, ostensibly from a broken home. Though there is the inference that Anakin is the result of a virgin birth – mirroring that other virgin birth. He is requested to help a princess and the Jedi knights, one of whom, Obi-Wan Kenobi (Ewan McGregor), will eventually become his mentor. Anakin accepts the quest and is transported through space with his mentor (departure) to face a test from the Jedi Council (initiation). The film ends with Anakin, as hero, destroying an enemy battlestation and emerging triumphant before his supporters (return) (26).

According to Young, Campbell believed that Lucas had clearly understood his books and had translated the key concepts and metaphors into contemporary terms. One of the central issues for Campbell was whether machines should be allowed to control humans. His notion of the machine includes the corporate state and to be fully human we should avoid becoming part of the larger machine; rather, we should 'listen to the still small voice within' (Young 2004). In the *Star Wars* films, technology is associated with the Empire whose machinic world is bereft of vegetation and whose spaceships are enormously destructive. In contrast, the rebels are associated with the forest, the colour green and with the organic 'force' that defeats the machines. Of course, a paradox of all *Star Wars* episodes is that their narratives set out to demonize the very technology and machines in which the films 'simultaneously relish and delight' (Roberts 2000, 87).

Heidegger writes of an 'era of technicity' and 'because the essence of technology is nothing technological, essential reflection on technology and decisive confrontation with it must happen in a realm that is ... akin to the essence of technology and ... fundamentally different from it. Such a realm is art' (1977, 35). The modern *techné*, in contrast to the original Greek meaning of the term which was a poetic and revealing art (1977, 27), causes us to refute the revelation that art can bring us. Thus rather than striving for an individuated existence where we are alienated aesthetically and culturally from technology as proposed by Campbell, Heidegger suggests to assure 'our redemption', art and presumably life and technology should be reintegrated.

Lucas has admitted to using the 'force' as a representation of God and the 'dark side' as a metaphor for evil that exists within all humans. According to Tom Kisken, 'with recurring themes of good and evil, redemption and the power of faith, the movies are at the very least the embryo of theological and philosophical forum' (1999). However, although Darth Vader is a metaphor for evil and for the dark side, he eventually gains redemption and returns once again to the light aided by his son Luke Skywalker (Mark Hamill) in *Episode VI – The Return of the Jedi*, who reminds him that even though he has been seduced by the dark side, he is still Anakin Skywalker and still carries the light within (Darth Vader in *Star Wars* episodes IV–VI is played by David Prowse and voiced by James Earl Jones). Concepts of planes, becoming, intensities, flows and connections (Deleuze and Guattari 1999a, 88), would prove useful tools in analysing *Star Wars* with the above blurring of the borders between good and evil and between light and dark.

It would seem that sensitivity to the force depends on the amount of 'midi-chlorians' that are present in the blood stream. In *Phantom Menace*, Qui-Gon Jinn (Liam Neeson) explains that midi-chlorians are present in every cell in the body and life could not exist without them, and that Anakin's blood stream contains an extremely high proportion of them. Midi-chlorians are described by George Lucas as being, 'a loose depiction of mitochondria', cellular components that are necessary for cell division (Knight 2000). Lucas wanted to provide an explanation of the symbiotic relationship between bodily cells and the force based on actual biochemical functions of the body. However, although mitochondrial DNA has proved an important tool in disciplines ranging from 'cellular biology to some branches of archeology' (Knight 2000), one obvious difficulty with the analogy of midi-chorians with mitochondria is the fact that mitochondria are strictly maternally inherited that would preclude Anakin's mythical father from passing on his exceptionally high concentration of midi-chlorians to Anakin, in the same way that Anakin would be unable to pass the organelles on to his own children, which would refute the fundamental premise of the *Star Wars* story. Nevertheless, within the films, midi-chlorians whether related to mitochondria or not are present within all living things, and behave as a medium for the force.

In *Episode I*, the catalyst for Anakin's transformation into Darth Vader takes place during an intergalactic trade conflict centring on the planet of Naboo. This seemingly insignificant event is eventually revealed to be a key element in an ingeniously contrived plot that ultimately leads to an intergalactic wide confrontation between good and evil, and between the force and the dark side. It is in this episode that Anakin first meets his mentor Obi-Wan Kenobi and also his future wife, a seeming maidservant, who is later revealed to be Queen Padme Amidala (Natalie Portman).

Together with its human characters, *Phantom Menace* presents a variety of non-human characters. According to Rob Coleman, the film's animation director, 'most of the nonhuman characters are CG.' Sixty-six non-human characters, including some that talk with full lip-sync, appear in 812 of the film's approximately 1900 shots (Robertson 1999b, 25–6). One such character created specially for the *Star Wars* prequels is Jar Jar Binks who is completely computer generated (voiced by Ahmed Best). A Gungan, Binks resembles a lizard with ears down to his waist and eyes on the top of his head. Although heavily criticized for his features and behaviour, and more importantly for providing a seemingly racial stereotyping of Caribbean people that proved, if not offensive, insensitive to many reviewers (Carson 2002, 168; O'Hehir 1999, 34), Binks was intended to provide some light comic relief (Robertson 1999b, 25). It is telling that Binks although ubiquitous in *Episode I* was very much relegated to the sidelines in the following prequels. Another character who caused similar concerns by displaying an apparent anti-Semitic caricature was Watto (voiced by Andy Secombe), a Tatooine junk dealer who is the slave owner of Anakin and his mother, Shmi (Pernilla August). Rather than accusing Lucas of having a conscious racist agenda, Andrew O'Hehir claims that Lucas cannot 'tell the difference between a sensitive depiction of cultural difference and offensive stereotypes' (1999, 34). However, whatever the problems with the characterizations of these non-human creatures, both proved to be feats of new technologies.

Several techniques were used to create the animation of these characters. For instance, procedural animation, dynamics and simulation programs were used for Binks's ears and similarly for Watto's phone which hangs from his waist. Likewise, both characters wear clothes, sometimes several layers that need to be animated. For Coleman 'simulation gives the characters extra realism. This isn't an all CG environment. Our CG characters are in the real world dealing with physics' (Robertson 1999b, 26). Watto's wings were also created with animation techniques, using several cycles of flapping wings which were rendered separately with motion blur and then blended with his body.

Binks's movements were created by animators from motion captured data taken from the actor, Ahmed Best, who wore Vicon optical markers. Mocap or motion capture was an important technology used in *Phantom Menace* and was piloted at ILM's motion capture studio. Of course now, the use of motion capture is fairly commonplace in helping create filmic special effects as in other areas of performance; but before the first *Star Wars* prequel, it had proved largely unworkable and unmanageable in the film-making process. For *Episode I*, multiple performances were captured using a 20-camera Vicon optical motion capture system. The resultant mocap data was utilized in a variety of ways, for instance, to help create animated storyboards for previsualization purposes; to provide reference material for keyframe animators; and also to provide motion cycles for non-human creatures such as the droids and Gungan armies. In order to create the film's animated storyboard, Jeff Light, the film's motion-capture supervisor, even acted out the entire film while wearing a wireless magnetic motion capture system (Robertson 1999c, 44).

In the *Star Wars* prequels, as with a number of digital practices, virtual bodies that are generated by physical movement through the mediation of digital technology are seen together with live performers. The prequels with their interface and interaction between physical and virtual bodies can be seen to displace fixed categories of identity. Within the films each carries a 'trace' of the other, given that the virtual performers are the digital reincarnation of the human bodies. However, the embodied self is delimited and external objects can be appropriated by the body. In such digital practices as the prequels with their use of Mocap technologies, the motions of a performer's body, captured technologically, result in a modified extension of that physical body.

Phantom Menace was followed in 2002 by *Episode II: Attack of the Clones*, which was set 10 years after *Episode I*. The main innovation for this film was high-definition (HD) digital cameras with their ability to download a 'response curve' or 'gamma', which allows increased control over filmic detail. On the film's set a 'video village' was created, containing over 50 hi-res plasma monitors which were linked to digital cameras, allowing instant preview and editing (Knoll 2005, 189). According to visual effects supervisor John Knoll, in comparing *Episode II* to *Episode I*, 'we have more digital characters in the shots, more digital environments, and the shots themselves are more technically challenging' (Robertson 2002a, 16). ILM created 2817 shots for this film, of which 2000 were used; in the entire film there are only 161 shots that were not visual effects shots (16).

In *Episode II*, the characters that were completely digital were the clones themselves who at all times were CG. Their performances were created from motion captured data with animation later applied. The battle scene, which was the penultimate moment in the film, was made up of a 'matte-painted sky, rendered terrain, film taken of miniatures, and scanned photographs,' together with still images taken from an actual desert. CG elements droids, clones, ships and so on were then added to the scene (Robinson 2002b, 22). A side effect of shooting the film in HD meant that it was necessary to artificially create a 'Z-depth'. According to Knoll, 'the HD chip is about the size of a 16mm frame, so you get four times the depth of field at the same f-stop.' Therefore, in order to create the illusion of distance, 'increasing amounts of haze' and various other digital paint effects were later added (Robinson 2002b, 24).

The *Attack of the Clones* begins with an assassination attempt on the life of Padme Amidala who is now a senator. The Jedi knight, Obi-Wan Kenobi, and his apprentice, Anakin Skywalker (now acted by Hayden Christensen), are sent to investigate and protect the former Queen of Naboo. Obi-Wan discovers that a clone army is being manufactured covertly for the Jedi on the remote watery planet of Kamino and also that a separatist group seemingly hostile to the republic have formed, led by Count Dooku (Christopher Lee). At the same time, a clandestine romance develops between Anakin and Padme which culminates in a secret marriage at a secluded lake retreat on the planet of Naboo.

Ironically, in the making of the prequels, new technologies caused unexpected problems in depicting some of the well-known characters from the original *Star Wars* trilogy. For instance, characters such as Yoda, the ancient and revered Jedi Master (voiced by Frank Oz) and Chewbacca, a Wookiee (Peter Mayhew), needed to look younger than in the original trilogy since the prequels were set approximately 20 years in the past. This transition could now be accomplished with the help of new animation and animatronic techniques. However, the concern was that the characters would now appear to be too different from the original characters. In *Attack of the Clones*, Yoda became entirely digital for the first time. Recreated by Rob Coleman and modelling supervisor, Geoff Campbell, work on the CG model began with scanned data from a maquette of Yoda's head. For Yoda's body and clothes, Campbell and his team of modellers worked in 'ILM's I-Sculpt, Alias Wavefront's Power Animator and Maya, and Avid's Softimage 3D'. Though, it became necessary to restrict the computer graphic possibilities in order to avoid Yoda looking like 'a little green talking man' (Robertson 2002a, 18). According to Coleman, Frank Oz believed that Yoda's face was now over-articulated since the original Yoda did little more than open and close his mouth. However, 'people have a memory of what they thought they saw Yoda doing. They projected a personality onto the puppet' (Coleman quoted by Robertson 2002a, 18). Therefore, 'the digital Yoda's facial expressions had to match expressions people thought they saw on the puppet' (Robertson 2002a, 18).

For Kosslyn and Koenig, perception is differentiated from imagery in as much as in the former, a perceived object is physically present. In the latter, perceived objects are not being actually viewed and these images can be changed at will. Memory plays a role since visual images are built on visual memories, just as visual images of Yoda's expressions from the original *Star Wars* trilogy were based on visual memories of what spectators thought they remembered. Although these images are immediate and transient, they can be used at different times to form new imagery. In fact, visual imagery is important to cognition due to its ability to create and be creative (1992, 129), even if the result can be, as in the case of Yoda, a false recollection.

The prequels' final episode, *Revenge of the Sith*, made in 2005, was also the most popular for movie-going audiences and critics alike. The technology used, although essentially the same as for the previous episodes, was again more sophisticated and highly evolved. For instance, the next generation of cameras was now available and substantially improved in all respects, providing even better signal-to-noise ratio and clearer pictures. According to Knoll,

> The images from the high definition (HD) cameras were so sharp we had to put Pro-Mist filters on them ... We'd discovered pretty early on while shooting Episode II digitally that things you can get away with on film ... would appear fake because the images were too crisp; you could see too much.
>
> (2005, 278)

Higher bandwidth recorders were also available which meant less compression and again superior image. Recording could now be undertaken in 12-bit rather than 8-bit that had been used in the previous episodes, leading to improved blue screen extraction (Knoll 2005, 278). Blue screen and green screen were widely used in all the *Star Wars* prequels. However, actors, in particular, have problems with this technology since on many occasions they are required to act solely to and in front of a blank screen. This is especially true for *Episode III*, where many of the characters and environments were CG. According to Ewan McGregor (Obi-Wan Kenobi) in speaking on *Revenge of the Sith*, 'we had as you say an enormous amount of blue screen and green screen ... at work in this film and I will never get used to that. It is really, really hard' (Lucas 2005c).

For Deleuze, cinema creates new affects and produces new possibilities for perception. Flows and connections of images are not fixed in time and do not combine to make complete wholes; 'there is always out-of-field, even in the most closed image. And there are always simultaneously the two aspects of the out-of-field, the actualizable relation with other sets, and the virtual relation with the whole' (Deleuze 1986, 18). Instead, cinema represents a challenge to perception and rather than offering a theory on cinema, philosophy responds to the new perceptive forces resulting from this new art form; 'it took the modern cinema to re-read the whole of cinema as already made up of aberrant movements and false continuity shots. ... This image is virtual' (Deleuze 1989, 41).

The story for *Revenge of the Sith* is set three years after the onset of the clone wars and the Jedi Knights have assembled an immense army to do battle with the Separatists. The Republic is falling, to be replaced by the evil Galactic Empire ruled over by the Emperor Palpatine, who reveals himself to Anakin as the Sith Lord Sidious. Anakin is seduced by Palpatine/Sidious into becoming his apprentice and takes the name of Darth Vader. The climax of the film is a light sabre duel between Darth Vader and Obi-Wan Kenobi on the lava planet of Mustafar. Vader sustains such critical injuries as a result of the duel that cybernetic enhancements and replacements are needed to keep him alive. Anakin in going over to the dark side, and becoming Sith ultimately loses what he most fears to lose, his wife Padme whose death he in effect causes. Padme lives long enough to give birth to twins, Luke and Leia. *Revenge of the Sith* although in reality the last *Star Wars* film to be made, sets the scene for the original *Star Wars* trilogy.

For this episode, Lucas concentrated on primarily creating complex environments rather than characters as had been his emphasis in the previous two episodes (Robertson 2005, 11). An example of this is Mustafar where the above duel took place. Much of this world was created with a complex giant miniature, approximately 20-by-30 feet. According to Knoll, 'the lava was created with Methylcel, which is a food additive … mixed with kitty litter, which forms into good-looking clumps in the lava streams' (2005, 338) In creating Mustafar's volcanic landscape, shots from this model were used together with digi-matte paintings for the background. An actual volcanic eruption fortuitously also provided footage. At Lucas's behest, the films' producer Rick McCallum and cinematographer Ron Fricke spent five days shooting volcanic lava flows in Sicily to help create the lava planet (Lucas 2005c).[6] The Mustafar sequence was supervised by Roger Guyett and provided 10–15 minutes of 'fiery eruptions, flaming waterfall, and blazing geysers'. Because the lava is central to the sequence it had to be art-directed in ways that fluid simulation would not allow. Instead, a crew led by Willi Geiger used Maya particle effects to create multiple shots of 'splashing, falling, flowing, erupting fiery lava that matched the real Mt. Etna lava and interacted with the methylcel lava' (Robertson 2005, 15).

An innovative device introduced in *Episode III* was a new camera-mapping tool called Zenviro. This digital implement allows an artist to position a camera in a simple 3-D scene, move the camera view into Photoshop as a flat line drawing, paint it, project the painted texture back onto the 3-D geometry, move the camera to an unpainted spot and continue. The images projected can be live action photography, 3-D renderings, digital photographs, motion captured shots of miniatures and so on. The system allows multiple projections so that all surfaces seen by the camera have projected images with the correct amount of detail included. According to Knoll, 'people began using it for all kinds of things since it is really easy to use. If they had a shot that didn't hold up in the foreground they'd fix it with Zenviro rather than sending a little thing like that to the matte-painting department' (Robertson 2005, 14). In short, Zenviro makes it possible to have synthetic environments in which the camera can follow 'fast action without needing to model and render an entire 3-D scene for every frame' (14).

For *Revenge of the Sith*, Lucas assembled one of the most highly developed previsualization teams ever. As already mentioned, previz for directors is a very practical way of allowing them to find out if what they imagine will function in the real world. A director can direct the previz in real time and take risks without having to involve the film crew or physical set. In this environment, the director is also more likely to investigate and explore more innovative ideas and possibilities that would be achievable in the directing of the actual film. At Lucas's Skywalker Ranch, a new art department containing a dedicated group of computer artists had evolved considerably since its inception prior to *Episode I*. The group's main objectives were to design digital special effects and streamline the design process. To this end, story board artists, whose designs were used in the construction of sets, costumes, special effects, props, landscapes and so on, worked closely with the previz team.

Previsualization has been around in some form or other since the beginning of film-making, but it is only in recent years due to the proliferation of new technologies that allow increased inventiveness and immediacy that it has become progressively more essential and central to the film-making process. The main tenets of contemporary previz are that it is created for the director rather than the visual effects department; it is composed of fully edited sequences offered in narrative form, complete with sound effects and dialogue; it is based on actual locations with digital sets built to scale; and finally, it contains sophisticated modelled characters. In short, as its name implies, it is a way of viewing an entire film together with its special effects before the film is made; 'essentially providing a digital viewfinder' (Katz 2005, 16).

According to Romanyshyn, technology allows us to 'increasingly practice a distancing and detached vision' (1989, 117), a way of viewing the world without seeing ourselves as being implicated in it; previsualization techniques epitomize this practice. Similarly, when Telotte suggests that computer-generated imagery takes this notion even further by allowing film-makers to '"reproduce" that which has never been "produced," that which has no existence separate from the movies, as is the case of *Star Wars: Episode I – Phantom Menace* and its digitized characters, particularly the infamous Jar-Jar Binks' (2001, 146), he is echoing Baudrillard who expounded his notion of simulation within *Simulacra and Simulation* (1994). In this phase, the image draws increasingly away from reality until it bears no relation to reality whatsoever. It is where the image loses its referent altogether and where production is superseded by simulation (Baudrillard 1983, 11).

According to Paul Virilio, 'representation now stretches beyond the real', together with the 'de-realization of sensory appearances'. This, quintessentially, is realized in film technologies where for Virilio 'cinematographic and videographic techniques' are 'symptoms' that we can respond to (1991, 111). He believes if we ignore these 'premonitory signs', then we are in danger of ourselves replicating the invisibility of our film technology and similarly becoming invisible, constructed only by our technological world (111–12). David Lavery argues that technological based film is not a fulfilment of 'total cinema' but rather it is opposed to that essentialist humanist vision; 'it has become increasingly clear that virtual reality may well be driven by a very different mythos than the one Bazin suggested was operative in films. It is a more sinister and less human project ... The movies and virtual reality ... may belong to different cultures' (Lavery 2001, 152), one where technological based film narrative becomes 'an ever recursive game' (156).

The discussions on film theory and practice until the early 1970s were the preserve of film-makers and theorists such as André Bazin and Jean Mitry. Such intellectual voices incorporated film-makers' perspectives into their views of how new technologies control change in film history (Mitry was himself a film-maker). This position is illustrated in both Mitry's *Esthétique et psychologie du cinéma* and Bazin's essay 'The Myth of Total Cinema'.[7] However, when Althusserian Marxism investigated the relation between ideology and technology (Althusser 1971, 170–7), an attack on this position was predictable. These writers now spoke from the 'position of the spectator', from what can be seen and heard on screen, rather, than from 'tainted' histories generated by film producers (Heath 1981, 226–69). However, the Marxist focus on historical change proved to be largely ineffectual, since it was theorized only from the 'spectator's position', and new production practices are often made deliberately 'invisible and inaudible' to general film audiences (Eidsvik 1988–9, 19).

Digital film concentrates on subject positions, but no position is fixed and unalterable; rather, it is a *vacant* place that may be filled by different individuals at varying times, for instance, the 'speaking subject', the 'viewing subject', the 'listening subject' or the 'questioning subject' (Foucault 1972, 54–5). The digital is not concerned with historical change through technical means; instead, it celebrates the multiplicity of codes produced as a result. For instance, the prequels' DVDs present multiple subject positions with their interactive games, commentaries, translations in multiple languages and their very comprehensive behind-the-scenes documentaries that demystify the film-making process, and at the same time allow viewers to explore and investigate key technologies used in the making of the films.

For Merleau-Ponty, perception is not an intentional act but rather simply a being in the world or a 'being at' in the world, 'the seeing and the visible, the touching and the touchable ... does not go beyond a sort of *imminence*, it terminates in the invisible' (2000, 249). Visibility always involves non-visibility; it is what consciousness does not see (248). Merleau-Ponty's theorization on the visible and invisible provides useful tools in exploring the interface between the physical and virtual, so integral to the prequels. Instead of either the physical or the virtual being prioritized over the other in these performances, the relationship between both could perhaps be seen as a system of inventiveness and 'possible actions'.

Finally, the *Star Wars* prequels are exemplary in their emphasis on cutting-edge technologies that have been, to a large part, developed during the production process of these films. However, although much interest in the prequels is directed towards these new technologies, it is my contention that the most important contribution of all digital practices, including film-making, is the enhancement and reconfiguration of an aesthetic creativity that fundamentally alters our being in the world.

Notes

1. See Baudrillard's *Simulcra and Simulations* (1994).
2. See Lewis Carroll's *The Adventures of Alice in Wonderland* (1950).
3. According to Derrida, 'there is such a general text everywhere that ... this discourse and its order ... are *overflowed* ... This general text is not limited of course ... to writings on the page' (1981b, 59–60).
4. A blue screen composite image begins with a subject or object being photographed or filmed in front of an evenly lit, bright-blue background. The compositing process, whether photographic or electronic, replaces all the blue in the picture with another image. Blue screen composites can be made optically for still photos or films, electronically for live video, or digitally for computer images. In addition to blue, other colours can be used, green is the most common, although sometimes red has been used for special purposes, but blue has been favoured for several reasons. Blue is the complementary colour to flesh tone since it is the most common colour in most scenes, and thus avoids conflicts of colour. Moreover, cameras and film have been on the whole more sensitive to blue light, although this is less true today.

5. See Derrida for a detailed discussion of metaphor and metaphoricity (1982, 209–71).

6. Mount Etna had opened six new fissures in 2001 giving the film-makers ample opportunity to film the necessary shots. Luckily, most of the lava flowed towards the uninhabited Valle de Bove.

7. This view presupposes an 'Idealist' and 'technologically determinist' appraisal of history, with film technology allowing film-makers ever greater means to manipulate images of reality (Mitry 1965; Bazin 1967).

7
Bioart

Bioart centres on the artistic investigation of biotechnology and raises complex ethical issues, such as those relating to the patenting and sale of genes. At the same time, genetic engineering is transforming forever our notions of and relationships to life forms including our own. Moreover, the discipline of biological studies is increasingly changing from a life science into an information science. For instance, 'biosemiotics' is an interdisciplinary science that studies communication and signification in living systems. Contemporary artists have responded to these changes by working with transgenics, cloning, inter and intraspecies communication, reproductive technologies, genotype and phenotype reprogramming, tissue culture engineering and hybridization techniques that reconfigure the borders of artwork and life.

Transformation and communication: Eduardo Kac's transgenic art

> Organisms created in the context of transgenic art can be taken home by the public to be grown in the backyard or raised as human companions. With at least one endangered species becoming extinct every day, I suggest that artists can contribute to increase global biodiversity by inventing new life forms ... Ethical concerns are paramount in any artwork, and they become more crucial than ever in the context of bio art.
>
> (Kac 1998)

> I will never forget the moment when I first held her in my arms, in Jouy-en-Josas, France, on April 29, 2000. My apprehensive anticipation was replaced by joy and excitement. Alba [the GFP Bunny] ...

was lovable and affectionate and an absolute delight to play with.…
She immediately awoke in me a strong and urgent sense of responsi-
bility for her well-being.

(Kac 2003, 97)

For Eduardo Kac, 'transgenic art … is a new art form based on the use of
genetic engineering techniques to transfer synthetic genes to an organism or to transfer natural genetic material from one species into another,
to create unique living beings' (1998). Kac (pronounced 'Katz'), whose
works date from the 1980s when he pioneered telecommunication art
(pre-Internet), has over the years concentrated on exploring the 'fluidity
of subject positions in the post-digital age', by means of a combination
of 'robotics and networking', 'telepresence', 'biotelematics' (combining
networking with a biological process), and more recently 'transgenics'
(Kac 2005a).

Originally from Rio de Janeiro in Brazil, Kac is currently based at the
School of the Art Institute of Chicago. In Rio he worked as an interven-
tionist performer, protesting against the military dictatorship that ruled
the country at the time before concentrating on telecommunications as
a form of art practice. He studied philosophy, semiotics and linguistics
at universities in Rio de Janeiro and later gained an MA in Fine Arts from
Chicago. He presented his first telepresence performance, *Ornitorrinco,
the Webot, travels around the world in eighty nanoseconds going from Turkey
to Peru and back*, shown at the Otso Gallery, in Espoo, Finland, in 1996
and his first transgenic performance *Genesis*, at Ars Electronica, Linz,
Austria, in 1999.

The primary emphasis throughout Kac's work has been an investigation of the philosophical and political aspects of communication, both
verbal and non-verbal. He explores and examines linguistic systems,
human communicative interaction and communication with and between
species. Multimedia and biological processes are combined to create
hybrids from existing communication systems. Frequently linking virtual
and physical spaces, Kac questions how processes of communication help
create shared 'realities'. Rejecting closure, his work encourages active audience participation and confronts issues concerning identity and agency
(Kac 2005a).

Lyotard with his emphasis on the political and experimentation, and
his interpretation of the Kantian sublime has provided vital knowledge
in this area. However, his recent linguistic bias lacks a satisfactory
account of non-verbal signification (1988; 1991). In such works as Kac's,
as with other digital practices, the physical and virtual are emphasized
and therefore, Lyotard's 'linguistic turn' needs to be adjusted to allow for

this technical interface and accompanying corporeal prominence. I am suggesting that this can be remedied by a retheorization using an inter-semiotic approach, that is, a significatory practice which involves such non-linguistic modes as those provided by the semiotics of body gesture (virtual, human and/or animal) and thus provide an appropriate inter-pretation of such digital practices as Kac's biotechnology artworks.

Kac's work has been exhibited internationally at venues such as Exit Art and New York Media Arts Centre, New York; InterCommunication Centre (ICC), Tokyo; Chicago Art Fair and Julia Friedman Gallery, Chicago; and the Museum of Modern Art, Rio de Janeiro. He has also published widely in various journals such as *Leonardo*, MIT Press, where he is a member of the editorial board and has been featured in such contem-porary art publications as *Flash Art* and *Artforum and* also in the mass media: ABC, BBC, *New York Times* and many others. However, it was with Alba, the transgenic GFP (green fluorescent protein) Bunny that Kac made his mark on the contemporary bioart scene by provoking heated debate relating to the sociocultural and ethical concerns resulting from his controversial creation of a living art work.

One of Kac's early biotelematic works was an interactive installation, titled *Teleporting an Unknown State* (1996) that linked a presentation at the New Orleans Museum of Contemporary Arts to the Internet. The installation consisted of a seed planted in soil in a completely darkened room, with the only means of light emitting from a video projector that received its lit image from the Internet. That light allowed the seed to photosynthesize and grow – the Internet becoming a 'life-supporting sys-tem' sustained by the real-time interaction of remote individuals as they logged in to the installation website. These individuals had captured images of the sky and transmitted the sunlight via cameras to produce a steady flow of photons aimed at the developing plant. The videoed images were converted into 'actual wavefronts of light' (Kac 1999, 90–1). The growth of the plant was in turn captured and transmitted via the Internet so that the participating audience could view the plant's growth, which they had enabled. For Kac, the piece operated as a rever-sal to the normal unidirectional image broadcast by regulated media where the audience passively receives a specific message; instead the audience of *Teleporting an Unknown State* actively transmitted light by their videoed image, at the same participating in the growth and devel-opment of a life form. According to Kac, 'the exhibition ended on August 9 1996. On that day the plant was 18 inches tall' (91).

This installation consisted of Kac's key investigative concerns such as interaction (in this instance, interspecies), issues of identity and the very possibility of communication. It also demonstrated other traits in common with digital practices, such as indeterminacy, contingency and active audience participation.

Kac's first transgenic performance work was *Genesis* and premiered at the O.K. Centre for Contemporary Art, Linz, Austria, 4–9 September 1999 as part of Life Science, Ars Electronica 99.[1] It is Kac's belief that art has progressively moved 'away from pictorial representation, object crafting and visual contemplation'; instead, there is now a more direct response to social transformations that emphasize 'process, concept, action, interaction, new media, environments, and critical discourse' (Kac 2003, 100). Transgenic art whilst acknowledging this shift in emphasis offers a radical departure by 'placing the question of actual creation of life at the centre of the debate' (100). As such, it accentuates the social existence of organisms by reminding us 'that communication and interaction between sentient and non-sentient actants lies at the core of what we call life' (101).

Genesis explores issues that relate to the cultural impact of biotechnology. Taking the biblical sentence from the book of *Genesis*: 'LET MAN HAVE DOMINION OVER THE FISH OF THE SEA, AND OVER THE FOWL OF THE AIR, AND OVER EVERY LIVING THING THAT MOVES UPON THE EARTH', as a starting point, Kac investigates 'the intricate relationship between biology, belief systems, information technology, dialogical interaction, ethics and the Internet' (1999). The above sentence from *Genesis*, which signifies a 'dubious', divinely ordained 'humanity's supremacy over nature', was chosen since it reflects a key concern of Kac's relating to interspecies relations. Thus echoing Deleuze and Guattari's belief that, 'in a way we much start at the end: all becomings are already molecular. That is because becoming is not to imitate or identify with something or someone' (1999a, 272).

Genesis was intended to 'playfully' consider the 'ambiguity of the Genesis gene itself', at the same time it reflects the absurdity of reducing human life and choice to 'a simple DNA sequence' (Kac, 2001). It also explores the belief that biological processes can be 'writerly and programmable' and can 'store and process data' in a similar way to computers (Kac 2005b). The project centres on the production of a 'synthetic artistic gene' that was created by Kac after translating the above biblical sentence into Morse Code and then converting the Morse Code into DNA base pairs, according to a conversion principle specially developed for this work. The gene was cloned into plasmids and transformed into bacteria that coded for cyan fluorescence (Enhanced Cyan Fluorescent Protein or ECFP). Another form of bacteria without the synthetic gene was also used in the performance, a plasmid that coded for yellow fluorescence (Enhanced Yellow Fluorescent Protein or EYFP). The two types of bacteria, one containing the 'Genesis' gene and one without, grew and mutated in petri dishes, exposed intermittently to ultraviolet light and observed by the audience by means of a digitally enlarged video projection. The audience was able to view the various new colour combinations of the mutating bacteria since as they make contact with each other, plasmid conjugal transfer took place and new colour combinations occurred as a result of this intraspecies communication (Kac 2005b).

The display was also made available to the Internet by means of two computers located in the installation space. One computer was interactive, allowing observers to increase the UV light leading to accelerated mutation rates of the Plasmids due to the disruption of their DNA sequencing. The other computer synthesized music that was transcribed from the physiological processes of the DNA by means of a software programme that responded to the growth rate of the bacteria. In effect, the audience to a certain extent, controlled the development and mutation of the bacteria but at the same time the music which was played to the audience was created by those same bacteria creating a real-time dialogic interaction between two diverse species. On the last day of the exhibition, Kac took the altered code back to the lab, translating the DNA back into Morse Code and then into English and posted the translation on the Genesis website. The new sentence read: 'LET AAN HAVE DOMINION OVER THE FISH OF THE SEA AND OVER THE FOWL OF THE AIR AND OVER EVERY LIVING THING THAT IOVES UA EON THE EARTH' (Kac 2005b), thus leaving Kac's audience to contemplate the consequences of interfering with evolution.

Transgenic artworks underscore the underlying concerns relating to genetic engineering and raise questions that are moral, ethical and political. For instance, although genetic changes to humans can correct various genetic disorders that may be life threatening, at the same time this process can also be used for selective breeding. As a result of genetic coding, individual traits can now be identified, such as intelligence, behaviour and race, that can potentially lead to the undermining of 'concepts of equality of opportunity'. For example, policies could be adopted that would prevent the birth of children with genetic disorders with the risk that parents who do not terminate such a pregnancy would be liable to be prosecuted for child abuse. Such a legal case has already been heard in California in 1980 where the court decided that 'a child with a genetic defect could bring suit against her parents for not undergoing prenatal screening and aborting her' (Andrews 1999, 91–2).

Kac's more recent transgenic event, Alba the *GFP Bunny* (2000), is an ongoing project that has intentionally provoked intense international scrutiny centring on the creation of a living artwork in the form of a transgenic albino rabbit.[2] According to Kac, although Alba is a 'very special animal', her genetic makeup is only one element in this artwork. Rather, the project is 'a complex social event that starts with the creation of a chimerical animal that does not exist in nature (i.e., "chimerical" in the sense of a cultural tradition of imaginary animals, not in the scientific connotation of an organism in which there is a mixture of cells in the body)' (2003, 97).

For this project, Kac collaborated with geneticist Louis-Marie Houdebine to create a 'GFP rabbit', whose genetic makeup was altered with a gene obtained from a Pacific Northwest jellyfish (*Aequorea Victoria*) that contains green fluorescent protein. The phenotype[3] expression of this is that the albino rabbit would glow green when illuminated with blue light (maximum excitation at 488nm). In fact, Alba was created with a 'synthetic mutated' form of the gene known as EGFP, which enhances the original gene and gives greater magnitude to the fluorescence in order to increase the observable green glow in the rabbit. This protein has already been used in experiments in the past to track genetic changes in mice and frogs. Originally, Kac wanted to create a 'GFP K-9', a dog that would have similar observable traits. However, he faced several obstacles in trying to accomplish this, the chief one being that at that time the dog genome had not been mapped (Kac 1998). Therefore, Kac decided to pursue the same idea with a rabbit since the Institut National de la Recherche Agronomique-INRA (National Institute of Agronomic Research) had already integrated GFP into rabbit DNA.[4] Alba is not the first transgenic rabbit; several have already been created in laboratory conditions, but she is the first one to be created as part of an artwork. Kac emphasizes that the alteration to Alba's genetic makeup has no detrimental effect on the rabbit whatsoever and 'she is healthy and gentle' and it is 'impossible for anyone who is not aware that Alba is a glowing rabbit to notice anything unusual about her' (2003, 100). Kac also notes that the human role in rabbit evolution is a natural element and domesticity is 'bidirectional' since, 'as humans domesticate rabbits, so do rabbits domesticate their humans' (100).

The first phase of *GFP Bunny* was completed in February 2000 'with the birth of "Alba" in Jouy-en-Josas, France' (Kac 2003, 97). Alba's name was chosen by Kac's family. However, the second and third phases of the project have not turned out so well. It was intended that Alba would be taken home and become part of Kac's family, since what is most important for Kac is not 'the creation of genetic objects, but the invention of transgenic social subjects' (98–9). In short, the 'completely integrated process of creating the bunny' and 'bringing her to society at large' by means of a 'loving, caring and nurturing' family (99). However, Kac was thwarted in this ambition when the then director of INRA, Paul Vial, refused to allow him to take Alba home. According to Vial, the rabbit belonged to INRA and Kac had nothing to do with the 'research object' (Allmendinger 2001). Since then a wide debate has ensued as to the implications of creating a living artwork, with Kac carrying out an extensive media campaign to draw attention to Alba's 'situation and to obtain her freedom' (Kac 2003, 102). At the same time the international press were outraged by an artwork that 'fuelled existing fears of global genetic mutation'. Importantly: 'Was Alba Art? What did she mean?' (Allmendinger 2001).

Kac believes that art can assist in revealing the cultural implications of genetic engineering and offer 'different ways of thinking about and with biotechnology' (2003, 101). He cautions that there is a difference between using biotech tools and adopting the 'corporate biotechnology worldview' (2001). However, Kac's approach reflects the notion that complicity goes hand in hand with critique, since we can never escape being complicit with what is being argued against without also giving up that same critique (Derrida 1978a, 281).

For Kac, biotechnology operates through sign systems that are not verbal or visual but are all the same changing the way we see the world and when these tools are appropriated and other views are added then instead of merely 'illustrating the world of biotech', more complex issues are brought to the fore (2001). In any artwork, ethical concerns are crucial and they become even more so in the context of bioart. Transgenic art by integrating the 'lessons of dialogical philosophy' and 'cognitive ethology', is obliged 'to promote awareness and respect for the spiritual (mental) life of the transgenic animal' (Kac 2003, 99).

In assessing our relationship with animals, it is important to think about agency without anthropomorphizing it. In this project, the relationship with Alba moves from one of interactivity into one of inter-subjectivity, which for Kac is to acknowledge 'the social dimension of consciousness' and 'the complexity of animal minds' since each individual is 'unique' (2003, 100). In detailing particular physical and intellectual traits of Alba and rabbits in general,[5] Kac believes that this should provide some understanding on how a rabbit sees the world though not 'enough to appreciate its consciousness' (100).

Since the exploration of consciousness may well be the final challenge for the human need to make sense of ourselves and by implication our world, what does this mean for a rabbit? Does it too have consciousness? If so, how would a rabbit's consciousness manifest itself? Would it be able to think in first person and experience 'qualia', that is, the subjective quality of a mental experience, such as 'the redness of red' (given that rabbits, like most mammals, see solely in monochrome, we already know it would only be able to see various shades of grey).[6] In exploring intersubjectivity between various species questions like these need to be taken into account, in order to fully appreciate each individual life form. As Kac argues, 'molecular biology has demonstrated that the human genome is not particularly important, special or different' and can only 'be seen as part of a larger genomic continuum rich in variation and diversity' (2003, 100) Artworks, such as *GFP Bunny* remind us of this, bridging the gap between humans and other species. As Ulli Allmendinger very aptly remarks:

> One small hop for Alba, one large hop for mankind.
>
> (2001)

Wetware and GMOs: Critical Art Ensemble's recombinant theatre

RH: Do you believe in originality?
SK: No, only recombination and invention.
(Steve Kurtz from CAE interviewed by Hirsch 2005, 30)

When we do projects concerning transgenics, one of the most common questions participants ask is whether CAE is for or against genetically modified organisms (GMOs). The reply from group members is always the same: We have no general position ... The real question of GMOs is how to create models of risk assessment that are accessible to those not trained in biology so people can tell the difference between a product that amounts to little more than pollutants for profit and those which have a practical and desirable function, while at the same time have no environmental impact ... individuals are left with the implied obligation that they should just have faith in scientific, government and corporate authorities that allegedly always act with only the public interest in mind.
(Critical Art Ensemble 2002b, 3)

Critical Art Ensemble (CAE), through their 'recombinant theatre', have made technology, wetware and transgenics, the focus of their work. For CAE, recombination 'typically denotes esoterica pertinent to molecular biology',[7] whereas the digital is associated with 'information and communications technology'. However, for CAE, both are not specialized and are in fact 'the foundations of a new cosmology'(Critical Art Ensemble 2000a, 151). They maintain that digital cultural resistances have evolved over the last century that use 'recombinant methods in various forms of combines'. For instance, 'sampling', 'detournement', 'bricolage', 'readymades', 'plagiarism', the 'theatre of everyday life', and so on (152). For CAE, recombinant theatre denies the privileged position of the auteur, director, genius or any other 'reductive, privatizing category' (158).

Although originally working with multimedia, CAE, since 1996, have concentrated on responding to the debates surrounding biotechnology. As 'tactical' mediaists, the group have presented various interactive performance projects. These projects are underpinned by their concerns with the representation, development and deployment of social policies regarding this technology. For CAE, tacticality includes a willingness to be amateurs, to try anything, and to resist specialization. They see all media as useful, as each mode can be effective within a given context (Critical Art Ensemble 2000b, 144). They propose that individuals will be empowered by gaining experiential knowledge of routine scientific processes that are central to biotechnology, and performativity plays a key role (142).

CAE is made up of a transient collective of artists with diverse specializations, for instance, performance, book art, text art, film, video, computer graphics and critical theory. Their work draws inspiration from such resistance practices as Dada, Guerrilla Art Action Group, the Living Theatre, Rebel Chicano Art Front and the Situationists; 'performances that invent ephemeral, autonomous situations from which temporary public relationships emerge, whereby the participants can engage in critical dialogue on a given issue' (Critical Art Ensemble 2000a, 157). For instance, CAE claim that their interest in the Living Theatre stemmed from a belief that it offered:

A proto-postmodern model of cultural production. The group quite consciously located itself in the *liminal* position between the real and the simulated. The Living Theatre ... contributed to the conceptual foundation now used to understand and create virtual theatre. It helped make it clear that for virtual theatre to have any contestational value, it must loop back into the materiality of everyday life.

(Critical Art Ensemble 1997; italics mine)

CAE was founded in 1986 by Steve Kurtz and Steve Barnes; they met whilst at film school in Tallahassee, Florida. Other members have included Hope Kurtz (Kurtz's late wife), Dorian Burr, Claudia Bucher, George Barker, Ricardo Dominguez and Bev Schlee. The present members are Kurtz, Barnes and Schlee. Kurtz is an associate professor of Art at the University of Buffalo, Barnes runs a media centre at Florida State University and Schlee works in a bookbindery. For Kurtz, the formation of CAE was a response to a 'localized problem of cultural alienation' (Hirsch 2005, 28–9).

Through the years, CAE have sought to address concerns regarding the commodification and consumerism of technology owned and provided by national and multinational corporations, by attempting to critique the dominant means of digital representation. They claim that digital technology has allowed power itself to go 'nomadic' through electronic networks. Therefore, resistance must go digital too (Critical Art Ensemble 1994). Deleuze, influenced by Nietzsche, posits the nomadic as an anti-dialectical tool to refute the Hegelian recuperation of negation and difference – an approach that is rhizomatic (root-like) rather than arboreal (tree-like) (Deleuze and Guattari 1999a, (11–12). According to CAE:

> As the electronic information-cores overflow with files of electronic people (those transformed into credit histories, consumer types, patterns and tendencies, etc.), electronic research, electronic money and other forms of information power, the nomad is free to wander the electronic net, able to cross national boundaries with minimal resistance from national bureaucracies.
>
> (1994, 16)

CAE's primary resistance strategy consists of making art that intersects with activist practices. In resisting naming locations in relation to their performance, together with identifying genres and even participating artists, their work interrogates politics of identity and authorship. However, as I have argued elsewhere, such blurring of the boundaries of performance points to a more general problematization of genres since the stipulation of an 'open genre' makes demands, which neither heterogeneity nor an emphasis on the local are able to meet (1999a, 20). A work of art cannot be identified unless it carries the mark of some genre, since there can be 'no genreless text ... yet, such participation never amounts to belonging' (Derrida 1980, 211–12). In a similar way, CAE's individual performances participate in various performance genres, such as bioart and digital performance, whilst not completely belonging to those genres.

Another strategy practiced by CAE is to disseminate their works as widely as possible by publishing collectively and anonymously, in order to underline their resistance to privatization. Although not against revealing their names, they do not use their signatures in relation to their works. In the same way, they feel they are free to plagiarize other artists' work. Between 1988 and 1994, they published five artists' books containing plagiarized poetry which have been sold to various libraries, universities and museum collections (Schneider 2000, 124). A precursor to this strategy was the development of collage and cut-up techniques by Andre Breton and William Burroughs, where pre-existing texts or artwork were cut, re-ordered and juxtaposed to create new works with new meanings, all aimed against the privatization of art and cultural practices.

CAE's works consist of various configurations even for the same event, for example, lecture presentations, performances that are participatory and books that contextualize their particular areas of interest. For instance, one of their projects, *Flesh Machine* (1997–8), focuses on eugenics in the discourse and practice of current reproductive technologies. It features the genetic screening of audience members, the diary of a couple going through in vitro fertilization, 'embryo murder' and involves lecture presentations, participatory performance and a published book, *Flesh Machine: Cyborgs, Designer Babies, and New Eugenic Consciousness* (1998), which contextualizes and critically analyses 'reprotech'. Although the book functions well in this capacity, for CAE it cannot solve 'the problem of there being no lived experience – critical texts have very definite limits' (CAE 2000a, 164).

Flesh Machine was first performed at Public Netbase in Vienna (1997), followed by performances in Ljubljana, Graz, Brussels and Helsinki. It begins with a lecture that discusses and explores various sociocultural issues, particularly in relation to women, concerning reproduction and reproductive technologies. This is followed by a section of the performance where the audience members become far more active in their participation. For example, they take part in laboratory experiments and are introduced to various sexual reproductive models and technology. For this event, CAE created its own cryolab to accommodate living human tissue for possible cloning purposes – leading to performers and audience alike taking up roles as genetic engineers. The audience members were genetically screened to assess their suitability for surrogacy and/or donating DNA and cytoplasm – the donor-screening test was appropriated from an actual clinic. Computers were used to deliver and seductively display information on medical procedures by means of a CD-Rom. Unsurprisingly, the individuals that were allowed to reproduce themselves were consistent in regards to appearance, sex and sociocultural background, being mainly white, middle class and usually male. For CAE, this result underscores the political and social inequalities implicated in eugenics.

As a culmination of the performance, donations were requested from the audience to continue to allow a frozen embryo to remain in its cryotank. A life-size video image of the embryo was projected, together with a clocked countdown of the time left for the embryo to remain in the cryotank. If no payment was received, which has been the usual practice to date, the embryo is removed from the tank and allowed to defrost and as a result dies. This event has been repeated during each performance, the audience in effect participating in the 'murder' of an embryo. A consequence that for CAE 'speaks for itself – though on more than one occasion CAE has had to speak in the wake of their actions ... debating the ethical implications of "embryo murder"' (Schneider 2000, 123).

Another work, *Society for Reproductive Anachronisms* (1999), also engaged the audience in dialogue about the problems of medical intervention in reproduction. However, CAE's more recent performances have attempted to critically evaluate and respond to concerns regarding genetic engineering and the creation and release of new life forms into the ecosystem. One such work is *GenTerra* (2001–5), which addresses the creation of genetically modified organisms (GMOs).[8] For this project, CAE collaborated with Bob Ferrell from the Department of Genetics, University of Pittsburgh; Linda Kauffman from the Department of Molecular Biology, the Mellon Institute; and Beatriz da Costa from the University of California, Irvine, an interdisciplinary artist, robotic art researcher and co-founder of Preemptive Media – an art, activism and technology group.

The aim of the work was to do a 'participatory theatre project' that would allow individuals to be involved in the clinical production of transgenic organisms. Transgenics is the recombination of genetic material at a molecular and cellular level, and as a result new entities are created which cross previous species boundaries. The release of transgenics into the environment raises widespread concerns relating to 'authority, nature, purity, danger and profit'. The performance's primary goal was an attempt to dispel the fear of GMOs within the general community, which for CAE is non-conducive to resistance. It was intended at the same time to empower people to assess for themselves which GMOs were essentially good and which were pollutants. Therefore, *Genterra*, which focuses on a fictional biotechnology company, was concerned with creating 'those dialogues around policies that deal with transgenics' (Critical Art Ensemble 2002a). In short, by setting itself up as a profit-driven corporate company, which is also socially responsible, CAE'S

Figure 7.1   GenTerra. Performance at St. Norbert Art and Culture Center, Winnipeg, Manitoba, Canada (2001)

Genterra accentuates the conflicting debates which surround transgenics research.

At the performance I attended, which was at the Working with Wetware Forum, organized by The Arts Catalyst (the science art agency) in London (2003), there were apparent laboratory technicians wearing white coats (CAE and collaborators), a plastic tent containing lab equipment including microscopes, together with machines and paraphernalia to store and release transgenic bacteria. There was also a video playing on a monitor and computers presenting various 'pedagogical' multimedia. For CAE, pedagogical and political actions are not identical since 'pedagogy requires performance, spectacle and *presence*. You want people to see it and then talk about it' (Critical Art Ensemble 2000b 144; italics mine).

There is the assumption that pure expression can be present in an unmediated and therefore certain way as expressed by CAE in the above quote. However, Derrida denies this possibility with its belief in a single definable moment since the trace is 'the *pure* movement' that 'produces difference' (1976, 62). In other words there can be no presence without absence.

On entering *Genterra's* performance space, audience members are introduced to the facts and issues surrounding transgenics by the 'technicians'.

They are also provided with containers and materials that allow them to make and store their own transgenic bacteria, later becoming actively involved in the area of risk assessment by deciding whether or not to release bacteria from the individual petri dishes. The majority of the dishes had non-transgenic bacteria samples taken locally but one contained the transgenic bacteria. If the dish with the transgenic bacteria was chosen, a robotic arm would pick up the lid of the dish, leave it open for about five seconds to allow the bacteria to be released and then replace the lid on the dish. As an audience member, I chose to release the bacteria, which turned out to be the transgenic bacteria. I have to admit, I was relieved to be later reassured by Kurtz that the bacteria were harmless.

In their latest publication *The Molecular Invasion* (2002), CAE claim that 'the power of transgenics and its knowledge-base remains in the hands of bureaucrats (the regulating agencies) and the scientists, and therefore is outside democratic process' (65). Since they believe that the biotechnology industry is impervious to traditional forms of resistance they argue for a 'contestational biology', which involves participatory,

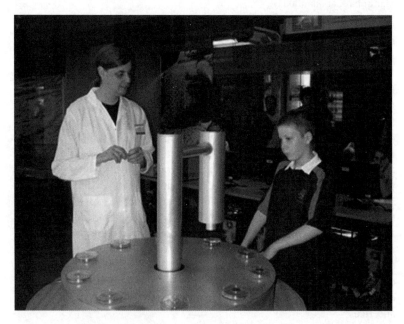

Figure 7.2   GenTerra. The photo was taken at the Darwin Centre, Natural History Museum, London (2001)

pedagogical performances that combine everyday experience with critical reflection on the socioeconomic and political issues concerning biotechnology. Their aim for cultural resistance is to create temporary public spaces where education and 'intersubcultural labour exchange' can take place with the key intention of 'opening knowledge bases' and 'dissolving boundaries of specialization'. And in order for this to occur, the 'hierarchy of the expert over amateur' must be suspended (2002, 65–6), that is, no longer should the scientists' discourse take precedence over that of the layperson. According to Michel Foucault, 'discourse is not the majestically unfolding manifestation of a thinking, knowing, speaking subject' but 'a space of exteriority in which a network of distinct sites is deployed' (1972, 49–55); the subject's position is a '*vacant*' place that may in fact be filled by different individuals. CAE in their performances problematize subject positions and challenge who is speaking and who is allowed to speak. They also reject transcendental categories and call for a Deleuzian rhizomatic model of resistance that harmonizes visual pleasure with critical discourse and does not need 'to exist at the expense of the transparent representation of power relationships within a given process/object' (Critical Art Ensemble 2002, 71).

CAE's most recent performance, *Free Range Grain*, has added another unplanned dimension to their intention of creating a 'theatre of everyday life', in as much as they have found themselves in the midst of an aggressive investigation launched under the United States' bioterrorism laws. As Alisa Solomon writes, 'no doubt members of the Critical Art Ensemble had no desire to prove their point by personal example when they wrote ... "In the era of pancapitalism, only the corporations have the right to manage and control the food supply. If anyone else intervenes, it's terrorism"' (2005). Kurtz himself has been fighting bioterrorism accusations following the tragic death of his wife, Hope, on 11 May 2004. Police were called to investigate the circumstances surrounding the death mainly due to it being sudden and unexpected. When police found what they believed at the time to be questionable scientific material Kurtz was arrested on suspicion of bioterrorism. In reality what they had found was equipment and materials that were to be used in a performance/exhibition of *Free Range Grain* as part of Interventionists: Art in the Social Sphere at the Massachussets Museum of Contemporary Arts (opened 30 May 2004). Although it was soon realized that the sequestered materials were harmless, charges were brought against Kurtz. The charges have since ranged from bioterrorism to 'mail fraud', and now apparently to bioterrorism once more, with others being implicated, including Bob Ferrell who allegedly helped Kurtz obtain

$256 shipment of scientific supplies. Subpoenas have been issued to various theorists and artists including: Beatriz da Costa; Steven Barnes; Dorian Burr; Beverly Schlee; Claire Pentecost; Julie Perini; Adele Henderson, Chair of the Art Department, University of Buffalo; Andrew Johnson Professor of Art, University of Buffalo; and Paul Vanouse, Professor of Art, University of Buffalo. Authorities have also subpoenaed Autonomedia, CAE's publisher.

Free Range Grain was a collaboration with Beatriz da Costa and Shyh-shiun Shyu,[9] and had already been presented to a European audience at Schirn Kunsthalle, Frankfurt, Germany (September 2003). CAE's aim in this project was to test foods for the more common genetic modifications. In order to do so, they constructed a portable, public laboratory where people could bring in foods that they found suspect for whatever reason, and CAE would test them. CAE's intention was to create a forum where issues of food purity and global trade could filtrate into the realm of public discourse.

Following the arrest and confiscation of the project's equipment, the planned performance for the Massachussets MOCA was abandoned. Over the last 12 months there has been widespread international support for CAE from a diverse range of areas including scientific journals such as *Nature*, whose front page notes:

> As with the prosecution of some scientists in recent years, it seems that government lawyers are singling Kurtz out as a warning to the broader artistic community. Kurtz's work is at times critical of science, but researchers should nevertheless be willing to support him … Art and science are forms of human enquiry that can be illuminating and controversial, and the freedoms of both must be preserved as part of a healthy democracy – as must a sense of proportion.
>
> ('On with show' 2004, 685)

Since the above event, CAE have spoken about their ordeal at many conferences and symposia around the world to raise awareness at the attempted suppression of artistic freedom, including at a Defence Fund arranged by the Arts Catalyst in London.[10] It is still unclear what charges, if any, will ultimately be laid against Kurtz and others as a result of a certain state-implemented paranoia, following the 9/11 attacks on New York in 2001, and the ensuing military operations in Afghanistan and Iraq. However, what is certain in this instance is that CAE have blurred the distinction between performance and everyday life, and in keeping with all their projects have also endeavoured to open up dubious government practices to public scrutiny.

Butterflies, FISH and functional portraits: Marta De Menezes's aestheticizing of evolution

> A whole series of scientific dimensions, like biomedicine, genetic engineering ... have outgrown the limits of their field and are ready to become society's aesthetic objects. Thereafter, in the near future we must expect the appearance of artists working with moist media (pixels + molecules) in various social spheres.
>
> (Bulatov 2004)

> Modern biology and biotechnology offer the opportunity to create art using biology as new media. We are witnessing the birth of a new form of art: art created in test-tubes, using laboratories as art studios.
>
> (De Menezes 2005c)

Marta de Menezes is a Portuguese artist who describes herself as 'working at the intersection between Art and Biology' (2005a). It is her belief that emerging biological technologies can form the basis for new art forms and new ways of thinking about the perceived cultural divide between art and science and it is De Menezes's objective to work with scientists in order to bridge this divide; 'DNA, proteins and cells offer an opportunity to explore novel ways of representation and communication' (De Menezes 2002a). Her first bioart project *Nature?* (2000) involved the microsurgical modification of live butterfly-wing patterns;[11] since then De Menezes has employed a variety of scientific technologies which include brain fMRI in *Functional Portraits* (2002b); fluorescent DNA in *NucleArt* (2001); and protein synthesis in *Proteic Portrait* (2002c); to produce a broad range of bioart works. Her work has been presented at international exhibitions, conferences, and in leading journals, such as *Leonardo*.[12]

According to De Menezes, the development in biological techniques and technology has allowed intervention in the normal developmental processes of living organisms, and although DNA is 'the central feature of biological life', it is not the only one. She emphasizes her opposition to the reduction of 'biological art' to merely art practices that utilize DNA technologies, since 'transgenics and genetics' are just 'a small (though important) field of biological sciences and biotechnology' (2005b). Although 'genetics offer immense possibilities for artists', other areas of biology have similar potential, for example, 'proteins, cells, supra-cellular systems and organisms can also be used as an art medium' (2002a). She argues that it not necessary to change the gene of an organism to modify its phenotypical features, that is, its external appearance and behaviour; rather, changes made either at cell or protein level can also cause such modification (2003a, 29).

The *Nature?* project resulted from De Menezes working as an artist at the Institute for Evolutionary and Ecological Sciences, University of Leiden, 1999. Scientists there had been studying the evolution and development of butterfly wing patterns, in order to discover the evolutionary significance of this process. Their research had involved interfering with the normal development of butterflies and as a result, ways had been found to alter wing patterns without altering the genes of those butterflies. The consequence of this was that the modified butterflies displayed unusual wing patterns, which only existed for their life span without being passed on to future generations, at the same time allowing them to lead an apparently normal existence.

De Menezes appropriated these techniques to create 'butterflies with wing patterns modified for artistic purposes' (2003a, 29). In this project she used two butterfly species: *Bicyclus anynana* and *Heliconius melpomeme*. During the pupal stage of a butterfly's life cycle, it is possible to interfere with its developmental processes by microcauterizing specific areas of its wing, thus damaging areas of tissue. This results in the usual wing-pattern configurations being modified or deleted. It is also possible to transfer tissue from different wing areas belonging to the same butterfly and to transfer tissue between various individual butterflies. For her project, De Menezes chose to modify patterns on only one wing, allowing the other wing to develop normally. According to De Menezes, one of her objectives in this study was to explore concepts relating to the perception of shapes in biological systems. She mentions that by modifying wing patterns asymmetrically (one wing being left unmodified), for example, adding or deleting eyespots on the modified wing, allows for our 'imagination to create shapes and rhythms familiar to our senses' (2003a, 30). The 'process' of creating contemporary art is as important as the final 'outcome'; 'the "doing" is as relevant as the "seeing"' (De Menezes 2003b).

For Merleau-Ponty, 'consciousness ... is not a matter of "I think that" but "I can"' (1962, 137). The body interprets itself and it is to be 'compared, not to a physical object, but rather to a work of art ... It is a focal point of living meanings' (1962, 150–1). As demonstrated by De Menezes's artworks, perception is not only intertwined with the scientific and rationalistic but also with the 'aesthetological', the 'mute' artistic, and the 'primordial' (Merleau-Ponty 1974b, 209).

De Menezes believes that her work differs from scientists, inasmuch as at Leiden the scientists were only interested in 'the outcome of a single

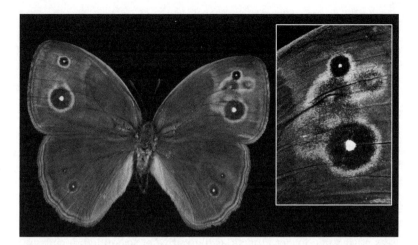

Figure 7.3 Marta de Menezes, *Nature?* Live *Bicyclus anynana* butterfly with modified wing pattern. Part of *Genes and Genius: The Inheritance of Gregor Mendel*, The Mendel Museum (2005) © Marta de Menezes

stimulus', and their resultant wing modification was very simple. In contrast, by applying multiple interventions, De Menezes creates much 'more complex designs' (2003a, 30). According to De Menezes, it is not her intention to enhance 'nature's design', nor for that matter to make something that is 'already beautiful even more beautiful'; rather, her aim is to investigate the limitations of a biological system by creating changes that are not the result of an 'evolutionary process' (31).

Lyotard's notion of the figural as the figuration of creativity and elusiveness, mirrors the bioart of De Menezes, whilst at the same time placing this work within the context of a libidinal economy. A libidinal economy is central to the belief that 'industrial and post-industrial technosciences ... implies the meticulous programming, of beautiful images.' In fact, these images are not only beautiful, but 'too beautiful', not as an indeterminate sentiment but rather the result of 'the infinite realization of the sciences, technology and capitalism' (Lyotard 1993a, 122).

De Menezes notes that all her procedures have followed existing laboratory guidelines with the 'same concern' for the butterflies' 'wellbeing'. Since there are no nerves in the butterfly's wing, the procedure causes no pain. Also, since the damage to the pupal tissue is at cellular level, the tissue regenerates, leaving no visible scars. In fact, according to De Menezes, the modified wing is 'indistinguishable' from a normal butterfly wing other than there is a reconfiguration of the pattern (2003a, 31). Interestingly enough, apart from stating how such works create 'novel ethical problems, for example, concerning the use of live organisms or potentially hazardous substances for art production,' and how individual scientific procedures are required to be evaluated as to 'appropriate' methodology and minimization of associated 'risks' (De Menezes 2003b), there is hardly any mention by De Menezes of the larger ethical issues arising from the manipulation and modification of a living organism as a means of producing an artwork. Rather, her focus is more on the formal and aesthetic features of the artwork. She believes that 'interactions with scientists can be fruitful for all parties concerned' (2003a, 29) and that 'society ... can only benefit from this kind of inter-action through the resulting increase of awareness and understanding of scientific issues' (31). However, as Catts and Zurr remark, 'De Menezes "sees great value in her artwork as illustrative of scientific principles ... Although Menezes avoids the ethical and epistemological issue of her work, the artwork itself generates these discussions regardless or in spite of her intent. Thus [as a result] issues concerning the well being of the but-terflies have overshadowed aesthetic discussions"' (Zurr and Catts 2003).

Following *Nature?* De Menezes's next project, *Nucleart* 2001, took place at the MRC-Sciences Centre at Imperial College, where she used DNA labelled with fluorochromes to paint the nuclei of human cells.[13] This process is known as FISH (Fluorescence In-Situ Hybridization) and is a process where chromosomes or portions of chromosomes are vividly painted with fluorescent molecules. The technique is used for identifying chromosomal abnormalities and gene mapping. Short sequences of single-stranded DNA known as 'probes' hybridize or bind to DNA and because they are labelled with fluorescent tags, allow researchers to see the location of those sequences of DNA. De Menezes used this process on human chromosomes and genes to create 'aesthetically interesting microsculptures' (2003b). Since the ensuing artworks require microscopes in order to be visualized, they were displayed using enlarged computer projections in order to present their 3-D structure. According to De Menezes, the laser microscope used to visualize the cells also destroyed the artwork as it led to the fading of the colours (2003b). As a result, the 3-D projected image referred to an artwork that had ceased to exist.

For her project *Proteic Portrait* (2002c), De Menezes created a self-portrait using proteins as an art medium. Since proteins are made up of 20 amino acids, with each one being represented by a letter-code, she designed a protein whose amino acids corresponded to her own name in order to create a 3-D sculpture. Using her full name,

'MARTAISAVELRIVEIRDEMENESESDASILVAGRACA', she was able, with the aid of computer modelling, to create several possible configurations for the 'marta protein', based on the structure of similar amino-acid sequences in known proteins. The exact configuration of this new protein could only be determined experimentally 'by solving its structure using nuclear magnetic resonance (NMR) or crystallography'; the portrait only being complete 'when the true structure of marta is uncovered' (2002a).

In *Functional Portraits* (2002b), De Menezes used fMRI,[14] to create artworks from the real-time visualizations of brain activity in order to realize 'who/how the person is'. She has created portraits of individuals (including her own) involved in various activities whilst at the same time undergoing brain imaging. The first portrait was of 'Patricia's' brain activity whilst playing a piano,[15] followed by De Menezes's own brain function when drawing. As a development of this work, she is planning to paint the brain while manipulating its activity. According to De Menezes, it is possible to devise tasks and activities that will stimulate various parts of the brain, in short, 'to "paint" a defined pattern of brain activity'. Although the artwork itself has a short life span, since it can only occur whilst the subject is performing the activity, it can nevertheless be documented by the mean of fMRI, the resulting art being created 'simply by thought' (2002a).

In De Menezes's most recent work, *Tree of Knowledge* (2004–5), she uses a combination of cell imaging and tissue culture technologies in order to create living sculptures. Since in this project she wants to represent the 3-D structure of human neurons (brain cells), she has decided that the most appropriate art medium would be the neuronal cells themselves. According to De Menezes, 'by covering a scaffold with live neurons, or by filling glass tubes with these cells', a representation of the neuron can be obtained whilst at the same time maintaining the dynamic nature of a neuron as it continually changes and establishes new connections (2004). For De Menezes, this is not an attempt to represent the actuality of the neuron, but rather to explore the neuron as a living object. In her quest to explore neuronal processes, De Menezes joins a long list of neuro-scientists who have also sought to investigate and examine neuronal cells, since they are believed, by many, to form the basis of consciousness itself.

A perspective on consciousness is proffered by Francis Crick, who prioritizes a scientific approach over the philosophical; his research centres on the correlation between consciousness and active neuronal processes (Crick 1994, 207). The 'neuronal correlate of consciousness', usually referred to as the NCC, generally refers to the correlation between neuronal activity and the sensation, thought or action that relates to that mental activity, as De Menezes with the aid of fMRI has attempted to demonstrate within her *Functional Portraits*. Central to the NCC has been the suggestion that consciousness occurs as a result of an emergent property of several interacting cortical neurons (Libet 1995). A further hypothesis is that there are specific sets of 'consciousness' neurons, whose subsets perhaps consist of distinctive physiological and structural characteristics and demonstrate specific behaviour (Crick and Koch 1995a, 121–3). There is yet another possibility that all cortical neuronal cells are capable of participating in representing conscious experience at different times and in a variety of ways (Zeki 1999, 67).

When viewing an object such as *Nature?* more than one set of neurons will fire in various regions of the brain's cortex as we take in the colour, form and motion of that artwork. Colour is perceived before form, which in turn is perceived before motion, yet all visual attributes are combined to provides us with an integrated experience (66). For instance, De Menezes's modified living butterflies are vividly colourful, two or three-dimensional in form and even capable of movement, yet this work provides us with a unified perceptual experience. This experience of perceptual unity suggests that the brain binds together neurons that are responding to different aspects of a perceived object in a 'mutually coherent way' (Crick 1994, 208).

For De Menezes, 'aestheticizing evolution' is not new, since as she mentions, many animals and plants have been the result of selective breeding programs that have sought to enhance certain valued aesthetic features. Biotechnology provides the means to take this evolutionary process much further and artists are seeking to use this technology in order to create artworks that reflect those developments. However, 'molecular biology tools' still remain very much within laboratory settings and therefore artists have restrictive access, with the result that there are far fewer 'bioartists' than 'computer artists' (De Menezes 2005b) – a situation that is not likely to change very much in the near future.

Finally, as with all digital performance practices, bioart both reflects and is an experimental extension of our contemporary culture and times. As De Menezes claims

Artists are reacting to society when producing artworks ... people need to react to artworks that represent what they hope or fear ... The great danger, as with any other technology, comes from people that are not informed: these are the ones more prone to misuse technology or ban altogether some harmless and beneficial uses.

(2005b)

Notes

1. For further information see *Genesis* (Kac 2005b).
2. For more details see *GFP Bunny* (Kac 2005c).
3. Phenotype is the outward, physical manifestation of an organism, in short, its observable traits. In contrast, genotype is the internally coded, inheritable information carried by all living organism and is used as a set of instructions for building and maintaining all living creatures. These instructions are found within almost all cells; they are written in a coded language (the genetic code) and they are copied at the time of cell division being passed from one generation to the next.
4. The method of integrating the GFP into the rabbit's genotype has been by direct microinjection of DNA into the male pronucleus of a rabbit zygote. The zygote is the fertilized cell formed by the union of two gametes or reproductive cells (male sperm and female egg). See Kac (2005c, n.18) for more detailed information and references.
5. See Kac (2003, 100).
6. David Lodge (2002, 8).
7. Recombination is the rearrangement of the genes in a chromosome of an organism that differs from either of that of its parents.
8. *GenTerra* has been performed at several venues worldwide including the Magasin, National Center for Contemporary Art, Grenoble, France (2001); twice in Winnipeg, Canada, at St. Norbert Center for the Arts and a farmer's market (2001); at the Adelaide Biennial of Australian Art (2002); at the Henry Art Gallery, Seattle (April 2002); at the Oldham Gallery, Manchester, UK (October 2002); and at Working with Wetware: a forum on art using living biological systems, organized by The Arts Catalyst (the science art agency) as part of *CLEAN ROOMS:* Art meets biotechnology, the Natural History Museum, London (2003).
9. See Critical Art Ensemble (2004), *Free Range Grain* http://www.critical-art.net/biotech/free/index.html. Accessed 10 August 2005.
10. I attended this event which was held at the Royal Institution of Great Britain, London, February 2005.
11. *Nature?* was developed at the Institute of Evolutionary and Ecological Sciences, Leiden University, the Netherlands, 1999. It was exhibited at the 'Next Sex: Sex in the Age of Its Procreative Superfluousness', Ars Electronica, Linz, Austria (2000).
12. De Menezes is currently artist-in-residence at the Medical Research Council – Clinical Sciences Centre, Imperial College, London.
13. *Nucleart* has been exhibited at several venues including the BioFeel: Art and Technology Exhibition, Perth Institute of Contemporary Arts (PICA), curatored by Oron Catts from SymbioticA, UWA, integrated in the Biennale of Electronic Arts of Perth (BEAP), developed in collaboration

with the John Curtin Gallery at Curtin University, Perth, Western Australia, in August 2002.

14. FMRI is a technique for determining which parts of the brain are activated by different types of physical sensation or activity, such as sight, sound or movement. This 'brain mapping' is achieved by setting up an advanced MRI scanner in a special way so that the increased blood flow to the activated areas of the brain shows up. Raw input images from the MRI scanner need mathematical conversion to reconstruct the images so that they look like brains. Image distortions are then corrected by a series of tools. The final statistical image in those parts of the brain which were activated appears brighter with a variety of colours on top of the original high resolution scan. This combined activation image can be rendered in 3-D, and calculated from any angle (Smith 1998).

15. 'Functional Portrait: Patricia playing the piano' (De Menezes, 2002). Installation: audio (piano music) and video projection using a white canvas as screen. The functioning portraits including this one were the result of De Menezes's collaboration with Patricia Figueiredo, a physicist at the University of Oxford.

8
Conclusion: Digital Practices

> Because the essence of technology is nothing techno-
> logical, essential reflection upon technology and deci-
> sive confrontation with it must happen in a realm that
> is, on the one hand, akin to the essence of technology
> and, on the other, fundamentally different from it.
> Such a realm is art.
>
> (Heidegger 1977, 35)

Performance and technology in all its divergent forms is an emergent area of performance, which reflects a certain being in the world – a Zeitgeist; in short, it provides a reflection of our contemporary world at the beginning of the twenty-first century. In a relatively short period of time there has been an explosion of new technologies that have infiltrated all areas of life and irrevocably altered our lives. Consequences of this technological permeation are both ontological and epistemological, and not without problems as we see our world change from day to day.

It is my belief that digital practices, as experimental artworks and performances, both serve as critique and have an *indirect* effect on the social and political, though a redefinition of this term is certainly needed, inasmuch as they question the very nature of our accepted ideas and belief systems regarding new technologies. In this sense, the digital does what all avant-garde art does; it is an experimental extension of the socio-political and cultural of an epoch.

Contemporary performance practices that are exemplary of the digital are in live performance: *Blue Bloodshot Flowers* featuring an avatar called Jeremiah, Merce Cunningham's *BIPED* with its virtual dancers, and Stelarc's 'obsolete body'; in sound and new media interactive practices, the digitally manipulated sound of Optik, the 'intermedia' of Palindrome

185

and the 'electronic disturbance' of Troika Ranch; in film, the digital innovation and creativity of *The Matrix* trilogy and the *Star Wars* prequels; and in Bioart, the 'transgenic art' of Eduardo Kac, the 'recombinant theatre'of Critical Arts Ensemble and the 'phenotypical reprogramming' and 'functional portraits' of Marta de Menezes.

In my opinion, such works present innovation in art practices, being at the cutting edge of creative and technological experimentation. It is also my belief that tensions exist within the spaces created by the interface of body and technology and these spaces are 'liminal' inasmuch as they are located on the 'threshold' of the physical and virtual. I am suggesting that it is within these tension filled spaces that opportunities arise for new experimental forms and practices. As such, I identify certain features that are central to these new practices. First and foremost, the utilization of the latest digital technology is absolutely central since within these various art practices and performances there is an assortment of technologies employed. Another important trait is an accentuation of the corporeal in terms of both performance and perception with its emphasis on intersemiotic modes of signification,[1] since in much of this performance the body is primary and yet transient.

I believe that such quintessential features demand a new mode of analysis which foregrounds the inherent tensions between the physical and virtual. In my opinion, central to such an analysis is both an aesthetic perspective, a development from my previous liminal theorization and a neuroesthetic approach which relates to the biological processes that inform how we perceive.

These practices, in different ways, emphasize the body and technology in performance and they explode the margins between the physical and virtual and what is seen as dominant traditional art practices and innovative technical experimentation. Therefore, my main premise is the exploration and investigation into the physical/virtual interface so prevalent within the digital.

In digital practices, instrumentation is mutually implicated with the body in an epistemological sense. The body adapts and extends itself through external instruments. To have experience, to get used to an instrument, is to incorporate that instrument into the body. The experience of the corporal schema is not fixed or delimited, but extendable to the various tools and technologies which may be embodied. Our bodies are always open to and intertwined with the world. Instruments appropriated by embodied experience become part of that altered body experience in the world. In this way, 'the body is our general medium for having a world' (Merleau-Ponty 1963, 146).

Technology then would imply a reconfiguration of our embodied experience. When the meaning aimed at cannot be reached by the body alone, it builds its own instruments and projects around itself a mediated world. Rather, than being separate from the body, technology becomes part of that body and alters and recreates our experience in the world. Moreover, the body is a system of possible actions since when we point to an object, we refer to that object not as an object represented but as a specific thing towards which we 'project' ourselves (Merleau-Ponty 1962, 138), in fact a 'virtual body' with its phenomenal 'place' defined by task and location (25). This emphasis on a virtual body has resonance with and points to a deconstruction of the physical/virtual body of digital practices, a body of potential creativity.

Magnetic or optical motion capture is exemplary of this 'instrumentation' and has been used widely in performance and art practices for some time now. This involves the application of sensors or markers to the performer or artist's body. The movement of the body is captured and the resulting skeleton has animation applied to it. This data-projected image or avatar then becomes some part of a performance or art practice. Motion tracking is used especially in live performances, such as *BIPED* (2000a), where pre-recorded dancing avatars are rear-projected onto a translucent screen giving the effect of a direct interface between the physical and virtual bodies. In film it is used with Jar Jar Binks's movements in *Phantom Menace* (1999) which was created by animators, from motion captured data taken from an actor. In digital sound and new media interactive practices, motion tracking is used in Troika Ranch's dance theatre, where captured live or pre-recorded images freeze, fragment, speed up, slow down, or warp in a shimmering effect – all by means of Isadora software.

In Stelarc's performances the body is coupled with a variety of instrumental and technological devices that instead of being separate from the body become part of that body, at the same time altering and recreating its experience in the world. One such performance is *Muscle Machine* (2003a), where Stelarc constructed an interactive and operational system in the form of a walking robot. This intertwining of body, technology and world is important, since instead of abandoning the physical body, instrumentation and technology extends it by altering and recreating its embodied experience.

Artificial intelligence is also featured in these technological practices, where the challenge is to demarcate the delimited human body from an artificially intelligent life form, such as Jeremiah the avatar from *Blue Bloodshot Flowers* (2001), who was developed from surveillance technology. One of the most interesting aspects of this performance is how much the performer/spectator projects onto the avatar. This is of course, due to a large area of the human brain being devoted to face recognition (Zeman 2002, 216). The ability of humans to recognize facial expressions is so sophisticated that even very slight differences are noticed and made meaningful and that is why faces such as Jeremiah's and the super-high resolution-mediated face of Agent Smith in *The Matrix: Revolutions* (2003) have such a powerful effect on the spectator.

Likewise, Stelarc intends to introduce artificial intelligence into his *Movatar* prosthesis in order for it to perform in the real world, thus further blurring the distinctions between the virtual and actual. According to Stelarc, his avatar can be thought of as 'a kind of viral life form' or agent that lies dormant except when it is connected to a physical body, which causes it to become activated and it in turn reactivates the host body. Therefore, the body shares its agency with an artificial entity that has the ability to learn, developing its behaviour within the duration of a performance (2002a, 76).

In digital practices, virtual bodies that are generated by physical movement through the mediation of digital technology are seen together with live performers. The performances with their interface and interaction between physical and virtual bodies can be seen to displace fixed categories of identity; each carries a 'trace' of the other, given that the virtual performers are the digital reincarnation of the human bodies. However, limits of the embodied self are not fixed since embodied emotional response can also be due to the stimulation of external objects that have been appropriated by the body (Ramachandran and Blakeslee 1999, 61–2). Digital practices, with their use of Mocap (motion capture) and artificially intelligent technologies take this appropriation further since the motions of a performer's body captured technologically featuring avatars, such as Jeremiah and the movatar, results in a modified extension of that physical body. The implication is that the embodied self as any other aspect of the conscious self is transitory, indeterminate and hybridized.

A key influence on Cunningham's embodied practice is television with its effect on our 'modes of perception' (Reynolds 2000, 1). According to Cunningham, *BIPED* (2000) was about working with technology and also to do with the notion of television channel surfing, 'flicking through channels on TV' (Kaiser 2004a). This motif was evident in the presentation of the performance where 'movement phases are combined and recombined, and scale and pacing are in constant flux' (Scarry 1999). However, as Derrida writes, although a 'live' image broadcast on a television channel can never be uncontaminated by its 'censor, frame, filter', in a similar way, neither can a 'live' humanoid representation that is projected on a scrim. However, knowing or believing that the live or direct is possible is enough to transform 'the field of perception and experience in general' (2002, 40).

Again, in the digital there is a proliferation of performances that utilize electronic sound technology for real-time interaction. A performance group that explores the use of this technology is Optik, who have performed at various national and international venues and now prioritize the use of digitally manipulated sound in their movement-based performance. Sound technologies central to their performances are MIDI and Max, a real-time programming environment that has the special advantage of being interactive with visual and network technologies. Established as an agreed universal standard method for sending and receiving musical controller information digitally, the application of the basic MIDI interface has expanded in a variety of ways. It provides a standardized interface for a wide variety of control devices. Its codes have also been adapted to control various non-musical devices to coordinate with video and graphics. The development of MIDI has had a strong impact on the accessibility and variety of interactions that can be utilized in performance. However, the accompanying necessary restriction of data means that important musical information is lost and the processing methods of MIDI are restrictive for real-time interaction, as they are particularly weak at handling continuously changing data. This in turn has led to the proliferation of numerous highly programmable interactive MIDI systems that can offer immediate feedback – Max being the most widely used. It has also led to the development of OSC, which is a protocol that allows the real-time control of computer-synthesis processes from gestural devices.

MIDI, Max and OSC are central to the performances of Troika Ranch who fuse traditional elements of music, dance and theatre with real-time interactive digital technology. They are pioneers in their use of MidiDancer and Isadora software, which can interpret physical movements of performers, and as a result that information can be used to manipulate the accompanying sound, media and visual imagery in a variety of ways, thus providing a new creative potential for performance. Likewise, Palindrome, who focus on the interface and interaction between virtual sound and the physical body, also utilize such sound technologies. Artistic directors Robert Wechler and Frieder Weiss have designed and developed interactive software and hardware, including Eyecon, a camera-based motion-sensing system.

Their choreography is affected by the live generation of sound through the use of sensors and real-time synthesis, and those movements in turn shape the resulting music.

When looking at objects in performance, colour is perceived before form, which in turn is perceived before motion (Zeki 1999, 66). The consequence of this is that the brain over very short periods of time is unable to combine what happens in real time; instead, it unifies the results of its own processing systems though not in real time. Nevertheless all visual attributes are combined to provide us with an integrated experience. Palindrome's shadows performances, as a result of their multilayered, distorted and delayed effects, challenge this 'integrated experience', at the same time they ensure the audience's active participation in the production of meaning. The shadows shift seamlessly between what is '*known*' and what is '*surprising*' making 'the piece fascinating to watch' (Dowling, Wechsler and Weiss, 2004, 78).

In digital practices, there is also an accentuation on the chthonic or primordial though this is not a feature shared by all digital practices. For example, *The Matrix* trilogy abounds with chthonic symbols, iconic imagery and mythological beings. They provide a visual cacophony of dreamscapes and primordial worlds where violence, terrorism, passion, affirmation through love, all take place; representing 'a kind of parthenogenic – which is to say autochthonous – mother,' a way of reproducing life without the need for sexual intercourse; analogical to the various myths and fables that relate to humans arising from the earth instead of being born (Kimball 2001, 191–4).

Paradoxically, films like *The Matrix* trilogy and *Star Wars* prequels fetishize technology while at the same time treating technology as the enemy. For example, within *The Matrix* films, the city of Zion, together with the post-apocalyptic earth landscape, is created with the aid of virtual cinematography and computer imagery, whilst the supposedly simulated world of the matrix, set in 1999, is far less dependent on technology and special effects for its representation. An important technical effect created for *The Matrix* was 'Bullet time' or 'Flo-Mo' that has the ability to capture both super-slow and high-speed motions at the same time on film. Likewise, in the *Star Wars* films, technology is associated with the Empire whose machinic world is bereft of vegetation and whose spaceships are enormously destructive. In contrast, the rebels are associated with the forest, the colour green and with the organic 'force' that defeats the machines. Blue- and green screen technologies were also widely used in all the *Star Wars* prequels. The compositing process, whether photographic or electronic, replaces all the blue or green in a picture with another image. However, actors, in particular, have problems with this technology since on many occasions they are required to act solely to and in front of a blank screen. This is especially true for *Episode III* (2005), where many of the characters and environments were computer generated.

Other aesthetic features within the digital are heterogeneity, indeterminacy, fragmentation, hybridization and repetition. Due to the hybridization of these practices and the diversity of media employed, various intensities are at play. It is these imperceptible intensities, together with their ontological status that give rise to new modes of perception and consciousness. Central to becoming and making new connections is the body without organs. It is 'the field of immanence of desire' (Deleuze and Guattari 1999a, 191) and an 'intense and intensive body' (Deleuze 2003, 44). Desiring machines and BwO can be seen as 'two states of the same "thing", a functioning multiplicity one moment, a pure, unextended zero-intensity the next' (Bogue 1989, 93). In Troika Ranch's performance of *The Electronic Disturbance* (1994), the ebb and flow between the organic and electronic is in a continual process of becoming and making new connections.

In both the *Star Wars* prequels and sequels, Lucas has admitted to using the 'force' as a representation of God, and the 'dark side' as a metaphor for evil that exists within all humans. According to Tom Kisken, 'with recurring themes of good and evil, redemption and the power of faith, the movies are at the very least the embryo of theological and philosophical forum' (1999). However, for Deleuze, orthodox tools of philosophy such as dualisms are replaced by the concepts of planes, becoming, intensities, flows and connections. Rigid binary oppositions, such as the above, are avoided in favour of a 'continuum of interacting embodied subjectivities', and 'machinic assemblage of bodies, of actions and passions' (Deleuze and Guattari 1991a, 88), notions that prove useful in theorizing the *Star Wars* films with their blurring of the borders between good and evil and between light and dark.

Likewise, for Lyotard, instead of a conceptual interpretation of meaning, the 'figural', a territory of form, colour and the visual, indicates flows and drives of 'intensities' which continually displace the identity of the reader (or spectator). The aim is to eliminate oppositions in favour of intensities; it is useful in a description of such digital practices as *Blue Bloodshot Flowers*, with its diverse elements that often escape meaningful interpretation.

'Defamiliarizing' devices are also employed within digital practices, such as the juxtaposition of disparate elements that in creating a distancing effect, causes the audience to actively participate in the activity of producing meaning. The employment of wide, jarring metaphors is another central characteristic of the digital. The colourful and figurative use of aural and visual imagery and the juxtaposition of metaphors evoke surreal dreamscapes. The interaction of the physical and virtual also creates inclusive, jarring metaphors. This mixture produces an aesthetic effect caused by the interplay of various mental sense-impressions, which unsettle the audience by frustrating their expectations of any simple interpretation and in turn produce a new type of synaesthetic effect that is analogous to the experience caused by cross-wiring or cross-activation of discrete areas of the brain in certain perceptual conditions (Ramachandran and Hubbard 2001, 9).

Troika Ranch's *The Future of Memory* explores memory and the act of remembering – by means of a multilayered collage of imagery and sound; the technology acting as a 'metaphor for memory' itself (Coniglio and Stoppiello 2005). Metaphor has been identified with the Freudian notion of 'condensation', and metonymy with 'displacement' (Lyotard 1989e). However, for Lyotard, there is a certain futility in bring everything back to the linguistic, when it is 'clear that language, at least in its poetic usage, is possessed ... by the figure' (30). The figural, is not the figuration of representational art but is instead that of creativity and elusiveness and it is important since it mirrors many digital practices.

Other forms of digital practices are those that incorporate biotechnology within their creative experimentation. Such art works are commonly referred to as 'Bioart'. The Tissue, Culture and Arts Project are such a group, whose tissue engineering exploration, exemplified by Stelarc's *Extra Ear* (2004c), is integral to their art installations, resulting in works of varying geometrical complexity thereby creating a living 'artistic palette'.

For Eduardo Kac, 'transgenic art ... is a new art form based on the use of genetic engineering techniques to transfer synthetic genes to an organism or to transfer natural genetic material from one species into another, to create unique living beings' (1998). One such artwork is Alba the *GFP Bunny* (2000), a genetically engineered rabbit that glows green when illuminated with the correct light. In detailing particular physical and intellectual traits of Alba and rabbits in general,[2] Kac believes that this should provide some understanding on how a rabbit sees the world though not 'enough to appreciate its consciousness' (100). Since the exploration of consciousness may well be the final frontier of our very human need to both understand and to be meaningful, what does this mean for a rabbit? Does it too have consciousness? If so how would a rabbit's consciousness manifest itself? Would it be able to think in first person and experience 'qualia', that is, the subjective quality of a mental experience.[3] In exploring intersubjectivity between various species, questions like this need to be taken into account, in order to fully appreciate each individual life form.

CAE through their 'recombinant theatre', have made technology, wetware and transgenics, the focus of their work. For CAE, recombination 'typically denotes esoterica pertinent to molecular biology'. Although originally working with multimedia, CAE over recent years have concentrated on responding to the debates surrounding biotechnology. As 'tactical' mediaists the group have presented various interactive performance projects. For CAE, tacticality includes a willingness to be amateurs, to try anything and to resist specialization. CAE's recent performance, *Free Range Grain*, has added another unplanned dimension to their intention of creating a 'theatre of everyday life', in as much as they have found themselves in the midst of an aggressive investigation launched under the United States' bioterrorism laws. In reality, what was found during a search of a member's property was equipment and materials that were to be used in a performance/exhibition of *Free Range Grain* as part of Interventionists: Art in the Social Sphere at the Massachussets Museum of Contemporary Arts (2004). Although the sequestered materials were harmless, charges were still brought. It is still unclear what charges if any will ultimately be laid as a result of a certain state-implemented paranoia. However, what is certain in this instance is that CAE have blurred the distinction between performance and everyday life, and in keeping with all their projects have also attempted to open up dubious government practices to public scrutiny.

Marta de Menezes is an artist who also works with biotechnology. For her project *Nature?* (1999), she reprogrammed patterns on butterfly wings by injecting the pupa in development. She has also applied various colours to elementary parts of brain cells and through projections in 3-D has created live sculptures. Her work *Functional Portraits* (2002) employs fMRI, which visualizes in real time the operation of the brain, the resulting art being created 'simply by thought' (De Menezes 2002a). In so doing, de Menezes attempts to demonstrate the 'neuronal correlate of consciousness', which generally refers to the correlation between neuronal activity and the sensation, thought or action that relates to that mental activity (Crick 1994, 208).

The bioart of De Menezes is mirrored in Lyotard's notion of the figural as the figuration of creativity and elusiveness, whilst at the same time placing this work within the context of a libidinal economy. A libidinal economy is central to the belief that 'industrial and post-industrial technosciences … implies the meticulous programming, of beautiful images.' In fact, these images are not only beautiful, but 'too beautiful', not as an indeterminate sentiment but rather the result of 'the infinite realization of the sciences, technology and capitalism' (Lyotard 1993a, 122). Artworks such as De Menezes's can also be seen as critical deconstructive practices since 'metaphysical complicity' cannot be given up without also giving up the critique of the complicity that is being argued against (Derrida, 1978a, 281). These performances whilst apparently complicit with dominant means of digital representation, attempt at the same time to destabilize those dominant structures by focusing on areas of concern relating to the commodification and consumerism of such technology.

In conclusion, whilst the central distinctive aesthetic trait of digital practices is the utilization of the latest digital technology, the digital as a discourse cannot convert phenomena directly but depends on a preceding production of meaning by the non-digital. For instance, the avatar in *Blue Bloodshot Flowers* emulates the graphic design and animation of an anthropomorphic representation, which is in this case a human head. The digital, like all formal systems, has no inherent semantics unless one is added. One must add meaning. Thus digitally processed contents require reading habits different from ordinary habits of reading – reading digital contents demands thinking in terms of 'indifferent differentiation'. A thinking that makes little distinction between the referent and meaning, between 'reality' and representation or for that matter between fact and fiction.[4]

Finally, although much interest is directed towards new technologies, it is my belief that technology's most important contribution to art is the enhancement and reconfiguration of an aesthetic creative potential that consists of interacting with and reacting to a physical body. For, it is within these tension-filled (liminal) spaces of physical and virtual interface that opportunities arise for new experimental forms and practice. As Philip Auslander remarks:

> Technology cannot take the place of human presence at the heart of performance … it is best used to extend the capabilities of human performers, to express humanistic themes more fully, and to allow performance to explore or evoke responses from realms of human physical and psychological experience not directly accessible otherwise … Perhaps, then, our anthropocentrism is the territory we are not

willing to cede to the dominance of the digital, at least not now. Or not yet.

(2006, 299)

Notes

1. A significatory practice which involves such non-linguistic modes as those provided by the semiotics of corporeal gesture. See (Broadhurst 1999a, 1999b, 2002, 2004a, 2004b).
2. See Kac (2003, 100).
3. David Lodge (2002, 8).
4. For a more detailed discussion of the concepts of 'differentiation' and 'de differentiation', see Scott Lash (1990, 5–15). See also Broadhurst (1999a, 177).

Bibliography

Albrecht, Thomas D. and Helen J. Neville. 2001. 'Neurosciences'. In *The MIT Encyclopedia of The Cognitive Sciences*, eds Robert Wilson and Frank Keil, li–lxxii. Cambridge, MA: MIT Press.

Allmendinger, Ulli. 2001. 'One small hop for Alba, one large hop for mankind'. Eduardo Kac's website (Originally published in *New York Arts Magazine* 6, no. 6, June 2001) http://www.ekac.org/ulli.html, accessed 20 August 2005.

Althusser, Louis. 1971. 'Ideology and Ideological State Apparatuses'. In *Lenin and Philosophy and Other Essays*, trans. Ben Brewster, 136–70. New York: Monthly Review Press.

Andrews, Lori B. 1999. 'Genetic Predictions and Social Responses'. In *Ars Electronica 99: Life Sciences*, eds Gerfried Stocker and Christine Schopf, pp. 86–92. New York: Springer Wein.

Auslander, Philip. 2006. 'An Afterword: Is There Life after *Liveness*?' In *Performance and Technology: Practices of Virtual Embodiment and Interactivity*, eds Susan Broadhurst and Josephine Machon, 292–9. London: Palgrave Macmillan.

Ballora, Mark. 2004. 'Get with the Interation'. *Electronic Musician* (Feb 1) http://emusician.com/mag/square_one/emusic_interaction/index.html, accessed 6 March 6.

Batson, Quinn. 2004. 'Seamless Surfaces'. *Offoffoff Dance*. http://www.offoffoff.com/dance/2004/surfacing.php, accessed 20 May 2005.

Baudrillard, Jean.1983. *Simulations*. Trans. Paul Foss and Paul Patton. New York: Semiotext(e).

———. 1988. 'Fatal Strategies'. In *Jean Baudrillard: Selected Writings*, ed. Mark Poster, 185–206. California: Stanford University Press.

———. 1990. *Cool Memories*. Trans. Chris Turner. London: Verso.

———. 1994. *Simulacra and Simulation*. Trans. Sheila Glaser. Ann Arbor, MI: University of Michigan Press.

———. 2004. 'The Matrix Decoded: Le Nouvel Observateru Interview with Jean Baudrillard'. Trans. Gary Genosko and Adam Bryx (Baudrillard was interviewed by Aude Lance for *Le Nouvel Observateur* – 19–25 June 2003). *International Journal of Baudrillard Studies* 1, no. 2 (July). http://www.ubishops.ca/baudrillardstudies/vol. 1–2/genosko.htm accessed 21 October 2005.

Bazin, André. (1967) 'The Myth of Total Cinema'. In *What is Cinema? Vol 1*, trans. Hugh Gray, 17–22. Berkeley, CA: University of California Press.

Bogue, Ronald. 1989. *Deleuze and Guattari*. London/New York: Routledge.

———. 2003. *Deleuze on Music, Painting and the Arts*. London: Routledge.

Bowden, Richard and Susan B roadhurst. 2001. *Interaction, Reaction and Performance*. Brunel University http://www.brunel.ac.uk/jeremiah accessed 23 March 2003.

Bowden, Richard, Pakorn Kaewtrakulpong and Martin Lewin. 2002. 'Jeremiah: The Face of Computer Vision'. *Smart Graphics*, 2nd International Symposium on Smart Graphics. Hawthorn, NY: ACM International Conference Proceedings Series: 124–8.

Broadhurst, Susan. 1999a. *Liminal Acts: A Critical Overview of Contemporary Performance and Theory*. London: Cassell/New York: Continuum.
————. 1999b. 'The (Im)mediate Body: A Transvaluation of Corporeality'. *Body & Society* 5, no. 1 (March): 17–29.
————, dir. 2001. *Blue Bloodshot Flowers*. Performer Elodie Berland. Music by David Bessell. Technology provided by Richard Bowden, University of Surrey. Brunel University (June); The 291Gallery, London (August).
————. 2002. 'Blue Bloodshot Flowers: Interaction, Reaction and Performance'. *Digital Creativity* 13, no. 3: 157–63.
————, dir. 2003. *Dead East, Dead West*. Choreography: Jeffrey Longstaff. Performers: Katsura Isobe and Tom Wilton. Percussionist and composer: Dave Smith. Technology provided by Martin Dupras, Jez Hattosh-Nemeth and Paul Verity Smith, University of the West of England. 3-D realization: Brian McClave (Film-maker). Institute of Contemporary Arts, London (August).
————. 2004a. 'Interaction, Reaction and Performance: The Jeremiah Project,' *The Drama Review* 48, no. 4 (Winter): 47–57.
————. 2004b. 'Liminal Spaces'. In *Mapping the Threshold: Essays in Liminal Analysis (Studies in Liminality and Literature* 4), ed. Nancy Bredendick, 57–73. Madrid: Gateway Press. ISBN 84-931843-2-2.
Broadhurst, Susan and Josephine Machon, eds. (2006). *Performance and Technology: Practices of Virtual Embodiment and Interactivity*. London: Palgrave Macmillan.
Brown, Dan. 2003. *The Da Vinci Code*. London: Corgi Books.
Bulatov, Dmitry. 2004. 'Introduction'. Website for *Biomediale Contemporary Society and Genomic Culture*, edited and curated by Dmitry Bulatov, trans. Tatiana Mishunina, The National Centre for Contemporary art (Kaliningrad branch, Russia). Kaliningrad: The National Publishing House 'Yantarny Skaz'. ISBN 5-7406-0853-7. http://ncca-kaliningrad.ru/biomediale/accessed 6 September 2005.
Campbell, Joseph. 1968. *The Hero with a Thousand Faces* 2nd edition. Princeton, NJ: Princeton University Press.
Carroll, David. 1987. *Paraesthetics: Foucault, Lyotard, Derrida*. New York: Methuen.
————. 1950. *The Adventures of Alice in Wonderland*. London: James Brodie.
Carson, Tom. 2002. 'Jedi Uber Alles'. In *A Galaxy Not So Far Away: Writers and Artists on Twenty-Five Years of Star Wars*, ed. Glenn Kenny, pp. 160–71. New York: Henry Holt.
Catts, Oron and Ionat Zurr. 2002. 'Growing Semi-Living Sculptures: The Tissue Culture & Arts Project'. *Leonardo* 35, no. 4: 365–70.
————. 2003. The Art of the Semi-Living and Partial Life: Extra Ear – ¼ Scale (Catalogue Essay: Art in the Biotech Era, Adelaide International Arts Festival 2003). The Tissue Culture & Art Project website hosted by SymbioticA, University of Western Australia. http://www.tca.uwa.edu.au/publication/TheArtoftheSemi-LivingandPartialLife.pdf, accessed 1 September 2005.
————. 2004. 'Extra Ear – ¼ scale: The Tissue Culture & Art in Collaboration with Stelarc'. The Tissue Culture & Art Project website hosted by SymbioticA, University of Western Australia, http://www.tca.uwa.edu.au/extra/extra_ear.html, accessed 21 November 2004.
Chalmers, David J. 1998. 'Facing Up to the Problem of Consciousness'. In *Explaining Consciousness The Hard Problem*, ed. Jonathan Shear, 9–30. Cambridge, MA: MIT Press.

Clarke, Julie. 2002. 'The Human/Not Human in the Work of Orlan and Stelarc'. In *The Cyborg Experiments: The Extensions of the Body in the Media Age*, eds Joanna Zylinska and Gary Hall, 33–55. London/New York: Continuum.

Clover, Joshua. 2004 *The Matrix*. London: British Film Institute.

Clynes, Manfred E. and Nathan S. Kline. 1995. 'Cyborgs and space'. In *The Cyborg Handbook*, ed. Chris Hables Gray, 29–33. London: Routledge.

Colebrook, Claire. 2002a. *Gilles Deleuze*. London: Routledge.

———. 2002b. *Understanding Deleuze*. London: Allen & Unwin.

Coniglio, Mark. 2004. 'The Importance of Being Interactive'. In *New Visions in Performance: The Impact of Digital Technologies*, eds Gavin Carver and Colin Beardon, 5–12. Lisse, the Netherlands: Swets & Zeitlinger.

Coniglio, Mark and Dawn Stoppiello. 2005. Troika Ranch Website. www. troikaranch.org/, accessed 1 May 2005.

Copeland, Roger. 2002. 'Merce Cunningham and the Aesthetic of Collage'. *The Drama Review* 46, no.1 (Spring): 11–28.

———. 2004. *Merce Cunningham: The Modernizing of Modern Dance*. London/New York: Routledge.

Crick, Francis. 1994. *The Astonishing Hypothesis*. London: Simon & Schuster Ltd.

Crick, Francis and Christof Koch. 1990. 'Towards a Neurobiological Theory of Consciousness'. *Seminars in the Neurosciences* 2: 263–75.

———. 1995a. 'Are We Aware of Neural Activity in Primary Visual Cortex?' *Nature* 375: 121–3.

———. 1995b. 'Why Neuroscience May be Able to Explain Consciousness'. *Sci Am* 273: 84–5.

———. 1998. 'Consciousness and Neuroscience'. *Cerebral Cortex* 8: 97–107.

———. 2001. 'Neurobiology of. Consciousness'. In *The MIT Encyclopedia Of The Cognitive Sciences*, eds Robert A. Wilson and Frank C. Keil, 193–5. Cambridge, MA/London: MIT Press.

Crick Francis and James Watson. 1953. 'A Structure for Deoxyribose Nucleic Acid'. *Nature* 171: 737.

Critical Art Ensemble. 1994. *The Electronic Disturbance*. New York: Autonomedia.

———. 1997. 'Conversation between CAE and Mark Dery – Part 1'. Critical Art Ensemble interviewed by Mark Dery. Net Theory. http://old.thing.net/wwwboard1/messages/415.html, accessed 18 August 2005.

———.1997–8. *Flesh Machine*. Public Netbase Museumsquartier, Vienna; Beursschouwburg (Art and Science Collusion), Brussels; Kiasma Museum of Contemporary Art, Helsinki; Labor Gallery, Graz; and Kapellica Gallery, Ljubljana.

———. 1998. *Flesh Machine: Cyborgs, Designer Babies and New Eugenic Consciousness*. New York. Autonomedia.

———. 1999. *The Society for Reproductive Anachronisms*. Expo Destructo, London.

———. 2000a. 'Recombinant Theatre and Digital Resistance'. *The Drama Review* 44, no. 4 (Winter): 151–65.

———. 2000b. 'Critical Art Ensemble: Tactical Media Practitioners'. Interview by Jon McKenzie and Rebecca Schneider. *The Drama Review* 44, no. 4 (Winter): 136–50.

———. 2001–5. *GenTerra*. A live performance in collaboration with Bob Ferrell from the Department of Genetics, University of Pittsburgh; Linda Kauffman from the Department of Molecular Biology, the Mellon Institute; and Beatriz da Costa, an interdisciplinary artist, robotic art researcher and co-founder of

Preemptive Media. Presented at Magasin, National Centre for Contemporary Art, Grenoble, France (2001); other venues include St. Norbert Centre for the Arts, Winnipeg, Canada, the Henry Art Gallery, Seattle (April 2002); the Oldham Gallery, Manchester, UK (October 2002); and Working with Wetware: a forum on art using living biological systems, organized by The Arts Catalyst (the science art agency) as part of *CLEAN ROOMS: Art meets biotechnology*, the Natural History Museum, London (2003).

———. 2002a. 'Critical Art Ensemble: GenTerra'. Interview with Steve Kurtz from CAE. *Creative Capital Channel: Granting Innovation in the Arts* http://channel. creative-capital.org/project_69.html, accessed 10 August 2005.

———. 2002b. *Molecular Invasion*. New York: Autonomedia.

Critical Art Ensemble, Beatriz da Costa and Shyh-shiun Shyu. 2004. 'Free Range Grain' http://www.critical-art.net/biotech/free/index.html, accessed 10 August 2005.

Cunningham, Merce. 1968. *Changes: Notes on Choreography*. New York: Something Else Press.

———. 1997a. 'Four Events That Have Led To Large Discoveries, 1994'. In *Merce Cunningham: Fifty Years*, ed. Melissa Harris, 276. New York: Aperture.

———. 1997b. 'The Impermanent Art'. In *Merce Cunningham: Fifty Years*, ed. Melissa Harris, 86–7. New York: Aperture.

———, chor. 1998. *Hand-drawn Spaces*. Computer-enhanced graphics: Paul Kaiser and Shelley Eshkar. Sound: Ron Kuivila. Siggraph Electronic Theatre, Orlando, Florida.

———, chor. 2000a. *Biped*. Computer-enhanced graphics: Paul Kaiser and Shelley Eshkar. Music: Gavin Bryars. Costume Designer: Suzanne Gallo. Barbican Centre, London, October 11 (Premiered at Zellerbach Hall, Berkeley, CA, April 23 1999).

———. 2000b. *Summer Dance: Merce Cunningham*. Interview. Dir: Charles Atlas, Executive Producer: Sheldon Schwartz. BBC 2 television (August 26).

———. 2001. 'Merce Cunningham'. Interview by Janet Lynn Roseman. In *Dance Masters: Interviews with Legends of Dance*, 35–56. London/New York: Routledge.

———, chor. 2002. Loops. Computer-enhanced graphics: Paul Kaiser, Shelley Eshkar and Marc Downie, ICA New Media Centre, London 25 September (Premiered at the Media Lab, MIT, 2001).

———, chor. 2004. *Split Sides*. Music: Radiohead, Sigur Rós. Décor: Robert Heishman and Catherine Yass. Costumes: James Hall. Lighting: James F. Ingalls. Barbican Centre, London, October 6 (Premiere at Brooklyn Academy of Music's Next Wave Festival, October 2003).

Cunningham, Merce with Jacqueline Lesschaeve. 1999. 'Torse: There are no Fixed Points in Space'. In *The Routledge Dance Studies Reader*, ed. Alexandra Carter, 29–34. London/NewYork: Routledge.

Deleuze, Gilles. 1986. *Cinema 1: The Movement Image*. Trans. Hugh Tomlinson and Barbara Habberjam. London: Athlone Press.

———. 1989. *Cinema 2: The Time-Image*. Trans. Hugh Tomlinson and Robert Galeta. Minneapolis, MN: University of Minnesota Press.

———. 1994. *Difference and Repetition*. Trans. Paul Patton. New York: The Athlone Press.

———. 2003. *Francis Bacon: The Logic of Sensation*. Trans. Daniel W. Smith. London/New York: Continuum.

Deleuze, Gilles, and Félix Guattari. 1984. *Anti-Oedipus: Capitalism and Schizophrenia*. Trans. Robert Hurley, Mark Seem and Helen R. Lewis. London: Athlone.

———. 1999a. *A Thousand Plateaus: Capitalism and Schizophrenia*. Trans. Brian Massumi. London: Athlone.

———. 1999b. *What is Philosophy?* Trans. Graham Burchell and Hugh Tomlinson. London/New York: Verso.

De Menezes, Marta. 2000. *Nature?* Developed at the Institute of Evolutionary and Ecological Sciences, Leiden University, the Netherlands and exhibited at the 'Next Sex: Sex in the Age of Its Procreative Superfluousness,' Ars Electronica, Linz, Austria.

———. 2001. 'Nucleart'. Marta De Menezes's website http://www.martademenezes. com/, accessed 1 September 2005.

———. 2002a. 'The Laboratory as an Art Studio'. In *Aesthetics of Care*, ed. Oron Catts, 53–8. Perth, WA: SybioticA, University of Western Australia.

———. 2002b. 'Functional Portraits'. Marta De Menezes's website http://www. martademenezes.com/, accessed 1 September 2005.

———. 2002c. 'Proteic Portrait'. Marta De Menezes's website http://www. martademenezes.com/, accessed 1 September 2005.

———. 2003a. 'The Artificial Natural: Manipulating Butterfly Wing Patterns for Artistic Purposes'. *Leonardo* 36, no. 1: 29–32.

———. 2003b. 'L'Art Biotech – Catalogue'. Le Lieu Unique, curated by Jens Hauser. Nantes Marta De Menezes's website.http://www.martademenezes.com/, accessed 1 September 2005.

———. 2004. 'Marta De Menezes'. Cultura 2000 website. http://cultura2000. min-cultura.pt/, accessed 11 September 2005.

———. 2005a. 'Biography'. Marta De Menezes's website http://www. martademenezes.com/, accessed 6 September 2005.

———. 2005b. 'Interview with Melanitis Yiannis'. Marta De Menezes's website http://www.martademenezes.com/, accessed 6 September 2005.

———. 2005c. Marta De Menezes's website http://www.martademenezes.com/, accessed 6 September 2005.

Demircioglu, Beliz. 2006. 'Hold the Line Troika, Evolutions'. *The Dance Insider*. Flash Review (January), http://www.danceinsider.com/flshMain.html, accessed 28 January 2006.

Dennett, Daniel. 1991. *Consciousness Explained*. London: Penguin Press.

Derrida, Jacques. 1972. 'Discussion'. In *The Languages of Criticism and the Sciences of Man: The Structuralist Controversy*, eds Richard Macksey and Eugenio Donato, 265–72. Baltimore: John Hopkins Press.

———. 1973. *Speech and Phenomena and Other Essays on Husserl's Theory of Signs*. Trans. David Allison. Evanston: Northwestern University Press.

———. 1976. *Of Grammatology*. Trans. Gayatri Spivak. Baltimore: Johns Hopkins University Press.

———. 1977. 'Limited Inc abc'. Trans. Samuel Weber. *Glyph* 2: 162–254.

———. 1978a. 'Structure, Sign and Play in the Discourse of the Human Sciences'. In *Writing and Difference*, trans. Alan Bass, 278–93. Chicago, IL: University of Chicago Press.

——— 1978b. 'The Theatre of Cruelty and the Closure of Representation'. In *Writing and Difference*, trans. Alan Bass, 232–50. Chicago, IL: University of Chicago Press.

———. 1980. 'The Law of Genre'. 1980. Trans. Avital Ronell, *Glyph* 7: 202–32.

———. 1981a. *Dissemination*. Trans. Barbara Johnson. Chicago, IL: University of Chicago Press.

———. 1981b. *Positions*. Trans. Alan Bass. Chicago, IL: University of Chicago Press.

———. 1982. *Margins of Philosophy*. Trans. Alan Bass. Chicago, IL: University of Chicago Press.

———. 1986. *Glas*. Trans. John P. Leavey and Richard Rand. Lincoln: University of Nebraska Press.

———. 1987. *The Truth in Painting*, trans. Geoff Bennington and Ian McLeod. Chicago, IL: University of Chicago Press.

———. 1991. 'Of Grammatology'. In *A Derrida Reader: Between The Blinds*, ed. Peggy Kamuf, trans. Gayatri Spivak, 34–58. New York: Columbia University Press.

———. 1993. *Memoirs of The Blind: The Self-Portrait and Other Ruins*. Trans. Pascale-Anne Brault and Michael Naas. Chicago, IL: University of Chicago Press.

———. 1998. 'To Unsense the Subjectile'. In Derrida Jacques and Paul Thévenin, *The Secret Art of Antonin Artaud*, trans. Mary Ann Caws, 59–157. Massachusetts: MIT Press.

Derrida, Jacques and Bernard Stiegler. 2002. *Echographies of Television*. Trans. Jennifer Bajoreck. Cambridge, UK: Polity Press.

Dery, Mark. 1996. *Escape Velocity: Cyberculture at the End of the Twentieth Century*. London: Hodder and Lucas Stoughton.

Dews, Peter. 1984. 'The Letter And The Line: Discourse And Its Other In Lyotard'. *Diacritics* 14, no. 3: 40–9.

Dils, Ann. 2002. 'The Ghost in The Machine: Merce Cunningham and Bill Jones'. *PAJ: A Journal of Performance and Art* 42, no. 1: 94–104.

Dixon, Steve. 2004. 'The Digital Double'. In *New Visions in Performance: The Impact of Digital Technologies*, eds Gavin Carver and Colin Beardon, 13–30. Lisse, the Netherlands: Swets & Zeitlinger.

Dowling, Peter, Robert Wechsler and Frieder Weiss. 2004. 'EyeCon – A motion sensing tool for creating interactive dance, music and video projections'. Proceedings of the Society for the Study of Artificial Intelligence and the Simulation of Behavior (SSAISB)'s convention: Motion, Emotion and Cognition at University of Leeds, England, (March): 74–9.

Doyle, Audrey. 2003. 'MATRIX: Anime-ted'. *Computer Graphics World*. 26, no. 6: 18–22.

Edwards, Barry. (1999). 'Performing Presence'. In *Reframing Consciousness: Art, Mind and Technology*, ed. Roy Ascott, 191–5. Exeter, UK/Portland, US: Intellect.

———, dir. 2000. *In the Presence of People*. Collaborating artists: Simon Edgoose (live percussion). Performers: Clare Allsop, Simon Humm, Hannah Seaton. Sound Engineer: Ben Jarlett. Curated by Tracey Warr (London) and Renato Cohen (Sao Paulo). Performed indoors at the Karman – Kompanhia Teatro Multimedia and outdoors at the Placa da Se Sao Paulo, Brazil (October).

———, dir. 2001. *Takingbreath*. Collaborating artists: Ben Jarlett (granular synthesis, electronic sound, digital projection), Terence Tiernan (video documentation), Clare Allsop, Simon Humm, Jennifer Lewin (performers). Curated by Olga Glisin and Ivan Pravdic SKC, Belgrade (October).

———, dir. 2002. *Stream*. Collaborating artists: Billy Currie (live music), Howie Bailey (live video), Ben Jarlett (electro-acoustic sound), Clare (October) Allsop, Simon Humm, Jennifer Lewin (performers), Institute of Contemporary Arts, London.

———, dir. 2003. *Xstasis*. Collaborating artists: Howie Bailey (live video), Ben Jarlett (electro-acoustic sound) with Andrea-Jane Cornell, Kafri Rae Seekins, Philip Viel, David Zilbert, Clare Allsop, Simon Humm (performers) with Fajer

Al-Kaisi, Stephanie Bogue Kerr, Laura Burke, Joe Cobden, Lucas Fehr, Vanessa Johnson, Amanda Knapp, Sadia Mahmood, Elkahna Talbi and Jocelyn Wickett. Curatored by Kate Bligh and the Temenos Performance Group. In collaboration with La Place des Arts and Concordia University. Performed outdoors in La Place des Arts Montréal and the Black Watch Drill Hall Montréal (May).

——, dir. 2004. *Space*. Collaborating artists: Howie Bailey (live video), Ben Jarlett (electro-acoustic sound), Performers, actors, dancers: Clare Allsop, Simon Humm, Jeremy Killick, Jennifer Lewin, Hannah Seaton, Nam Eun Song and Alison Williams-Bailey. Curatored by Kerry Irvine. A collaboration with London Borough of Camden and Total Theatre Network. Performed at the Camden Centre (18–19 February).

——. 2001. 'A Telepresence Experiment: Optik in Sao Paulo + London'. *Body, Space, & Technology* 1, no.2. Brunel University http://www.brunel.ac.uk/bst/, accessed 1 June 2005.

——. 2005. Interview by author, Brunel University, West London, UK, June 20.

Edwards, Barry and Ben Jarlett. (2003). 'Sound Capture and Real-Time Composing in Inter-Disciplinary Live Performance'. In MAXIS$_{11}$ 2003: Proceedings of the 2nd Festival & Symposium of Sound and Experimental Music, eds Kia Ng and Scott Daniel Hawkins, 49–53, Interdisciplinary Centre for Scientific Research in Music, School of Music, University of Leeds, UK (April 10–13).

—— .2005. '2005 EDDY Award Winners announced'. *Entertainment Design*. PRIMEDIA Business Magazines & Media Inc (March 30). http://entertainment-designmag.com/masterclasses/eddy_awards_2005/, accessed 16 May 2005.

Eidsvik, Charles. 1988–9. 'Machines of the Invisible: Changes in Film Technology in the Age of Video'. *Film Quarterly* 42, no. 2 (Winter): 18–24.

Eliot, Thomas Stearns. 1994. *Four Quartets*. London: Faber and Faber.

Eshkar, Shelley. 2000. *Summer Dance: Merce Cunningham*. Interview. Dir. Charles Atlas, Executive Producer Sheldon Schwartz. BBC 2 television (August 26).

Farley, Kathryn. 2002. 'Digital Dance Theatre: The Marriage of Computers, Choreography and Techno/Human Reactivity'. *Body, Space & Technology* 3, no.1. Brunel University, http://www.brunel.ac.uk/bst/, accessed 3 May 2005.

Fleming, Chris. 2002. 'Performance as Guerrilla Ontology: The Case of Stelarc'. *Body & Society* 8, no. 3: 95–109.

Foucault, Michel. 1972. *The Archaeology of Knowledge*. Trans. Alan Sheridan. New York: Random House.

——. 1986. *Discipline and Punish: The Birth of The Prison*. Trans. Alan Sheridan. London: Penguin.

Gaeta, John. 1999. Interview, *The Matrix* DVD. Written and directed by Andy and Larry Wachowski, Warner Bros/Village Roadshow Films (BVI) Limited.

——. 2003. 'New Realties: The Matrix Revolutions Completes a Trilogy of Films that Introduced a New Style of Visual Effects'. Interview by Barbara Robertson. *Computer Graphics World* 26, no. 12: 56–4.

Gasché, Rodolphe. 1979. 'Deconstruction as Criticism,' *Glyph* 6: 177–215.

——. 1986. *The Tain of the Mirror: Derrida and the Philosophy of Reflection*. Cambridge, MA: Harvard University Press.

Gibson, William. 1984. *Necromancer*. New York: Ace Books.

Goodall, Jane. 1999. 'An Order of Pure Decision: Un-Natural Selection in the Work of Stelarc and Orlan'. *Body & Society* 5, no, 2–3: 149–170.

Gray, Charles and Wolf Singer. 1989. 'Stimulus-specific Neuronal Oscillations in Orientation Columns of Cat Visual Cortex'. *Proceedings of the National Academy of Sciences* USA 86: 1698–1702.

Gregory, Richard L. 1998. *Eye and Brain: The Psychology of Seeing.* 5th ed. Oxford: Oxford University Press.

Greskovic, Robert. 1999. 'Merce Cunningham'. In *Fifty Contemporary Choreographers*, ed Martha Bremser, pp. 72–4. New York: Routledge.

Harraway, D. 1991. 'A Cyborg Manifesto: Science, Technology and Socialist-Feminism in the Late Twentieth Century'. In *Simians, Cyborgs and Women*, 149–81. New York: Routledge.

Hayles, Katherine N. 1999. *How We Became Posthuman: Virtual Bodies in Cybernetics, Literature and Informatics.* Chicago/London: University of Chicago Press.

Heath, Stephen. 1981. *Questions of Cinema: Essays in Film Theory.* London: Palgrave Macmillan.

Heidegger, Martin. 1971. 'The Origin of The Work of Art'. In *Poetry, Language, Thought*, trans. Albert Hofstadter, 17–87. New York: Harper and Row.

———. 1977. *The Question Concerning Technology and Other Essays.* Trans. William Lovitt. New York: Harper and Row.

———. 1978. *Being and Time.* Trans. John Macquarrie and Edward Robinson. Oxford: Basil Blackwell.

Hirsch, Robert. 2005. 'The Strange Case of Steve Kurtz: Critical Art Ensemble and the Price of Freedom'. *Afterimage* (May–June): 22–32.

Jay, Martin. 1993. *Downcast Eyes: The Denigration of Vision in Twentieth-Century French Thought.* Berkeley, CA: University of California Press.

Jordan, Michael L. and Stuart Russell. 2001. 'Computational Intelligence'. In *The MIT Encyclopedia of the Cognitive Sciences*, eds Robert Wilson and Frank Keil, lxxiii–xc. Cambridge, MA: MIT Press.

Jorgl, Stephanie. 2003. 'Troika Ranch: MIDI-triggered, Mac-based Dance Troupe'. Apple Website www.apple.com/hotnews/articles/2003/03/troikaranch/, accessed 6 May 2005.

Kac, Eduardo. 1998. 'Transgenic Art'. Leonardo Electronic Almanac 6, no. 11, http://mitpress.mit.edu/e-journals/LEA, accessed 20 August 2005.

———. 1999. 'Genesis'. Life Science: Ars Electronica 99 website http://www.aec.at/lifescience/, accessed 27 August 2005.

———. 2001. 'Trans-Genesis: An Interview with Eduardo Kac'. Eduardo Kac interviewed by Lisa Lynch (originally published in *New Formations* 2001). Kac's website http://www.ekac.org/nabout.html, accessed 28 August 2005.

———. 2003. 'GFP Bunny'. *Leonardo.* 36, no. 2: 97–102.

———. 2005a. 'Eduardo Kac: Biographical Note'. Eduardo Kac's website http://www.ekac.org/kacbio600.html, accessed 20 August 2005.

———. 2005b. 'Genesis'. Eduardo Kac's website http://www.ekac.org/geninfo.html accessed 27 August 2005.

———. 2005c. 'GFP Bunny'. Eduardo Kac's website http://www.ekac.org/gfpbunny.html, accessed 28 August 2005.

Kaiser, Paul. 2000. *Summer Dance: Merce Cunningham.* Interview. Dir. Charles Atlas, Executive Producer Sheldon Schwartz. BBC 2 television (August 26).

———. 2004a. 'On Biped'. On-line essay http://www.kaiserworks.com/duoframe/duoonbiped.htm, accessed 10 September.

————. 2004b. Website. http://www.kaiserworks.com/artworks/loops/loopsmain. htm, accessed 12 October.

Kant, Immanuel. 1911. *Critique of Pure Reason*. Trans. Max Müller. London: Macmillan & Co. Ltd.

————. 1978. *The Critique of Judgment*. Trans. James Creed Meredith. Oxford: Clarendon Press.

Katz, S.D. 2005. 'Charting the Stars v.3: With the Lucas Dream Team at Skywalker Ranch'. *Millimeter – The Magazine of Motion Picture and Television Production* 33, no. 4 (April): 16–18, 20, 22, 24.

Kimball, Samuel A. 2001. 'Not Begetting the Future: Technological Autochthony, Sexual Reproduction and the Mythic Structure of *The Matrix*'. *Journal of Popular Culture* 35, no. 3 (Winter): 175–203.

————. 2002. 'Conceptions and Contraceptions of the Future: *Terminator 2, The Matrix and Alien Resurrection*'. *Camera Obscura* 17, no. 2: 69–107.

Kisken, Tom. 1999. 'The Book of "Star Wars"'. Jonathan Young's website www. folkstory.com, accessed 20 January 2006.

Knight, Chris. 2000. 'Midi-Chlorians: Physiology, Physics and the Force'. The Force Net website, http://www.theforce.net/midichlorians, accessed 29 January 2006.

Knoll, John with J.W. Rinzler. 2005. *Creating the Worlds of Star Wars: 365 days*. New York: Harry N. Abrams, Inc.

Kosslyn, Stephen, and Oliver Koenig. 1992. *Wet Mind: The New Cognitive Neuroscience*. New York: Macmillan.

Kosslyn, Stephen, William Thompson and Nathaniel Alpert. 1995. 'Topographical Representations of Mental Images in Primary Visual Cortex'. *Nature* 378: 496–8.

Kosslyn, Stephen and William Thompson. 2000. 'Imagery and Perception'. In *The New Cognitive Neurosciences*, ed. Michael S. Gazzaniga, 975–85. Cambridge MA: MIT Press.

Lancashire, Anne. 2000. '"The Phantom Menace": Repetition, Variation, Integration'. *Film Criticism* 24, no. 3 (Spring): 23–44.

Lane, Anthony. 2005. 'Star Wars: Episode III'. *The New Yorker* 81, no. 14 (May): 94–5.

Lash, Scott. 1990. *Sociology of Postmodernism*. London: Routledge.

Lavery, David. 2001. 'From Cinespace to Cyberspace: Zionists and Agents, Realists and Gamers in the The Matrix and eXistenZ'. *Journal of popular Film and Television*, 28, no. 4 (Winter): 150–7.

Lawrence, Matt. 2004. *Like A Splinter In Your Mind: The Philosophy Behind The Matrix Trilogy*. Maiden, MA/Oxford/Victoria Australia: Blackwell.

Lechte, John. 1994. *Fifty Key Contemporary Thinkers*. London: Routledge.

Lesschaeve, Jacqueline. 1985. *The Dancer and the Dance: In Conversation with Merce Cunningham*. New York: Marion Boyers.

Libet, Benjamin. 1985. 'Unconscious Cerebral Initiative and the Role of Conscious Will in Voluntary Action'. *The Behavioral And Brain Sciences* 8 no. 4: 529–39.

————. 1995, *Neurophysiology of Consciousness: Selected Papers and New Essays*. Boston: Birkhäuser.

Lodge, David. 2002. *Consciousness And The Novel*. London: Secker & Warburg.

Lucas, George, dir. 1999. *Star Wars: Episode I – Phantom Menace*. Written by George Lucas, produced by Rick McCallum, visual effects supervisors: John Knoll, Dennis Mure and Scott Squires, animation director: Rob Coleman, music: John Williams, costume designer: Trisha Biggar. Special visual effects and animation by Industrial Light & Magic. LucasFilm Ltd – Twentieth Century Fox.

———, dir. 2002. *Star Wars: Episode II – Attack of the Clones.* Story by George Lucas, screenplay by George Lucas and Jonathan Hales, produced by Rick McCallum, visual effects supervisors: John Knoll, Pablo Helman, Dennis Muren and Ben Snow, animation director: Rob Coleman, digital matte sequence supervisors: Jonathan Harb, Paul Huston and Yusei Uesugi, Pre-Visualization/Effects Supervisors: Daniel D. Gregoire and David Dozoretz, music: John Williams, costume designer Trisha Biggar. Special visual effects and animation by Industrial Light & Magic. LucasFilm Ltd – Twentieth Century Fox.

———, dir. 2005a. *Star Wars: Episode III –Revenge of the Sith.* Story and screenplay by George Lucas, produced by Rick McCallum, visual effects supervisors: John Knoll and Roger Guyet, animation director: Rob Coleman, digital matte sequence supervisor: Jonathan Harb, Pre-Visualization/Effects Supervisor: Daniel D. Gregoire, music: John Williams, costume designer Trisha Biggar. Special visual effects and animation by Industrial Light & Magic. LucasFilm Ltd – Twentieth Century Fox.

———, dir. 2005b. 'The Chosen One'. Documentary and Featurettes. *Star Wars: Episode III – Revenge of the Sith* DVD – Disc 2. LucasFilm Ltd – Twentieth Century Fox.

———, dir. 2005c. 'Within a Minute: The Making of Episode III'. Documentary and Featurettes. *Star Wars: Episode III – Revenge of the Sith* DVD – Disc 2. LucasFilm Ltd – Twentieth Century Fox.

Lyotard, Jean-François. 1971. *Discours, Figure.* Paris: Klincksieck.

———. 1984. 'Interview'. Interview by Georges Van Den Abbeele. *Diacritics* 14, no. 3 (February): 16–21.

———. 1986a. 'A Response to Philippe Lacoue-Labarthe'. Trans. Geoff Bennington. In *Postmodernism: ICA Documents 4 and 5*, ed. Lisa Appignanesi, 8. London: ICA.

——— 1986b. 'Complexity and the Sublime'. Trans. Geoff Bennington. In *Postmodernism: ICA Documents 4 and 5*, ed. Lisa Appignanesi, 10–12. London: ICA.

———. 1988a. *The Differend.* Trans. Georges Van Den Abbeele. Manchester: Manchester University Press.

———. 1988b. 'An Interview with Jean-François Lyotard'. Interview by Willem van Reijan and Dick Veerman. In *Theory, Culture and Society* 5, trans. Roy Boyne, nos 2–3 (June): 277–309.

———. 1988–9. 'Can Thought Go On Without A Body?' *Discourse* 11, no. 1: 74–87.

———. 1989a. 'Acinema'. Trans. Paisley N. Livingston. In *The Lyotard Reader*, ed. Andrew Benjamin, 169–80. Oxford: Basil Blackwell.

———. 1989b. 'Anamnesis of the Visible, or Candor'. Trans. David Macy. In *The Lyotard Reader*, ed. Andrew Benjamin, 220–39. Oxford: Basil Blackwell.

———. 1989c. 'Beyond Representation'. Trans. Jonathan Culler. In *The Lyotard Reader*, ed. Andrew Benjamin, 155–68. Oxford: Basil Blackwell.

———. 1989d. 'Philosophy and Painting in the Age of their Experimentation: Contribution to an Idea of Postmodernity'. Trans. Mária Minich Brewer and Daniel Brewer. In *The Lyotard Reader*, ed. Andrew Benjamin, 181–95. Oxford: Basil Blackwell.

———. 1989e. 'The Dream Work Does Not Think'. Trans. Mary Lydon. In *The Lyotard Reader*, ed. Andrew Benjamin, 19–55. Oxford: Basil Blackwell.

———. 1989f. 'The Tensor'. Trans. Sean Hand. In *The Lyotard Reader*, ed. Andrew Benjamin, 1–18. Oxford: Basil Blackwell.

————. 1991. *Lessons on the Analytic of the Sublime*. Trans. Elizabeth Rottenberg. Stanford, CA: Stanford University Press.

————. 1993a. *The Inhuman: Reflections on Time*. Trans. Geoffrey Bennington and Rachel Bowlby. Cambridge, UK: Polity Press.

————. 1993b. *The Postmodern Explained*. Trans. Julian Pefanis and Morgan Thomas. Minneapolis, MN: University of Minnesota Press.

Magrid, Ron. 1999. 'Techno Babel: An Exotic Blend of Photographic and Digital Effects Techniques Lend a Distinct Look to an Arcane World in "The Matrix"'. *American Cinematrographer – The International Journal of Film and Digital Production Techniques* 80, no. 4 (April): 46–8, 50, 52–5.

Marsh, Anne. 1993. *Body and Self*. Melbourne: Oxford University Press.

Maxwell, James Clerk. 1872. 'On Colour Vision'. *Proceedings of the Royal Institution of Great Britain* 6: 260–9.

Merleau-Ponty, Maurice. 1962. *Phenomenology of Perception*. Trans. Colin Smith. London: Routledge.

————. 1963. *The Structure of Behavior*. Trans. Alden L. Fisher. Boston: Beacon Press.

————. 1964. 'Cézanne's Doubt'. In *Sense and Non-Sense*, trans. Hubert L. Dreyfus and Patricia A. Dreyfus, 9–25. Evanston: Northwestern University Press.

————. 1974a. 'Eye and Mind'. Trans. Carlton Dallery. In *Phenomenology, Language and Sociology: Selected Essays of Maurice Merleau-Ponty*, ed. John O'Neill, 280–311. London: Heinemann.

————. 1974b. 'The Primacy of Perception'. Trans. James M. Edie. In *Phenomenology, Language and Sociology: Selected Essays of Maurice Merleau-Ponty*, ed. John O'Neill, 196–226. London: Heinemann.

————. 2000. *The Visible and the Invisible*. Ed. Claude Lefort. Trans. Alphonso Lingis. Evanston: Northwestern University Press.

Mitry, Jean. 1965. *Esthétique et psychologie du cinéma*. Vol 2. Paris: Editions Universitaires.

Moltenbray, Karen. 2004. 'Part II: *Making the Matrix*: Battle Plan: *The Matrix* directors previz the high-rev action of *Revolutions*'. *Computer World Graphics* 27, no. 1: 29–31.

Neville, Helen J. 1990. 'Intermodal Competition and Compensation in Development: Evidence from Studies of the Visual System in the Congenitally Deaf Adults'. *Annals of the New York Academy of Science* 608: 71–91.

————. 1995. 'Developmental specificity in neurocognitive development in humans'. In *The Cognitive Neurosciences*, ed. Michael S. Gazzaniga, 219–34. Cambridge MA: MIT Press.

Newman, Kim. 2005. 'Sith Happens: Lead Review: Star Wars Episode III Revenge of the Sith'. *Sight and Sound* 15, no. 7 (July): 38–9.

Nietzsche, Friedrich. 1956. *The Birth of Tragedy and The Genealogy of Morals*. Trans. by Francis Golffing. New York: Doubleday Anchor Books.

O'Hehir, Andrew. 1999. 'Soft War'. Reviews. *Sight and Sound* 9, no. 7: 34–5.

'On with the Show: Why Scientists Should Support an Artist in Trouble'. Editorial. *Nature* 429, no. 6993: 685.

Penfield, Wilder and Theodore Rasmussen. 1950. *The Cerebral Cortex of Man: A Clinical Study of Localization of Function*. New York: Mcmillan.

Pefanis, Julian. 1991. *Heterology and the Postmodern: Bataille, Baudrillard and Lyotard*. Sydney: Allen & Unwin.

Priest, Stephen. 2003. *Merleau-Ponty*. London: Routledge.

Probst, Christopher. 1999. 'Welcome to the Machine: Directors Larry and Andy Wachowski Reteam with Cinematographer Bill Pope on the Futuristic, Eye-Popping Action Thriller "The Matrix"'. *American Cinematographer – The International Journal of Film & Digital Production Techniques* 80, no. 4 (April 1999): 32–6, 38, 40, 42–4.

Puckette, Miller. 2005. 'Some Mathematical Tools for Music-Making'. In *Art + Mathematics = X*: International Conference Proceedings, ed. Carla Farsi. University of Colorado, Boulder, Colorado (June 2–5).

Ramachandran, V.S. 2003. 'Lecture 5: Neuroscience – The New Philosophy'. *BBC – Radio 4 – Reith Lectures – The Emerging Brain*, http://www.bbc.co.uk/radio4/reith2003/, accessed 6 May 2004.

———. 2004. *Horizon: Derek Tastes of Earwax*. Interview. Prod. Aidan Laverty, BBC television (Thursday 30 September).

Ramachandran, V.S. and Sandra Blakeslee. 1999. *Phantoms In The Brain*. New York: Quill.

Ramachandran, V.S. and William Hirstein. 1999. 'The Science of Art: A Neurological Theory of Aesthetic Experience'. *Journal of Consciousness Studies* 6–7: 15–51.

Ramachandran, V.S. and Edward M. Hubbard. 2001. Synaesthesia: A Window into Perception, Thought and Language'. *Journal of Consciousness Studies* 8, no. 12: 3–34.

Reynolds, Dee. 2000. 'Displacing "Humans": Merce Cunningham's Crowds'. *Body, Space, & Technology* 1, no.1. Brunel University http://www.brunel.ac.uk/bst/, accessed 24 November 2004.

Roberts, Adam. 2000. *Science Fiction*. London: Routledge.

Robertson, Barbara. 1999a. 'Living A Virtual Existence: New Visual-Effects Techniques Help Depict the Extreme Environments in *The Matrix*'. *Computer Graphics World* 22, no. 5 (May): 54–5.

———. 1999b. 'Star Wars: Super Models'. *Computer Graphics World* 22, no. 5 (May): 39–44.

———. 1999c. 'Star Wars: Using Digital Tools to Handcraft a Fantastic World'. *Computer Graphics World* 22, no. 6 (June): 24–34.

———. 2002a. 'Attack of the Clones: The First of a Two-Part Series'. *Computer Graphics World* 25, no. 6 (June): 16–21.

———. 2002b. 'Attack of the Clones: The Second of a Two-Part Series'. *Computer Graphics World* 25, no. 7 (July): 20–6.

———. 2003. 'Part I: *Making the Matrix: The Matrix*'. *Computer Graphics World* 26, no. 12 (December): 22–8.

———. 2005. 'Dark and Stormy Knight'. *Computer Graphics World* 28, no.6 (June): 10–15.

Rossing, Thomas D., F. Richard Moore and Paul A. Wheeler. 2002. *The Science of Sound*. 3rd edition. San Francisco: Addison Wesley.

Ryle, Gilbert. 1976. *The Concept of Mind*. Harmondsworth: Penguin.

Romanyshyn, Robert D. 1989. *Technology as Symptom and Dream*. London: Routledge.

Rovan, Joseph Butch, Robert Wechsler and Frieder Weiss. 2001. 'Artistic Collaboration in an Interactive Dance and Music Performance Environment: *Seine hohle Form*, a project report'. *Body Space and Technology Journal* 2, no. 1. Brunel University http://www.brunel.ac.uk/bst/, accessed 24 January 2005.

Rucker, Rudolf V.B. 1989. *Wetware*. Massachusetts: New English Library.

Ruthrof, Horst. 1997. *Semantics and The Body: Meaning from Frege to the Postmodern*. Toronto: University of Toronto Press.

Sacks, Oliver. 1986. *The Man Who Mistook his Wife for a Hat and Other Clinical Tales*. London: Picador.

Scarry, Siobhan. 1999. 'Devising the Digital Dance'. *Wired News*. http://www/wired/com/news/, accessed 20 April 2004.

Schneider, Rebecca. 2000. 'Nomadmedia: On Critical Art Ensemble'. *The Drama Review* 44, no. 4: 120–31.

Smith, Steve. 1998. 'Brief Introduction to FMRI'. University of Oxford website. http://www.fmrib.ox.ac.uk/fmri_intro/brief.html, accessed 28 August 2004.

Solomon, Alisa. 2005. 'Terror Hysteria Gone Absurdist'. *The Nation*. http://www.thenation.com/doc/20050801/solomon, accessed 10 August 2005.

Stanier, Philip. 2001. 'Blue Bloodshot Flowers: Text for Performance'. *Body, Space, & Technology* 1, no. 2. Brunel University http://www.brunel.ac.uk/bst/, accessed 27 January 2004.

Stelarc. 1996. *Fractal Flesh: Split Body: Voltage in/Voltage Out*. Presentation. Software developed by Gary Zebinton, Dimitri Arononv and the Merlin Group in Sydney. Perth Institute of Contemporary Art, courtesy of the Cyberminds Conference hosted by the School of Design, Curtin University, Western Australia, 28 November.

———. 1995. 'Electronic Voodoo'. Interview by Nicholas Zurbrugg. *21C* 2: 44–9.

———. 1999. 'In Dialogue with 'Posthuman' Bodies: Interview with Stelarc'. Interview by Ross Farnell. *Body & Society* 5, nos 2–3: 129–47.

———. 1997. 'From Psycho to Cyberstrategies: Prosthetics, Robotics and Remote Existence'. *Cultural Values* 1, no. 2: 241–9.

———. 1998. 'Telematic Tremors, Telematic Pleasures: Stelarc's Internet Performances'. Interview by Nicholas Zurbrugg. In *Carnal Pleasures: Desire, Public Space and Contemporary Arts*, ed. Anna Novakov. Berkeley, CA: Clamor.

———. 2000. *Movatar*. Construction of motion prosthesis: Stefan Doepner, Gwendoline Taub and Jan Cummerow; Controller and Programming: Lars Vaupel; Sound and System Design: Rainer Linz. Premier was for Cybercultures at the Casula Powerhouse Arts Centre, 19 September.

———. 2002a. 'Towards a Compliant Coupling: Pneumatic Projects, 1998–2001'. In *The Cyborg Experiments: The Extensions of the Body in the Media Age*, eds Joanna Zylinska and Gary Hall, 73–8. London/New York: Continuum.

———. 2002b. 'Probings: An Interview with Stelarc'. Interview by Joanna Zylinska and Gary Hall. In *The Cyborg Experiments: The Extensions of the Body in the Media Age*, eds Joanna Zylinska and Gary Hall, 114–30. London/New York: Continuum.

———. 2003a. *Muscle Machine*. Performance Premiere. A collaboration involving the Digital Research Unit, Nottingham Trent University and the Evolutionary and Adaptive Systems Group, COGS at Sussex University. Project coordinator: Barry Smith (DRU, TNTU); robot consultant: Inman Harvey (COGS, Sussex University); development/project manager: Philip Breedon (FaCCT, TNTU); choreography: Sophia Lycouris (DRU, TNTU); sensor technology & sound producer: Stan Wijnans (DRU, TNTU); Project support – Pneumatic circuits & systems – Kerry Truman (FaCCT, TNTU); Computer Aided Design – John Grimes (FaCCT, TNTU); Leg design – Lee Houston; Final year BSc Product Design Student. Manufacturing support – Alan Chambers

(FaCCT, TNTU); 3-D Model and Animation – Steve Middleton, Melbourne. 291 Gallery, East London July 1.

———. 2003b. *Prosthetic Head*. Collaboration involving Karen Marcelo – project coordination, system configuration, alicebot customization, Sam Trychin from Eyematic – customization of 3-D animation and test to speech software and Barrett Fox – 3-D modelling and animation. ICA, London, 12 March 2003.

———. 2003c. 'Stelarc, Robot and Mostafa'. Interview and video by Mostafa Yarmahmoudi. At the Premiere of *Muscle Man*, 291 Gallery, East London.

———. 2003d. 'Talking Heads: Listening to Stelarc'. Interview by Gary Hall and Joanna Zylinska. In *Live Art Letters: A Live Art Research Journal*. Nottingham: Live Art Archives at Nottingham Trent University.

———. 2004a. 'The Hum of the Hybrid,' Stelarc's website http://www.stelarc.va. com.au/hybhum/hybhum.html, accessed 23 November 2004.

———. 2004b. 'Stomach Sculpture'. Stelarc's website including video. http://www. stelarc.va.com.au/stomach/stomach.html, accessed 21 November 2004.

———. 2004c 'Stelarc ¼ Scale Ear'. Stelarc's website http://www.stelarc.va. com.au/extra_ear/index.htm, accessed 20 November 2004.

Stoppiello, Dawn. 2003. 'Fleshmotor'. *Leonardo Electronic Almanac* 11, no. 12 (December) http://mitpress2.mit.edu/e-journals/LEA, accessed 3 May 2005.

Thompson, Seth. 2003. 'Evolving Traditions'. *Afterimage* 31, no. 3 (Nov/Dec): 12–13.

Telotte, J.P. 2001. 'Film and/as Technology: Assessing a Bargain'. *Journal of Popular Film and Television* 28, no. 3 (Winter): 146–9.

Travers, Peter. 2002. 'Episode II – Attack of the Clones'. *Rolling Stone* 897 (June): 83.

Troika Ranch. 1996. *The Electronic Disturbance*. Created by Mark Coniglio and Dawn Stoppiello. Performed by Dawn Stoppiello, Gail Giovaniello, Lana Halvorsen, Rose Marie Hegenbart, Ernie Lafky and Joan La Barbara. The Kitchen, New York (April).

———. 2000. *The Chemical Wedding of Christian Rosenkreutz*. Created by Mark Coniglio and Dawn Stoppiello. Performed by Dawn Stoppiello, Mark Coniglio, Danielle Goldman, Anthony Gongora, Michou Szabo, Sandra Tillett, Diane Vivona and Pam Wagner. Premiered at HERE Art Centre, New York (June).

———. 2003. *The Future of Memory*. Created by Mark Coniglio and Dawn Stoppiello. Performed by Dawn Stoppiello, Danielle Goldman, Michou Szabo and Sandra Tillett. Premiered at The Duke, 42nd Street, New York (February).

———. 2004. *Surfacing*. Choreographer: Dawn Stoppiello. Music & Video: Mark Coniglio. Costume Design: Wendy Winters. Lighting Design: Susan Hamburger. Set Design: David Judelson. Performed by Danielle Goldman, Patrick Mueller, Michou Szaabo and Sandra Tillett. Premiered at Danspace Project, New York (May). I attended a performance at Chancellor Hall, Essex, 12 May 2005.

Turim, Maureen. 1984. 'Desire in Art and Politics: The Theories of Jean-François Lyotard'. *Camera Obscura* 12 (Summer): 90–106.

Turner, Victor. 1990. 'Are There Universals of Performance in Myth, Ritual and Drama?' In *By Means of Performance*, eds Richard Schechner and Willa Appel, 1–18. Cambridge: Cambridge University Press.

Vaughan, David. 1997. 'Chronicle and Commentary'. In *Merce Cunningham: Fifty Years*, ed. Melissa Harris. New York: Aperture.

———. 2000. '"A way of looking": Merce Cunningham & Biped'. *The Dancing Times* (Oct) 61–3.

Van Gennep, Arnold. 1960. *The Rites of Passage*. Trans. Monika B. Vizedom and Gabrielle L. Caffee. Chicago, IL: Chicago University Press.

Virilio, Paul. 1991. *The Lost Dimension*. Trans. Daniel Moshenberg. New York: Semitext(e).

Wachowski, Andy and Larry Wachowski, dirs. 1999. *The Matrix*. Written by the Wachowski brothers, produced by Joel Silver, director of photography: Bill Pope, visual effects: John Gaeta, Kung Fu choreographer: Yuen Wo Ping, music by Don Davis.

Warner Bros (US/Canada/Bahamas/Bermuda)/Village Roadshow (all other territories).

———. dirs. 2003a. *The Matrix Reloaded*. Written by the Wachowski brothers, produced by Joel Silver, director of photography: Bill Pope, visual effects: John Gaeta, Kung Fu choreographer: Yuen Wo Ping, music by Don Davis. Warner Bros (US/Canada/Bahamas/Bermuda)/Village Roadshow (all other territories).

———. dirs. 2003b. *The Matrix Revolutions*. Written by the Wachowski brothers, produced by Joel Silver, director of photography: Bill Pope, visual effects: John Gaeta, Kung Fu choreographer: Yuen Wo Ping, music by Don Davis. Warner Bros (US/Canada/Bahamas/Bermuda)/Village Roadshow (all other territories).

Ward, Jamie. 2004. *Horizon: Derek Tastes of Earwax*. Interview. Producer Aidan Laverty, BBC television (Thursday 30 September).

Warwick, Kevin. 2000. 'Cyborg 1.0'. *Wired* 8.02 (February). http://www.wired.com/wired/archive/8.02/warwick, accessed 12 December 2005.

Waters, Keith. 1987. 'A Muscle Model for Animating Three-Dimensional Facial Expressions'. *Computer Graphics* 21, no. 4: 17–24.

———. 1999–2004. 'Decface'. Mediaport.net. http://www.mediaport.net/CP/CyberScience/BDD/fich_055.en.html, accessed 27 March 2004.

Waters, Keith, James Rehg, Maria Loughlin, Sing Bing Kang and Demetri Terzopoulos. 1998. 'Visual Sensing of Humans for Active Public Interfaces. In *Computer Vision for Human-Machine Interaction*, eds R. Cipolla and A. Pentland, 83–96. Cambridge, UK: Cambridge University Press.

Wechsler, Robert. 2004. 'Palindrome: A Critical Perspective and Interview'. Interview by Jane Frere and Mostafa Yarmahmoudi. *Body, Space & Technology* 4. Brunel University http://www.brunel.ac.uk/bst/, accessed 6 January 2005.

Wechsler, Robert and Frieder Weiss. 2004a. 'Motion Sensing for Interactive Dance'. *IEEE-Pervasive Computing, Mobile and Ubiquitous Systems* 3, no. 1 (Jan–March) 35–7.

———. 2004b. Palindrome Inter.media Performance Group home page http://www.palindrome.de, accessed 12 December.

Wells, Jeffrey. 2002. 'The "Matrix" Sequels'. *Rolling Stone*, no. 906 (March 10): 75–7.

Winkler, Todd. 1999. *Composing Interactive Music: Techniques and Ideas Using Max*. Cambridge, MA: MIT Press.

Young, Jonathan. 2004. 'A Scholar's Life'. Jonathan Young website www.folkstory.com, accessed 20 January 2006.

Zeki, Semir. 1999. *Inner Vision: An Exploration of Art and the Brain*. Oxford: Oxford University Press.

Zeman, Adam. 2002. *Consciousness: A User's Guide*. London: Yale University Press.

Zurr, Ionat and Oron Catts. 2003. 'The Ethical Claims of Bioart: Killing the Other or Self-Cannibalism'. The Tissue Culture & Art Project website hosted by SymbioticA, University of Western Australia. http://www.tca.uwa.edu.au/publication/TheEthicalClaimsofBioart.pdf, accessed 1 September 2005.

Index

Achromatopsia, 48, 55
aesthetic theorization, 2, 7, 19–46
AI (artificial intelligence), 1, 6, 9, 11,
 13, 31, 69, 71, 72, 133, 140,
 187–8
Animatronic, 14, 146, 154
Andrews, Lori B, 165
art and perception, 57–60
Auslander, Philip, 194
Avatar, 11, 17 n.1, 18 n.18, 37, 41, 55,
 59, 66, 69, 70–6, 78, 84–7, 93,
 98 n.12, 185, 187–8, 194

Baudrillard, Jean, 14, 88, 132–7, 158,
 159 n.1
 Hyperreality, 15
 Simulation, 14, 132–4, 136–7,
  158,159 n.1
Bazin, André, 158, 160 n.7
 Total Cinema, 158
Bioart, 15, 20, 32, 41, 50, 64, 95,
 161–84, 186, 192–3
 and ethics, 96, 164
biosemiotics, 161
Blakeslee, Sandra, 7, 8, 9, 17 n.12, 18
 n.14, 51, 57, 59, 63–4, 66, 68
 n.15, 73, 97, 140, 188
Blue Bloodshot Flowers, 18 n.18, 25, 36,
 37, 41, 55, 56, 62, 66, 69–77,
 90, 97, 185, 187, 191, 194
 avatar, as extension and
  modification of human being,
  66, 73, 97
Berland, Elodie, 70–3
Bessel, David, 70–3
Bowden, Richard, 70, 71–2, 74, 76,
 97 n.1, n.4
 DECface, 71, 74
 face recognition, 54, 72, 188
 Gaussian mixture model
  of colour, 75
 Geoface technology, 71, 74
 Grimson motion tracker, 75, 97 n.4

'Intelligence, Interaction, Reaction,
 and Performance', 69–77
Jeremiah, 11, 37, 55, 67, 69–77, 97
 n.4, 185, 187–8
Kaewtrakulpong, Pakorn, 74
Lewin, Martin, 74
Stanier, Philip, 70, 97 n.2
surveillance technology, 11, 70–1,
 97 n.4, 187
Turing test, 76
Unpredictability, 73
body, delimited, 23, 69, 91, 97, 153,
 186–7
 of potential and infinite creativity,
  21, 24, 43, 79, 187, 194
 primary, 16, 66, 186
 transient, 16, 66, 186
 virtual, 1, 6, 1, 21, 64, 115,
  134, 187
brain, anatomy of, 8, 50–7
 fusiform gyrus, 54–5, 58, 67 n.6

cortex, 9, 48, 50–61, 67 n.3, n.4,
 89, 182
 and neurons, 8–9, 17 n.12, 18 n.14,
  50, 53–4, 60–4, 67 n.3, n.8,
  68 n.11, 84
 frontal lobe, 58–9, 117
 activation of the middle frontal
  convolution, 58–9, 117
 as location of thinking and
  planning, 57
 as response to elements of the
  unusual, 58–9
 when viewing non-
  representational colour, 58
 functional, functions of, 9, 48–57,
  61, 62, 66
 limbic system, 59, 63, 66, 84
 mapping, 50, 66, 67 n.1, 184 n.14
 regional encroachment of, 51
 visual areas of, 7, 50, 53–4, 57, 59,
  67 n. 8, 68 n.11, 84

211

cortex—*continued*
  unification of processing systems,
    50, 54, 61, 116, 182, 190
CGI (computer generated image), 14,
    143, 157
Chalmers, David, 60, 62–3
cognitive neuroscience, 6–8, 10, 17
    n.5, 6
Colebrook, Claire, 5, 17 n.10
Collage, 10–11, 13, 48, 81, 123,
    171, 192
Consciousness, as computational or
    neural mechanism, 62
  and the digital, 60–8
  as final frontier, 60, 192
  and free will, 8, 64–66, 139–40
    readiness potential, 65, 140
  integration of experience, 54, 61,
    116, 182, 190
  multiple consciousnesses, 50, 54
  NCC (neuronal correlate of
    consciousness), 9, 18 n.16,
    60–1, 63, 182
  neural binding, 62
  qualia, 8–9, 63–4, 168, 193
  self, emotional responses, 66,
    73, 148, 188
  as evolutionary device, 66
  appropriation of objects, 66,
    97, 188
  (GSR) galvanic skin response,
    7, 66
  love and identity, 66
  executive, 64–5, 140
  passionate, 64
  unified, 64
Copeland, Roger, 11, 79, 81, 83
  Collage, 11, 81
  Montage, 10, 81
Crick, Frances, 8–9, 18 n.15, 47–63,
    67 n.3, n.8, n.10, 68 n.11,
    181–2, 194
  NCC (neuronal correlate of
    consciousness), 9, 60–1, 182
  neural binding, 62
  working memory, 61
Critical Arts Ensemble (CAE), 15, 18
    n.24, 168–76, 193
  and multimedia, 16, 169, 173, 193

  as tactical mediaists, 15, 169, 193
  Barker, George, 170
  Barnes, Steve, 169–70, 176
  Bucher, Claudia, 170
  Burr, Dorian, 170, 176
  Costa, Beatriz da, 172, 176
  digital technology, 170
    electronic information, 170
    nomadic, 38, 170
  Dominguez, Ricardo, 170
  Ferrell, Bob, 172, 175
  Flesh Machine, 15, 18 n.24, 171
  Free Range Grain, 16, 175–6, 183
    n.9, 193
  Genterra, 16, 172–4, 183 n.8
  genetic engineering, 16, 172
  genetically modified organisms
    (GMOs), 168, 172
  Kauffman, Linda, 172
  Kurtz, Hope, 170, 175
  Kurtz, Steve, 169–76
    and bioterrorism, 175, 192–3
  Molecular Invasion, The, 174
    contestational biology, 174
  recombinant theatre, 15, 168–9,
    186, 193
  Schlee, Bev, 170, 176
  Shyu, Shyh-shiun, 176
  Society for Reproductive Anachronisms,
    15, 18 n.24, 172
  Transgenics, 168, 172–4, 193
Cunningham, Merce, 11, 29, 34, 37,
    59, 65, 77–86, 111, 185, 188
  and computer terminology, 83
  anti-dramatic, 81
  BIPED, 11, 18 n.19, 29, 34, 37, 41,
    59, 77–86, 111,
    185, 187–8
  Amkraut, Susan, 83
  and evolution, 83
  and television channel surfing,
    79, 188
  Biped (software), 84–5
  Bryers, Gavin, 85
  Character Studio, 83–4
  Collage, 81
  DanceForms, 78, 85
  Eshkar, Shelley, 11, 77–86
  Gallo, Suzanne, 85

Girard, Michael, 83
Kaiser, Paul, 11, 77–86
Philips, Jarad, 79
Steele, Jeannie, 79–83
Cage, John, 81–3, 85, 98 n.6
chance principle, 82
discrete elements of performance, 79
Hand-drawn Spaces, 78, 83–4
Loops, 83, 97 n.8
movement as non-reference, 80
polyvocal, 81
Rejection of traditional notions of space, 80
Sixteen Dancers for Soloist and Company of Three, 82
Split Sides, 82, 97 n.7
Trackers, 78
Walkaround Time, 83
Cybernetics, 86, 88, 91, 95, 97 n.9
Cyborg, 88–90

Danks, Mark, 109
Defamiliarization, 10, 14, 28, 49, 117, 140, 191
Deleuze, Gilles (with Guattari, Félix), 5, 37–46, 75, 86, 92, 99, 127–8, 131, 138, 146, 150, 155, 164, 170, 191
affects and percepts, 42
an experience, connections of, 39
and experimentation, 17 n.11, 41–3, 75, 99
arboreal, 38, 170
art as, sensation, 42–3, 46 n.20
force, 43, 75
becoming, 38–9, 41, 43, 80, 86, 92, 128, 150, 164, 191
aesthetic-becoming, 43
becoming-animal, 41
becoming-other, 43
becoming-woman, 41
BWO (bodies without organs), 5, 17 n11, 40, 41–3, 86, 92, 128, 191
intense and intensive body, 40, 86, 92, 128, 191
thresholds, 40–1, 86
cinema, movement image, 146
time-image, 146
desire, as affirmation, 43

deterritorialized, 39
difference, 5, 38, 41–2, 170
difference and repetition, 5, 37
everyday experience, 175
intensities, 5, 37–43, 75, 86, 154, 191
machinic metaphors, desiring-machines, 39–41, 128, 191
machinic assemblage of bodies, 37, 39, 191
paranoiac machine, 41
social machines, 38
Nietzsche, Friedrich, 38, 138, 170
Nomadology, 37, 45 n.17
Oedipalization, 39–40
Philosophy, as critical enterprise, 37
Reterritorialized, 39–40
Rhizomes, 38, 43, 45 n.18
Schizophrenics, 39–40
De Menezes, Marta, 16, 20, 28, 50, 60, 177–84, 186, 193–4
aestheticizing evolution, 182
functional magnetic resonance (fMRI), 16, 60
Functional Portraits, 16, 60, 177, 181–2, 186, 193
modification of phenotypical features, 185–6
Nature?, 16, 28, 177–83, 193
NucleArt, 177, 180, 183 n.13
and FISH (Fluorescence In-Situ Hybridization), 180
Proteic Portrait, 177, 180
Tree of Knowledge, 50, 181
and neuronal processes, 181
Derrida, Jacques, 2, 4–5, 19, 29–36, 46 n.16, 79, 80, 88, 102, 104, 137, 159 n.3, 160 n.5, 167, 170, 173, 188, 194
absence, 4, 34, 36, 137, 173
Artaud, Antonin, 5, 32–3, 40, 45 n.12, n.13
Theater of Cruelty, 33, 45 n.13
Augenblick, 30
contamination of 'virtual' and 'live', 4, 36
deconstruction, 4, 31–2, 36, 45 n.11, 148
de Saussure, Ferdinand, 33
difference, to differ and defer, 33

Derrida, Jacques—*continued*
  Gasché, Rodolphe, 32, 45 n.11,
    n.15, 80
  double nature of Derrida's decon-
    struction, 32
  Husserl, Edmund, 30, 35
  identity, formation and
    deformation, 4, 5, 36, 37
  interconnectedness of senses, 30
  interiority and exteriority of text,
    137
  Lévi-Strauss, Claude, 33
  mark, 34
  metaphor and metaphoricity, 36, 45
    n.16, 160 n.5
  metaphysical complicity, 31, 36, 191
  origin, 4–5,11, 29, 34–5, 37
  phonocentrism, 32–3
  plenitude of presence, 31
  presence, metaphysics of, 30
  primacy of perception, 30
  primacy of speech over writing, 30
  repetition, 33–4, 37, 45 n.13
  speech, 30–3, 35
  supplement, 34
  'The Theater of Cruelty and the
    Closure of Representation', 33
  Trace, 31–2, 34, 45 n.14, 79, 173
  Truth, 4, 32
  Writing, *écriture*, 31
    techné, 34
    teletechnology, 35
digital paint, 1, 14, 147, 153
digital practices, aesthetic features
    and traits of, 10, 12, 17 n.4, 33,
    75, 145, 190–1
  centrality of technology, 9, 131
  chthonic, 10, 13, 17 n.4, 18 n.17,
    23, 133, 140, 190
  corporeal prominence, 16, 163
  delimited body, 69, 91, 97, 153,
    186–7
  fragmentation, 1, 33, 75, 145, 191
  heterogeneity, heterogeneous,10,
    12, 17 n.4, 25, 27, 45 n.9, 66,
    75, 170, 191
  hybridization, 5, 10, 41, 69, 75,
    161, 180, 191
  immediacy, 10, 16, 30, 33, 64, 157

indeterminacy, 10, 12, 33, 65, 69,
    75, 164, 191
  indifferent differentiation, 194
  repetition, 10, 75, 85, 145, 191
Dixon, Steve, 126

electronic sound technology, 99–130
  GEM (Graphics Environment for
    Multimedia), 109
  Max, 12, 99, 107–9, 112,
    129 n.6, 189
  MIDI (musical instrument data
    interface), 12, 99, 106–7, 189
  OSC (open sound control), 99, 107,
    129 n.5, 189
  Pd (pure data), 109, 130 n.7
embodied experience, 3, 20, 23–4,
    117, 120, 186–7

Figueiredo, Patricia, 184 n.15
Foucault, Michel, 4, 146, 158–9, 175
  subject positions, 158–9, 175
  as vacant site, 158, 175
functional magnetic resonance
    (fMRI), 16, 60, 177, 181–2, 184
    n.14, 193

Gesamtkunstwerke (collective works of
    art), 10, 81, 107
Gibson, William, 90, 133
Goodall, Jane, 89, 91, 93
Guattari, Félix, 5, 17 n.11, 37–46, 75,
    86, 99, 127, 128, 138, 150, 164,
    170, 191–2

Harraway, Donna, 90
Hayles, Katherine, 86, 91, 14
  Cybernetics, 86, 91
  delimited body, 91, 134
  posthuman, 91, 134
Heidegger, Martin, 3, 4, 35, 150, 185
  era of technology, 35, 150
  gestell, 35
  techné, 35
Helmholtz, Herman von, 8, 49
  unconscious inference, 8, 49
Henschen, Salomon, 53
  retina and primary visual cortex
    (V1), 53

Hirstein, William, 59–60, 84
Hubbard, Edward M., 55, 57, 67 n.6,
     75, 144,192,
interactive design, 1
intersemiotic, 12, 64, 69, 76, 120,
     163, 186
Kac, Eduardo, 15, 41, 62, 64, 161–8,
     183 n.1, n.2, n.4, n.5, 186, 192,
     195 n.2
  Alba, 15, 64, 161–8, 192
  Biotelematics, 1, 162
  ethical concerns, 161, 163, 167
  Genesis, 41, 164–5, 183 n.1
  GFP (green fluorescent protein), 15,
     163
  Houdebine, Louis-Marie, 166
  networking, 15, 162
  *Ornitorrinco, the Webot, travels
     around the world in eighty
     nanoseconds going from Turkey to
     Peru and back*, 162
  Robotics, 15, 162
  Teleporting an Unknown State, 163
  Telepresence, 15, 162
  Transgenics, 15, 161
     transgenic art, 15, 161–2, 164–5,
       167, 186, 192
  verbal and non-verbal
     communication, 162
Kant, Immanuel, 2, 3, 4, 10, 17 n.13,
     24, 50, 162
  aesthetic judgment, 17 n.13,
     58–9
  complex judgment, 7
  reflective reason, 17 n.13
  sublime, 10, 59, 162
Kimball, Samuel, 13, 135, 138, 190
  Autochthony, 13, 13, 190
Koch, Christof, 9, 60–1, 62, 63, 182
Koenig, Olivier, 6–7, 48, 154
Kosslyn, Stephen, 6–7, 48, 53, 155
  perception differentiated from
     imagery, 6–7, 48, 154
  visual imagery, 6–7, 48, 154
     depictive imagery, 53
  wet mind, 6
  working memory, 61

Lacan, Jacques, desire as lack, 5
Lash, Scott, 195 n.4
  indifferent differentiation, 194,
     195 n.4
Lavery, David, 158
Libet, Benjamin, 61, 65, 140, 182
  free will, 65, 139– 40
  readiness potential, 65, 140
liminal, 1–2, 16–17 n.4, 67 n.2, 69,
     88, 149,169, 186, 194
  spaces, 1–2, 67 n.2, 69, 88, 194
  thresholds, 40, 41, 86
  Turner, Victor, 16–17 n.4
Lodge, David, 8, 9, 68 n.13
  consciousness, 8, 9
Logocentrism, 32, 33
Lucas, George, 13–14, 131,
     146–59, 191
  and Joseph Campbell,148–50
  the hero's journey, 148–9
  The Hero With a Thousand Faces,
     148–9
  animatronic models and
     techniques, 14, 146, 154
  Chewbacca, problems of
     ageing, 154
  blue and green screen composite
     imaging, 14, 155, 159 n.4, 190–1
  computer generated imagery, 14,
     147, 151, 191
  complex environments, 156
     Mustafar, 14, 147, 151, 191
  digital characters, 14, 146, 153
     animation of clothing, 52, 154
     clones, 147–8, 153
     Jar Jar Binks, 147, 151, 158, 187
     problems of age, 154
     Watto, 152
     Yoda, 154
  HD (high definition), 14, 153, 154
  Industrial, Light & Magic (ILM),
     131, 147, 152–4
  Knoll, John, 153, 155–7
  Lucasfilm, 147
  matte-digital paint, 14, 147, 153
  Maya (software), 154, 156
  midi-chlorians, 151
  Mocap (motion capture), 14,
     152–3, 188

Lucas, George—*continued*
previz (previsualization), 14, 152, 158
simulation, 152, 156, 158
Skywalker Ranch, 149, 157
Star Wars prequels, 13, 21, 26, 37,
131, 146–60, 186, 190–91
and technological culture, 148
Episode 1: Phantom Menace, 13,
146–7, 149, 151–3, 157, 187
*Episode11: Attack of the Clone*s, 13,
146–8, 153–4
Episode 111: Revenge of the Sith,
146–7, 154–7
organic versus technology, 150
3D modelling and animation, 13,
14, 131, 147, 156–7
Zenviro (camera mapping tool),
14, 156–7
Star Wars sequels, 148–51, 11
*Star Wars: Episode 1V - The New
Hope*, 146, 148
*Episode V - The Empire Strikes
Back*, 146
Episode V1 - The Return of the Jedi,
146
Lyotard, Jean-François, 3–4, 17 n.8,
19, 24–9, 44 n.6, n.7, n.8, 45
n.10, 70, 76, 88, 90, 123–4,
162, 179, 191–4
acinema, 28
aestheticization of the political, 24
anamnesis, 45 n.10
'Can Thought Go On Without A
Body?', 90
Cézanne, Paul, 26, 44 n.7, n.8
differend, 25, 28, 44 n.6
discourse, 3, 24–9, 44 n.6
Discours, figure, 25–7
'The Dream-Work Does Not
Think', 27
experimentation, 4, 2, 27, 29
figural, 3, 25–9
figure, figure-forme, 20
figure-image, 26
figure-matrix, 26
Freud, Sigmund, 27–8, 123–4, 192
industrial and postindustrial
technosciences, 4, 28–9,
179, 194

intensities, 3, 4, 26–8, 76, 191
Klee, Paul, 45 n.8
Lacan, Jacques, 27–8
libidinal economy, 4, 27–9, 44–45
n.8, 124, 179, 193–4
Merleau-Ponty, Maurice, 26, 44 n.7
Metaphor, 27–8, 123–4, 192
Metonymy, 27, 123–4, 192
Structuralism, 27
Sublime, 3–4, 24–5, 28–9, 162
Linguistic, 3–4, 28–9,162

Memory, hippocampus, 57–8
working memory, 61
Merleau-Ponty; Maurice, 2–3,
17 n.6, n.7, 19–24, 26, 43 n.1,
44 n.2, n.3, n.4, n.5, n.7, 90,
94, 98 n.10, 101, 111, 120, 159,
178, 187
Body, as 'mediator of a world', 23
as medium for creating a world
lived, 21
system of possible actions, 21, 23,
159, 187
chiasm, 3, 17 n.6, 21–2, 23, 26, 44
n.4, 101
consciousness, 2–3, 20, 22, 44 n.4
corporeal turn, 19
de Saussure, Ferdinand, 22
experience, embodied, 3, 20, 23–4,
120, 186–7
lived, 3, 20, 101
'Eye and Mind', 20
Flesh, 3, 17 n.6, 20–3, 44 n.2, n.3
flesh of the world, 17 n.6, 20
massive flesh, 21, 3
reversibility, 21, 23
instrumentation, 23, 24, 94, 186–7
interaction of language and
perception, 22
intertwining, 3, 17 n.6, 20–4, 44
n.4, 101, 187
Lacan, Jacques, 21
Mute, 20, 22–3, 26, 44 n.5, 178
thinking, 22
vision, 23
perception, 2–3, 19–23, 159, 178
The Phenomenology of Perception,
19, 22

Primordial, 20, 22–3, 27, 178
The Structure of Behaviour, 22
virtual body, 21, 187
visible, 17 n.6, 21–3, 44 n.2, n.7,
    159
    invisible, 17 n.6, 21–3, 159
    four layers of, 44 n.4
    non-visible, 44 n.4
The Visible and The Invisible, 20
Montage, 10–11, 13, 81
motion capture, 11, 13, 14, 16 n.1,
    69, 77, 79, 83–4, 87, 93, 141,
    152–3, 156, 187–8
motion tracking, 1, 126, 187
Muybridge, Edward, 141
Locomotion, 141

NCC (neuronal correlate of
    consciousness), 9, 18 n.16,
    60–1, 63, 182
Neville, Helen, 17 n.5, 51
visual encroachment of the
    auditory region, 5
Neuroesthetic, approach, 2, 10,
    47–68, 186
non-linguistic modes of signification
    (visual, kinetic, gravitational,
    proximic, aural), 10, 18 n.20,
    163, 195 n.1

Optik, 12, 20, 27, 35, 62, 65, 99–110,
    185, 189
Allsop, Clare, 102, 105, 107
A Short Tour of Ancient Sites, 100
An Experiment in Telepresence, 12
and improvisation, 100, 105–6, 108
Bailey, Howie, 107
Currie, Billy, 107
Diegetic, 101–2, 105
Edgoose, Simon, 102–4
Edwards, Barry, 2, 99–110, 129 n.2
granular synthesis, 105, 108
Humm, Simon, 102, 105, 107
In the Presence of People, 35, 100,
    102, 104, 129 n.2
Jarlett, Ben, 99–109
Lewin, Jennifer, 105, 107
One Spectacle, 100
performing presence, 100

Seaton, Hannah, 102
Stranded, 100
Taking Breath, 105
Tropic, 100
Xstasis, 100, 107–8

Palindrome, 12, 23, 25, 29, 49, 54, 58,
    65, 110–117, 129–30 n.8, 130
    n.11, 185, 189–90
Biosensors, 111
EyeCon, 111–13, 115, 189
Fernandez, Emily, 115–16
gestural coherence, 114
intermedia, 110, 112, 114, 129–30 n.8
real time interaction, 111–12
    between virtual sound and the
        physical body, 12, 111, 189
Rovan, Butch, 12, 110, 113–14
Seine hohle Form, 12, 23, 110, 130 n.9
shadow performances, 54, 115–16
Solo4>Three, 115–16
virtual architecture, 112
Wechsler, Robert, 12, 110–17, 130
    n.11, 189–90
Weiss, Frieder, 12, 110–17, 130
    n.11, 189–90
Zwiauer, Helena, 113–14
Penfield, Wilder, 66–7 n. 1
Homunculus, 66–7 n.1
perception, differentiated from
    imagery, 6–7, 48, 154
memory, 7, 48
phenotypical reprogramming,
    177–8, 186
posthuman, 10, 87, 90–1, 134
primordial, 10, 13, 16–17 n.4, 20, 22,
    23, 26, 30, 133, 178, 190
prosopagnosia, 48, 54
Puckette, Miller, 109
Max/MSP, 109
Pd (Pure Data), 109

Qualia, 8–9, 63–4, 168, 193

Ramachandran, V.S., 7–9, 17 n.12, 18
    n.14, 51, 55–7, 59–60, 63–6, 67
    n.6, 68 n.15, 73, 76, 84, 97,
    140, 144, 188, 192
blindsight, 57

Ramachandran, V.S.—*continued*
   peak shift effect, 59, 84
   phantom limb, 51
      emergence of new functionally
         effective brain pathways, 51
   self, emotional responses, 66
      as evolutionary device, 66
      appropriation of objects, 66
      embodied, delimited, 65–6
      executive, 64
      (GSR) galvanic skin response, 66
      love and identity, 66
      passionate, 65
      unified, 65
   synaesthesia, 55–7, 67 n.6, 75,
      144, 192
robotics, 1, 15, 87, 162
Romanyshyn, Robert, 14, 80, 157
   distancing and detached vision,
      14, 157
   vanishing point, 80
Ruthrof, Horst, 19, 68 n.4
Ryle, Gilbert, 8

Stelarc, 11, 20, 26, 32, 51, 62, 65,
      86–98, 185, 187, 188
   and gender, 90
   body, the body, 90–1
      as hollow, 92
      delimited, 91
      experience, 88
      interfaces of, 87–8
      suspended, 87
   BWO (body without organs), 92
   Cybernetics, 88
   Cyborg, 88
      for developing circuitry and
         feedback loops, 89
   embodiment, 90–1
   evolution, evolutionary, 90–1
   Exoskeleton, 87, 98 n.13
   Extended Arm, 87
   Extra Ear, 87, 94–6, 192
   Fractal Flesh, 26, 87, 91–2, 98 n.11
   human/machine interface, 88
   interface between virtual and
      physical, 88–9
   Movatar, 11, 87, 93, 187

Muscle Machine, 11, 87, 93–4, 98
   n.13, 187
Nanotechnology, 92–3
   obsolete body, 86, 87, 92, 185
   posthuman, 87
   prosthesis and prosthetic, 84, 87,
      91–4, 96, 98 n.15, 188
ParaSite performances, 87, 92
Ping Body, 26, 87, 92
Prosthetic Head, 87, 94, 96, 98
   n.15
Robotics, 87
   soft prothesis, 87, 94–6
Stomach Sculpture, 87, 92
   technologies as alternate
      strategies, 88
Third Hand, 87
'Tissue Culture & Art Project',
      94–5, 192
   Catts, Oron, 32, 94–6, 180,
      183–4 n.13
   Zurr, Ionat, 32, 94–6, 180
Virtual Arm, 87
   virus, viral agent, 93, 188
Stielger, Bernard, 29
Sublime, 2, 3, 10, 24, 25, 28, 43, 44
   n.4, 59, 60, 75
Synaesthesia, 20, 36, 44 n.1, 55–7, 67
   n.6, 75, 144, 192
   and creativity, 55–6
   cross wiring of regions in the brain,
      67 n.6, 75, 144, 192
   mixture of mental sense
      impressions, 36, 56, 75,
      144, 192
   Ramachandran, V.S., 55–7, 67 n.6,
      75, 144, 192
   Ward, James, 56

Thompson, Seth, 118
Thompson, William, 53
3 D modeling and animation, 1,
      13–14, 17 n.1, 69, 78–9, 83–4,
      131, 151–4
transgenics, 15, 161–2, 168, 172–4,
      178, 193
transgenic art, 15, 161–2, 164–5,
      167, 186, 192

Troika Ranch, 12–13, 23, 25, 27, 29,
41, 48, 58, 62, 65, 117–129,
130 n.13, n.14, n.15, 186, 187,
189, 191–2
*Chemical Wedding of Christian
Rosenkreutz*, 41, 125–6, 128,
130 n.17
Coniglio, Mark, 13, 118–29, 192
Electronic Disturbance, The, 42,
126,128, 191
Future of Memory, The, 28, 41, 48,
123–5, 128, 130 n16, 192
Goldman, Danielle, 123
Isadora, 121–3, 187, 189
Lagger, Alica, 124
'liveness' of technology, 120
MidiDancer, 23, 119–123, 189
Molitz, Julian, 124
Mueller, Patrick, 122
organic and electronic, 41, 119,
125, 128, 191
real-time interactive performances,
118, 121, 189
16 [R]evolutions, 41, 126–8
Stoppiello, Dawn, 117–29, 192
Stuart, Leigh, 124
Surfacing, 41, 122–3, 128, 130 n.13,
n.14
Szabo, Michou, 118, 122–3
Tillett, Sandra, 122–3
Turner, Victor, 16–17 n.4

Van Gennep, Arnold, 149
The Rites of Passage, 149
Virilio, Paul, 88, 158
visual perception, 3, 6, 30, 47–51
as integrated experience, 54
automatic computation, 58
blindsight, 57
face recognition, 54–5, 72,
144, 188
frontal lobe, 58–9
middle region of the frontal
lobe, 59
activation of the middle frontal
convolution, 58
as response to elements of the
unusual, 58

when viewing non-
representational colour, 58
resolution of perceptual/
experiential conflict, 58,117
retina, 47, 52–3, 67 n.3, n.8
search for constancies, 49
visual areas of the brain, 47–68
V1 (primary visual cortex), 53–5,
57–8, 67 n.3
during imagery, 53
visual gateway, 57
V2, 53–4, 55, 57–8, 67 n.3
V3, 53
V4, 53, 55
colour centre, 55
V5 (MT), 53, 58, 116
motion center, 53

Wachowski, Andy; Wachowski Larry,
13, 36, 90, 132–46
Agent Smith, 55, 134–5, 143–4, 188
and violence, 36, 133, 135,
144, 190
and Baudrillard, 132–4, 136–7,
159 n.1
Animatrix, The, 145
Autochthony, 13, 38, 190
bullet time (flo mo), 14, 132,
140–41, 143, 190
commodification, 145–6
computer generated imagery,
132, 143
DVD, and marketing, 145
and video-games, 145
facial capture, 55,144–5
fetishization of technology, 141, 190
Gaeta, John, 132, 141–3
green screen composite imaging,
142–3
and blue screen, 143, 159 n.4
Matrix, The, 13, 31, 65, 90, 131–3,
137–8, 147, 190
Matrix Reloaded, The, 13, 132,
138–39, 141, 143
Matrix Revolution, The, 13, 55, 132,
139, 140–4, 188
motion capture,13, 141
mythology, myth, 139

Wachowski, Andy; Wachowski
  Larry—*continued*
Neo, 14, 28, 31, 55, 65, 134–44
  and free will, 139–40
  posthuman, 134
  previz (previzualization), 142–3
Silver, Joel, 132
simulation, 132–4, 136–7
  simulacra, 134, 136
virtual cinema, 132, 142
virtual cinematography, 141–2, 190
Warwick, Kevin, 132

Wo Ping, Yuen, 138, 142
Zion, 13, 135, 137, 139–41, 190
Wetware, 15, 168, 193

Zeki, Semir, 2, 48–50, 52–6,
  58, 67 n.3 n.5,
  115, 182, 19
  microconscious events (opposed to
    unified whole), 50
  neuro-esthetics, 2
  time delay in the perception of
    colour, form and motion, 54